Forecasting in Business and Economics

Second Edition

C. W. J. GRANGER

Department of Economics
University of California, San Diego
La Jolla, California

Academic Press
San Diego New York Boston
London Sydney Tokyo Toronto

Find Us on the Web! http://www.apnet.com

ACADEMIC PRESS
A Division of Harcourt Brace & Company
525 B Street, Suite 1900, San Diego, California 92101-4495

United Kingdom Edition published by
ACADEMIC PRESS INC. (LONDON) LTD.
24–28 Oval Road, London NW1 7DX

Library of Congress Cataloging-in-Publication Data

Granger, C. W. J. (Clive William John). Date-
　　Forecasting in business and economics / C.W.J. Granger.— 2nd ed.
　　　p. cm.
　　Bibliography: p.
　　Includes index.
　　ISBN 0-12-295181-6
　　1. Economic forecasting. 2. Business forecasting. I. Title.
HB3730.G68 1989
338.5′442—dc19　　　　　　　　　　　　　　　　88-30262
　　　　　　　　　　　　　　　　　　　　　　　　　CIP

PRINTED IN THE UNITED STATES OF AMERICA
98 IBT 9 8 7 6

Forecasting in Business and Economics

Second Edition

Contents

Contents

Chapter 6 Survey Data: Anticipations and Expectations

Chapter 7 Leading Indicators

Chapter 8 Evaluation and Combination of Forecasts

Chapter 9 Population Forecasting

Preface to the Second Edition

In the eight years since the first edition appeared, practical techniques have evolved enough to require a new edition. The main changes are a considerable expansion of Chapter 5, dealing with regression models and large-scale econometric models, mentions of more advanced topics such as causality and cointegration, and the relevance of forecasting for policy and control questions. An empirical project, involving actual forecasts constructed by the students and evaluated by them, runs throughout the text. I have found in my economics classes that students learn a great deal from these projects; they particularly appreciate what they thought they understood but in fact do not.

To make the book self-contained, an appendix has been added that briefly covers the basic concepts of statistics, particularly the ideas underlying correlation and regression, which are so vital in building forecasting models.

Preface to the First Edition

This text arose from my being asked to give a course on economic and business forecasting to senior undergraduates in the Management Science sequence at the University of California, San Diego. My immediate reaction was to glance at the available texts, but, as so often seems to be the case, I found none that I viewed as acceptable. Some concentrated on just a single forecasting technique, others were just uncritical lists of alternative methods, some lacked depth or content, and some even were wrong. I have attempted to write a text that will provide a clear-cut strategy for tackling a forecasting problem. The importance of the selection of a relevant information set is emphasized together with the question of how to evaluate one's forecasts once they have been prepared. With this strategy in mind, a variety of forecasting techniques and problems, of increasing scope and complexity, are discussed.

I hope that the text will be suitable for senior undergraduates in economics, business, commerce, and management, and also for MBA and starting graduate students in these and other fields, such as operations research and production engineering. Some basic knowledge of statistics is assumed, and I have tried to treat the readers as being both intelligent and motivated. The layout of much of the first half of the book parallels, at a lower level, the recently published *Forecasting Economic Time Series* by Paul Newbold and myself, Academic Press, 1977. Because of the availability of this more advanced and rigorous book, I do not attempt to prove every statement made in this text.

The students in my forecasting course have certainly helped in the evolution of the contents of the book, and I would like to thank those who made constructive comments. I would like to thank Liz Burford for her excellent typing, and I also would like to thank Dennis Kraft and Mark Watson for their careful reading through the page proofs. They must share in the blame for any minor errors that remain; any gross errors must be attributed to the author.

1

Basic Concepts of Forecasting

Any astronomer can predict just where every star will be at half past eleven tonight; he can make no such prediction about his daughter.

James Truslow Adams

1.1   A SCENARIO

If a person hears that he or she is about to relocate to a new city, he or she might very well be interested in knowing what life will be like there. It is for the same reason that everyone should be highly interested in the future — for it is where they are going to spend the rest of their lives, and it is likely to be quite different from the past or present. However, for managers or economists, knowing about the future is not merely a matter of academic interest. Management and Economics are decision sciences; they are concerned with sensible decision making and the effects of decisions. Any decision has to take a viewpoint about what will occur in the future and thus comes the idea of forecasts. To begin our discussion of forecasts, consider this statement about a day in the future:

September 28, 1995, will be a Thursday. By 11 A.M. the sun will be shining brightly on the Scripps Beach at La Jolla, a few miles north of San Diego in California. The surf will consist of four-foot breakers from the southwest at fourteen-second intervals.

It will be high tide, with a height of $+2.3$ feet. After a brief spell of body surfing and enjoying the 20°C temperature, I shall put on my mask and snorkel and start exploring the kelp beds just beyond the pier. I will find a half dollar lost by another diver many months ago and find that a particularly attractive barnacle is attached to it. I use the half dollar to buy an *Evening Tribune* and get no change.

1

This little scenario or view about the future contains a number of predictions or forecasts.[1] These predictions are all time specific, in that a definite time and date are specified, together with a particular location.

There is absolutely no possibility of the scenario being fully accurate about what will occur. At this time one cannot forecast the future perfectly, that is, without error. It does not require much imagination to realize how dull and mentally debilitating life would be if everything about the future were known with complete accuracy. Fortunately, such a possibility is by no means in sight.

Let us now examine some of the details of the scenario:

(i) the date. September 28, 1995, merely specifies when the scenario is to occur.

(ii) the day. That this date will be a Thursday is not a forecast but merely a designation of a name to a date according to a widely accepted method of designating such names, known as the Gregorian calendar. This calendar has given such names to all dates into the indefinite future. An assumption is being made that the same calendar will be in use in 1995.

(iii) tide-height. The mechanism that causes tides is very well known and depends on the movement of the moon and various other members of the solar system. As these movements can be predicted with great accuracy, it is possible to calculate a tide height for virtually any beach in the world, although the calculation is not necessarily an easy one. Thus a forecast of tide height can be made, and one would expect very little error in the forecast, although previous wind conditions may affect the actual value somewhat. The only assumption required to make this forecast is that the tide-generating mechanism does not change in any significant fashion before 1995.

(iv) sun shining, surf conditions, ocean temperature. These can all be considered to be forecasts made by observing what typically happens at Scripps Beach in La Jolla on September 28. For example, one might record sea temperature at 11 A.M. on all previous September 28s for which readings exist, average these values, and use this average to forecast what will occur at the same date in the future. It would clearly be wrong to average temperatures over all past days, as ocean temperature varies greatly from one part of the year to the next, a feature known as the seasonal variation. Clearly such forecasts could be very wrong, but it is difficult to see how they might be improved. Local weather effects in 1995 depend so

---

[1] The words *prediction* and *forecast* will be considered to be completely interchangeable in what follows.

greatly on the future movements of air masses and the mechanism that moves these masses through the atmosphere is so complicated that there is virtually no hope of making a really accurate forecast of what will occur several years hence. Unlike the astronomers and oceanographers, who have a very high quality model for the movement of planets and oceans, the meteorologist has only a very imperfect model for the atmosphere due to the extra order of complexity involved.

(v) my personal behavior. Much of this is very doubtful, requiring not only that I be around in 1995 and sufficiently healthy to enjoy the ocean but also that I learn how to snorkel. Given that I am sufficiently healthy and wealthy, the prediction could be self-fulfilling, as I could ensure that I am in La Jolla and do body surf and so forth.

(vi) finding a half dollar with a barnacle. This is just pure fantasy. Such a thing could occur but is extremely unlikely. Any detail of this kind can be thought of as being merely the use of artistic license by the writer.

(vii) spending a half dollar to buy an *Evening Tribune*. The San Diego evening paper at this time is the *Evening Tribune* and currently costs 25 cents, having gone up from 15 cents fairly recently. By looking at the history of price increases in the economy at large, one might well forecast that what now costs 25 cents will be costing 50 cents by 1995. In fact, such a price is possibly optimistic. There has been a noticeable upward drift in prices, known as a trend, and, by simply assuming that this drift will continue, the price of the paper in 1995 may be estimated. The mechanism by which prices will change is by no means well understood, so the forecast is based on an extension, or extrapolation, of what has been observed in the past.

(viii) use of centigrade. There is one possibly implied forecast in the scenario, the temperatures will be officially measured in degrees centigrade in California in 1995, rather than in degrees Fahrenheit as now. This is an example of a forecast about a change in the way society operates, albeit a very minor one. It is not based on any model of the society or on a great deal of past data but is just a suggestion about the consequences of discussions that are now occurring. In this case, it is not a particularly important forecast, since one can easily convert from centigrade to Fahrenheit without any error, 20°C being equal to 68°F.

Even this simple scenario brings out a number of important points about forecasting. The most important of these is that things to be forecast vary greatly in their degree of predictability. One can have much greater confidence in the forecast for tide height than in that for ocean temperature, and even less confidence in the forecast of the price of an evening paper. Whereas some variables can be predicted with considerable accuracy, others are almost entirely unpredictable, as will be shown later. It should also be clear that the methods that can be used to forecast can vary greatly and will depend upon data availability, the quality of models available, and the kinds of assumptions made, amongst other things. This means that forecasting is generally not easy, which is one reason why the topic is so interesting.

1.2 SOME FORECASTING SITUATIONS

Many million dollars are spent annually on prediction in the United States alone, making forecasting big business. Who forecasts and why? The major consumers of specific forecasts are government officials and servants, federal, state, and local, together with management, particularly that part belonging to the higher echelons, in all types of business. Some typical forecast situations are the following:

(i)   A company has to forecast future sales of each of its products to ensure that its production and inventory are kept at economical levels while controlling the likelihood of being unable to meet orders.

(ii) A firm is considering putting capital into a new investment. To decide whether the investment is a worthwhile one, it has to forecast the returns that will result in each of the next few years.

(iii) A cigarette manufacturing company is considering introducing a new brand and has to predict the likely sales for this brand and also the effect of sales on its other brands.

(iv) A government wants to forecast the values of some important economic variable, such as the unemployment rate, if it takes no action or if it alters one of its controls, such as the marginal tax rate. Such forecasts are necessary for policy decision.

(v)   A town council forecasts the demand for junior school places in some part of the town in order to decide whether or not an extra school is required, or if an existing school should be expanded.

(vi) A government expects to have a substantial deficit in three years' time and would like to know if there will be a "crowding out" effect leading to increased interest rates.

Forecasting is by no means confined to business and government, as there are plenty of situations in which some kind of forecasting is needed in the lives of individuals. An example is deciding what career choice will give good total value in terms of job satisfaction and adequate monetary reward. One has to predict how well he or she will like a job, what kind of advancement possibilities exist, and whether the career is oversubscribed or not. Similarly, if one is making an investment such as buying a house, getting married, or having a further child, it is necessary to ask if the advantages will outweigh the disadvantages and to predict what these will be. These types of predictions are generally very difficult and liable to huge errors and are very rarely made in any formal or specific manner.

It is important to note one common feature of all these forecasting situations — that they lead to *decisions*. The government official, the manager, or the individual requires forecasts in order to decide what to do right now or how to plan for the near future. The forecaster is the producer of information, and the decision maker is the consumer. It is clearly important for there to be no misunderstanding between the forecaster and the decision maker about what is being forecast, what information is being utilized, and what assumptions underlie the forecast.

There are, of course, some forecasts that have nothing to do with decisions, such as those that might be contained in an article entitled "Religion in Iceland in 50 Years Time" or "What Life Will Be Like in the Year 3078." Such offerings may be highly entertaining and are sometimes useful in helping forecasters free their minds from unnecessary restrictions, but they have to be classified with most science fiction as not serious forecasting. The majority of forecasting techniques described in later chapters will be aimed at being useful in decision making.

Exercises

In order to get yourself in the mood for thinking about how the future can be investigated, consider each of the following personal questions and give forecasts:

(a) What will you be doing next weekend?
(b) How will you spend your next summer vacation?
(c) When will you get married, and how many children will you have, if any?
(d) If taking a forecasting course, what mark or grade will you receive in the course?

As a final example of a situation familiar to all students that requires a forecast, suppose you are taking a lecture course from a professor you have not had before. As his or her first introductory lecture drags on, one's mind naturally turns to the question of when the lecture will end. Suppose the time-table indicates that the lecture will start at 10 A.M. and finish by 11 A.M. So that students can get from one class to another, it is generally understood that teachers will finish by ten minutes to the hour. However, from experience you know that some professors so dislike teaching that they finish as early as they dare, while others are (expletive deleted) and so enjoy the sound of their own voice that they keep on going to within a minute or two of the hour, resulting in an unseemly rush to your next class. What forecast do you make about when the lecture will end? As you have very little information to go on, you will probably take a neutral course and guess at 10:50 A.M. but realize that the actual time of finishing will very likely lie in the period 10:40–10:59 A.M. After you have attended the course for a few weeks, you will have gathered some useful information in predicting the time the next lecture will finish. You may have observed, for example, that the lecture always ends between 10:46 and 10:52 A.M., with an average of 10:49 A.M. Thus, an appropriate forecast would be 10:49 A.M., and the expected interval within which the finish time will lie is now much smaller. Thus, the acquisition of relevant information can help greatly in improving the forecast. After a couple of more weeks observation, rather more subtle effects might be noticeable. You may notice, for instance, that the lecturer has the tendency to follow a longer than average lecture by one that is shorter than average, or you may find that the lectures are generally becoming longer as the sequence continues. Such patterns in the data can obviously be utilized in making improved forecasts. A great deal of attention will be paid in what follows to discussing what information should be gathered and how it should be used, particularly how patterns in the data sequence can be picked out and utilized to form better forecasts.

1.3 TYPES OF FORECASTS

It should already be clear that there are several types of forecasts that need to be made and that they each require different approaches.

The first classification depends on the length of time into the future one is looking. When making statements about the near future, the forecasts are called *short run,* when considering the very distant future, they are called *long run,* and the intermediate case involves *middle-run* forecasts. Such a statement having been made, it now has to be admitted that there is no precise definition of what constitutes short, middle, or long run, as this depends on the variable being forecast and the type of data available, amongst other things. In weather forecasting, the short run might be up to

24 hours ahead and the long run 2 weeks or more, whereas if one is forecasting an economic variable such as unemployment, short run is up to 10 – 15 months and long run 4 years and more, although these are purely personal views.

It is generally true that the further ahead one forecasts the less well one does, in that larger errors are likely to occur. The reason for this is that usually the information available for making a forecast is more relevant in the short run than in longer runs.

In the extremely short run, forecasting is often trivial. For instance, if you ask yourself, "Where will I be in two seconds time?" the answer will have to be "Right here, or extremely nearby," as it is impossible to move very far in a couple of seconds. There is frequently a certain momentum in the course of events and this helps greatly in forecasting in the short run but is of very little relevance in the long run. It is also possible to make quite a reputation "predicting" things that have already occurred or have been planned but which are not yet publicly known. Again, such an approach does not help in the long run.

Three important types of forecasts may be called event outcome, event timing, and time series forecasts. These will now be considered in turn.

1.3.1 Event Outcome Forecasts

You know that an event will occur in the future with virtual certainty, but what will be the outcome of the event? For example, consider the following:

  (i)   A baby is to be born. What sex will it be?
 (ii)   An election is to occur. Who will win?
(iii)   A new brand of soap is to be introduced. Will it succeed? What will its sales be?
 (iv)   A new premier is about to take over power in Moscow. How will this affect Russian foreign policy?
  (v)   A new law is about to come into operation legalizing the use and sale of marijuana for adults. What will be the consequences?
 (vi)   What grade will you get in your forecasting course?

The main problem with forecasting the outcome of a future event is that the event may be unique, so that really relevant information may be difficult or expensive to acquire. Take example (i), the sex of an unborn baby. It is very easy to note that in the United States in recent years 51.3% of all babies have been boys and, of course, 48.7% have been girls. Thus, one could make a forecast of the form "with probability 0.513 the baby will be a boy." By observing the proportions of boys and girls born in the families of the mother and father, one might want to alter this probability, since some families produce a predominance of girls, for instance. Much better information could be acquired by performing chemical tests on the mother-to-be and quite possibly a very definite prediction could be made with considerable confidence, particularly as the birth date draws near.

It is highly likely that in the next decade or so, potential parents will have the choice of whether a baby will be a boy or a girl. Such a statement is a *technological forecast,* that is, a forecast about a change in the basic technology of our society. This type of forecast is discussed in Chapter 10. The effects on society of this choice for parents is very uncertain, but it seems doubtful if the natural frequency of boys, 51.3%, will remain the same.

The main approach to event outcome forecasting is to seek or generate relevant data. For example, to predict the outcome of an election one conducts a poll of electors, and to forecast the success of the introduction of a new brand of soap the company will perform various market tests. These are examples of increasing one's information set; the usual limitations to doing this depend on the state of the relevant technology and the cost of gathering the information.

1.3.2   Event Timing Forecasts

This class of forecasts considers questions of the form, when, if ever, will an event occur. Examples are the following:

  (i)   When will the next British election occur?
 (ii)   When will the next turning point of the economy happen?
(iii)   When will our company's main competitor introduce a new brand?
 (iv)   When will the company president retire?
  (v)   When will the bank change its interest rate?
 (vi)   When will your sister get married?

In some of these cases there exists a sequence of similar events in the past, such as the timing of British elections. By observing the pattern of the times between the events, it might be possible to forecast when the next event will occur. However, the usual procedure is to look for *leading indicators,* which are events that are likely to precede the one we are trying to forecast. For instance, the competitor company may book an exceptional amount of television advertising time or be observed doing market testing, or one's sister may announce her engagement. This approach is used intensively when considering turning points in the economy, as will be discussed in Chapter 7.

1.3.3 Time Series Forecasts

A time series is a sequence of values usually recorded at equidistant time intervals. Examples are

(i)   hourly temperatures taken at the base of the Statue of Liberty,
(ii)   daily closing prices of IBM shares,
(iii) weekly automobile production by the Chevrolet division of General Motors,
(iv)   monthly unemployment rate or balance of payments deficit, and
(v)   annual births in California.

As an example of the appearance of a time series, Fig. 1.1 shows the plot of quarterly U.S. Government surplus or deficit figures, using an annual rate, in billions of current dollars, for the period 1952–1984.

Suppose one observes such a time series, denoted by x_t for the value at the time period t, over the period from $t = 0$ up to $t = n$, where $n \equiv$ now. In time series forecasting we are interested in making statements about what value the series will take at some future time period $n + h$, where $h \equiv$ hence. Thus h represents the number of time periods into the future the forecaster is looking. If $h = 1$, then one-step forecasts are being made. For example, if x_t represents the number of U.S. firms that go bankrupt in month t, this series might be observed over a 50 month period, $t = 1, \ldots, 50$, ending in August 198x, and one may want to forecast the values taken by this series for September 198x ($h = 1$) and December of the same year ($h = 4$). As the reasons for any individual company going bankrupt are so complex, the series x_t may be considered to be a sequence of random variables. In particular, when standing at time n and contemplating the value that will occur at time $n + h$, one has very little reason to suppose it possible to forecast this value with perfect accuracy, except by incredible luck. Thus x_{n+h} is a random variable, when viewed at time n, and so should be characterized in probability terms. In particular, one could talk about its distribution function or its probability density function, plus summary statistics such as mean and variance. As will be seen later, these

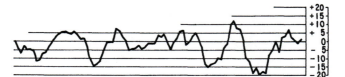

1952 53 54 55 56 57 58 59 60 61 62 63 64 65 66 67 68 69 70 71 72 73 1974

Fig. 1.1 Government surplus or deficit (quarterly).

distributions will be conditional ones, given the information available at time n upon which a forecast is based.

Figure 1.2 shows the situation being considered. To fully characterize x_{n+h}, the value to occur at time $n + h$, one needs a complete probability density function, so that statements such as prob($163 < x_{n+h} \leq 190$) = 0.42 can be made, for any interval. It will generally be quite impossible to completely determine the shape of the density function without making some very strong and highly unreal assumptions about the form of this function. A rather less ambitious procedure is to try to place confidence intervals about the forthcoming value x_{n+h}, so that a statement of the form

$$\text{prob}(B < x_{n+h} \leq A) = 0.95$$

can be made. The points A and B are shown in Fig. 1.2 and enable the forecaster to put limits on the value being forecast with a reasonably high degree of confidence of being correct. An example of such a forecast interval is to say, "I believe the price of potatoes in California will be in the range 6¢ – 8¢ per pound by the end of 198x, with probability 0.95." If your forecasting procedure were a good one and a whole sequence of such forecasts were made, you would expect that the true prices of potatoes or whatever would be outside the stated intervals only about 5% of the time. If you can go through life being wrong only 5% of the time, things should turn out very well for you. Such intervals are called *interval forecasts.* Confidence intervals are sometimes given in practice, although much less often than they should be, but forecasters are usually content with providing just a *point forecast,* that is, a single guess for x_{n+h} that in some way well represents the whole distribution of possible values. An obvious candidate for such a value is an average, such as the mean shown in Fig. 1.2. Some examples of point forecasts are the following:

(i)   My wife will drink 17 cups of coffee next week.
(ii) There will be 35 near misses by pairs of commercial airlines over the United States next year.

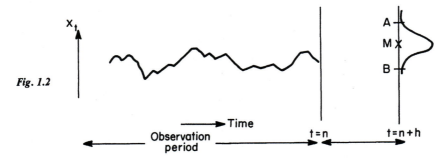

Fig. 1.2

(iii)   We expect 142 minor accidents in our manufacturing plant over the
next three months.

Most forecasts used in government and business are point forecasts. Chapters 3 and 4 will be particularly concerned with the formulation of such forecasts for a time series.

A whole sequence of point forecasts, for $h = 1, 2, 3, \ldots, H$, will be called a *trace forecast*, but the method of making such forecasts presents no new problem. As an example of the use of a trace forecast, consider the manager of a chocolate factory who has to buy cocoa on the international cocoa commodity market. Such markets are often very volatile, resulting in widely changing prices. If the manager has sufficient cocoa in his inventory to meet production needs in the near future, he or she may use a trace forecast to decide the best time to enter the cocoa market and purchase further stocks of the commodity, presumably trying to buy at the lowest available price.

Exercises

1.   Make point forecasts and also 95% confidence interval forecasts, if possible, of each of the following variables:
(a)   How many hours of television will you watch tomorrow? Next week?
(b)   How many books will you read purely for enjoyment over the next three months?
(c)   Over the next week, how many cans of beer (cups of tea, mugs of coffee, or whatever turns you on) will you drink?
(d)   How many head-turning girls (boys, cars, horses, or whatever) will you see tomorrow?
2.   Classify the type of forecast involved in each of the following situations:
(a)   A university announces it will admit a much larger proportion of "minority students." How will this affect the average grades of future graduating classes?
(b)   A company decides to lower the price of its product. How will sales be affected?
(c)   A manager is planning a new factory to be started in 5 years time and is interested in the possibility of nuclear power eventually providing very cheap electricity. Should he plan on putting electric or gas heating in the factory?
(d)   In order to decide whether or not a desalination plant to produce fresh water is required, a town council asks for a forecast of future water requirements for its area.

(e)   The date of the day of reckoning is required by a company considering making a very long-term loan.

1.4 INFORMATION SETS AND COST FUNCTIONS

Before forming a forecast, it is necessary to assemble the set of information that is to be used to make the forecast. For example, if time series forecasting, the forecast might be formed from the observed past and present values of the series. In this case, the *information set* available at time n, denoted I_n, will consist of

$$I_n: x_{n-j}, \qquad j \geq 0,$$

which will be called the single series information set. Most of the forecasts considered in Chapters 2 and 3 will use only this set. However, on other occasions wider information sets may be utilized, consisting of the past and present of the series to be forecast, together with the past and present values of other series that might be thought relevant, which can be written formally

$$I_n: x_{n-j}, y_{n-j}, z_{n-j}, \text{etc.}, \qquad j \geq 0.$$

Thus, for example, suppose a forecast of next month's unemployment rate is required. A forecast might be made from just the previous values of this series by utilizing some observed pattern. This would be the single-series forecast. However, it might be thought that the past and present values of an index of production and also of government expenditure, in real terms, would contain relevant information which, if it could be properly used together with past unemployment figures, would provide a better forecast. This would be a forecast based on a multi-series information set. In general, you would expect to forecast better the wider the information set used, provided the relevant information in the set has been fully extracted. Certainly, as the contents of the information set is increased you would not expect to do any worse at forecasting. At some point, any further extension of the information set is likely to provide such insignificant improvements in the forecasts that the work involved in trying to use the extra information will not be worthwhile, unless a particularly relevant series has previously been omitted, of course.

An information set will be called *proper* if it contains the past and present terms of the series to be forecast. The use of improper information sets will usually lead to suboptimal forecasts, although this is not inevitably so.

In most circumstances, the information set will be assumed to contain just numerical data. However, on occasions information of a nonnumerical kind may become available that appears particularly significant, such as rumors that an important government official is resigning, that a President is secretly seriously ill, that two rival companies are considering merging, or that your main competitor is about to introduce a new brand formulation. This type of information, including opinions about some situation by experienced managers, salesmen, or economists, is often extremely important but is very difficult to handle within a purely statistical framework. Some possible ways of using nonnumerical information will be discussed in Section 8.3.

On some occasions a very poor forecast can result due to a poor choice of information set. For example, in the late 1950s, a commission was set up in Britain to consider the future demand for medical school places. They decided that very few, if any, new places were required to meet the future demand for doctors in England. In fact, the number of doctors available in England fell far short of demand in the next decade or so. The reason for the inaccurate forecast is that it was not realized that about one in four of the doctors would emigrate. This mistake was due to two factors which were badly estimated, the number of doctors who would go to the United States, which proved to be a major market, and — a serious underestimate – the number of doctors who were already emigrating in the 1950s. This underestimate occurred because official estimates of this figure only considered those who emigrate by *sea* and totally ignored the large percentage who went by air. If the information set had included figures for air emigration, the forecast would have been much improved and a superior policy decision reached, leading to new medical schools being instituted.

In the discussion so far, statements of the kind "one procedure will produce better forecasts than another" have been used without defining what is meant by "better" or having a specific criterion by which forecasting methods can be ordered. As there is a natural desire to use the best available methods of forecasting that are affordable, it is imperative to have a criterion so that forecast methods can be compared.

Assume that someone is going to base a decision on your forecast. It follows that when you make an error, there will be in consequence a cost to the decision maker because he did not make the optimum decision. Generally, the larger the magnitude of the error, the larger will be this generated cost. For example, suppose that you work for a cake maker who uses no preservatives and advertises that he sells no cakes not made within the previous 24 hours. The cakes are actually made during the night hours and sold from the maker's shops the following day. Any cakes that are not sold are thrown away and have no value. Your task is to forecast sales for tomorrow, and the number of cakes made is always put equal to your forecast. If your forecast is too high, then more cakes will be made than can be sold, so that wastage will occur. If your forecast is too low, insufficient cakes will be made and so the profits that could have been made on those extra cakes would be lost. As you see, the forecaster cannot win except by making perfect forecasts, and this is virtually impossible to achieve. Let us put some figures to these costs. Suppose that each cake costs exactly 70¢ to make and that the cakes sell for $1 each. If you forecast that ten more cakes will be sold than actually are, the cost is $10 \times 70¢ = \$7$, which is cost of the cakes that were made unnecessarily. If you underestimate the number of cakes that could have been sold, the cost is $10 \times 30¢ = \$3$, since 30¢ profit is made per cake. In this example, the cost function of making an error e, denoted by $C(e)$, is given by

$$C(e) = \begin{cases} 70e & \text{if } e > 0 \\ 30(-e) & \text{if } e < 0 \\ 0 & \text{if } e = 0, \end{cases}$$

costs being in cents. In this case, it is seen that the cost function, which is plotted in Fig. 1.3, is not symmetric, takes the value zero when no error is made, is never negative, and is increasing in size as the errors become larger in magnitude. In more realistic situations, the cost functions will be expected to have similar properties, although they could be symmetric about $e = 0$ and need not consist of straight lines.

In practice, it is unlikely that the decision maker can provide you with a precise cost function partly because the company accountant may not be up to costing the effect of a single suboptimal decision amongst many and partly because the costs involved will occur in the future and so would have to be forecast. For this reason what is invariably done is that the forecaster assumes that a particular cost function, chosen for his own convenience, is a sufficiently good approximation to the decision maker's true cost function. The function usually chosen is

$$C(e) = Ae^2,$$

where A is some positive constant. It will be seen later that the value of A is quite irrelevant and so can be taken to be unity. Thus, the cost of an error is

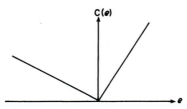

Fig. 1.3   Nonsymmetric cost function.

just the error squared. The obvious problem with this choice for $C(e)$ is that it is a symmetric function, whereas actual cost functions are often nonsymmetric. It is possible for the decision maker to take into account the fact that an incorrect cost function has been used, but to do this he has to have a good estimate of his true function, which is rarely the case in practice. Thus, the choice of an error-squared cost function is justifiable only on pragmatic grounds, but it is unclear how any additional costs that this may involve to the decision maker can be reduced.

With this preamble, it is now possible to give a criterion for choosing between forecasting methods, as follows:

Criterion.   For a given cost function $C(e)$, the best of a set of alternative forecasting methods is that which results in the lowest expected (or average) cost.

Suppose $f(1), f(2)$ are a pair of forecasting methods which when applied to a series of forecasting situations result in forecast errors $e_j(1)$, $e_j(2)$, $j = 1, \ldots, N$, respectively. Then using the squared-error criterion, $f(1)$ is the better method if

$$\frac{1}{N} \sum_{j=1}^{N} e_j^2(1) < \frac{1}{N} \sum_{j=1}^{N} e_j^2(2),$$

so that it produces the lower average squared error.[2] If both sides of this inequality were multiplied by the same positive constant, the inequality would not be altered, which is why the constant A is of no consequence in the preceding formula. Even the $1/N$ term can be dropped. The advantage of the squared-error cost function is that it corresponds to a *least-squares criterion* and so allows the use of much standard and well-understood statistical theory and practice relating to regression problems.

As an example of using this criterion, suppose you consider three alternative forecasting methods to predict daily cake sales and that the resulting errors over ten trading days are given in Table 1.1. The resulting average costs are shown in Table 1.2, using both the square error and the true cost function, as shown in Fig. 1.3.

Note that method (2) appears superior under both forms of the average least-cost criterion, whilst method (1) is consistently worst. The actual values in the cost table do not matter, as they are only used to find the method with the lowest figure in a column. To make a proper ranking of the methods, it is generally advisable to use more than ten error values if

[2] If a general cost function $C(e)$ were used, the criterion would read

$$\frac{1}{N} \sum_{j=1}^{N} C(e_j(1)) < \frac{1}{N} \sum_{j=1}^{N} C(e_j(2)).$$

TABLE 1.1

Forecast Errors from Three Forecasting Methods

Forecasting method	Day									
	1	2	3	4	5	6	7	8	9	10
(1)	−10	8	4	1	11	−2	4	6	−4	2
(2)	3	−2	5	−3	1	2	−1	0	−5	−2
(3)	6	5	−7	6	−2	1	−3	−1	6	4

possible. One may also wish to apply a test of significance to the average cost values, but discussion of how this can be done is delayed until Chapter 8.

Suppose that the number N of errors to be used in our least-squares criterion is very large and that a wide selection of possible forecasting methods are available. In fact, suppose that one can speak of all possible forecasting methods using a particular information set I_n. Then the method with the lowest average cost, that is, the smallest average squared error, may be called the *optimum forecast* based on I_n, although strictly it is the optimum least squares forecast. Some theoretical properties of optimum forecasts are discussed in Section 4.5. It is generally too difficult to consider all possible forecasts based on I_n, even if this information set contains just numerical data. The form of a forecast usually considered is that which uses the data in I_n in a linear fashion. Thus, for example, if a single-series information set is used, $I_n : x_{n-j}, j \geq 0$, then a forecast of x_{n+h} will be considered of the form

$$f_{n,h} = \sum_{j=0}^{m} \gamma_j x_{n-j}$$

and will be called a *linear forecast*.

If some appropriate m is chosen and the parameters γ_j are then chosen so

TABLE 1.2

Average Costs of Three Forecasting Methods

Method	Cost function	
	Squared error	True
(1)	37.8	$3
(2)	8.2	$1.16
(3)	18.3	$2.35

that the forecast is the best available according to our criterion, one has an optimal, linear, least-squares, single-series forecast.

Exercises

1. If you were asked to forecast how many students would graduate from a particular university, what information set would you ask for? What if you were asked to forecast the number of students entering the university in two years time?
2. Two methods of forecasting the number of companies going bankrupt in California per month produce the following errors:

	Month							
Method	1	2	3	4	5	6	7	8
(1)	16	11	−3	−14	9	−11	3	−3
(2)	12	−1	−8	−2	3	8	−6	−9

On this evidence, which method appears superior, using
(a)   a squared-error cost function and
(b)   the cost function

$$C(e) = \begin{cases} e, & e \geq 0, \\ -e, & e \leq 0? \end{cases}$$

1.5   A NOTE ON NOTATION

The following notation will be used frequently throughout this text, but particularly in the early chapters, and so is worth memorizing:

n now, the time period at which the forecast is made;

h hence, the number of time periods ahead one is forecasting;

x_t the basic time series under consideration;

x_n the latest value available in this time series;

I_n the information set upon which a forecast is based;

A_n the set of assumptions made by the forecaster;

x_{n+h} the value of the series to be forecast, the exact value of which is not known until time period $n + h$;

$f_{n,h}$ the forecast made at time n, looking ahead h periods, and so is a forecast of x_{n+h};

$e_{n,h}$ $x_{n+h} - f_{n,h}$, the resulting h-step forecast error, and not known until time $n + h$.

Strictly the forecast $f_{n,h}$ should be written $f_{n,h}(I_n, A_n)$, since it will depend on the information set used plus any assumptions made, but this extended notation is too uncomfortable for use. It is nevertheless worth noting whenever possible the form of I_n and of A_n being used. For example, I_n may consist of the past and present of a couple of time series, plus a batch of rumors, and A_n may contain assumptions that there will be no major breakdown in the running of society or in the physical laws operating in the universe, plus the belief that the economy can be well approximated by a linear model. These kinds of assumption are almost inevitably made, although they are dropped in Chapter 11.

1.6   THE FORECASTING PROJECT

1.6.1   The Plan

The only satisfactory way to learn how to forecast is to actually do it. It is also better to form forecasts and then to evaluate them in real time rather than using a contrived situation. Readers and students using this text are advised to undertake a forecasting project of the type outlined below.

Suppose that the project is for a ten-week college quarter. A basic outline of the timing of the project would be as follows:

Week 1:   Decide what real economic variable(s) to forecast and what other variables are to be used to form the forecast. Denote the variable being forecast by X_t and an explanatory variable by Y_t. These should be variables whose values are available weekly so that X_1 is the value taken by X in week one. Gather past data for the variables.

Week 4:   Forecast the value X_9, that is, the value that will be taken by X_t in Week 9.

Week 7:   Again forecast X_9 using more recent data and possibly a different forecasting method.

Week 10:   Compare the two forecasts made of X_9 with its actual value and perform a simple evaluation of the forecasts.

Clearly, there are many relevant variants of the outline. For a fifteen-week semester, the forecasts could be made of $X_9, X_{10}, \ldots, X_{14}$ in weeks 4 and 7 making the evaluation exercise much more meaningful. A reader not using the book in a course may want to use a daily interval rather than weeks.

1.6.2   The Data

The most important decision to be made is what variables to use in the project. The series should be available weekly and immediately after the end of the week. A good sequence of previous values must also be available. At least the previous 25 to 30 terms should be found. If the series has a strong seasonal, values for the corresponding period last year will also be needed.

If possible it is best to forecast a series in which one has some real interest. Examples could be weekly sales in some shop or gas station, the number of telephone calls made from an office, or hours of mainframe computer time used by a consultant. The financial press is an excellent source of weekly data. Journals and newspapers such as *Barrons, The Economist, The Wall Street Journal,* and *The Financial Times* have many pages of suitable series, such as interest rates, automobile sales, money supply, and the weekly volume of shares transacted on a stock market.

It is *strongly recommended* that the series to be forecast is *not* a price taken from a highly speculative market such as stock or bond prices, the prices of major commodities, such as copper, silver or gold, or exchange rates. Although such series are certainly readily available and are of general interest, it has been well established that changes in these prices are extremely difficult to forecast and so are inclined to make disappointing projects. The reasons for this observation are discussed in Chapter 5.

The other data to be gathered is information that might be helpful in forecasting the series of interest. For example, if one is attempting to forecast electricity sales to households in some region, then a measure of local temperature could be a good explanatory variable. The search should be for a "causal" series or a "leading indicator" of the series to be forecast. All series should have data available over the same period. One can use common sense or economic theory to choose likely explanatory series. Of course, several possible explanatory series could be utilized, but this would make the project rather more difficult.

1.6.3   Initial Analysis

All the series should first be plotted through time. These plots give a good indication of the general properties of the series: are they smooth or jagged; is there a monthly or annual swing in the series; and does the series contain a trend in mean? It is also very important to ask if the series contain strange values, called outliers. If they exist, they can be seen easily from the plot. Outliers can arise either from a genuine strange period in the data — due to a strike, typhoon, or heavy snow storm, for example — or can be found because the data was misrecorded or incorrectly plotted.

If an outlier is found, it is suggested that for the purposes of the project, a simple method of removal should be used, such as replacing the outlier by the previous, acceptable value or by the average of the two terms on each side of the extraordinary value.

1.6.4   The Various Forecasts

The text contains discussions of several forecasting methods. Some use just the past values of the series to be forecast as discussed in Chapters 2, 3, and 4, and others also use other series, as in Chapters 5, 6, and 7. At the end of most of these chapters there is a section discussing what is relevant in the chapter for the project. Chapter 8 has a discussion about evaluation of the results of the project.

1.6.5   An Example

In the discussions of the project in later chapters, the same data set will be used to illustrate the techniques. This data, which is constructed rather

TABLE 1.3

Data Used in Project Example

t (time)	x_t	y_t
1	−6	0.9
2	19	0.8
3	−5	0.7
4	10	−0.6
5	8	−2.4
6	−19	−2.0
7	46	−3.6
8	−29	−3.4
9	−67	−1.8
10	−33	−1.8
11	20	−0.1
12	15	−0.4
13	−3	−0.2
14	18	−0.1
15	−12	−1.7
16	−37	−1.8
17	−18	0
18	−20	0.2
19	−5	−0.4
20	6	0.9
21	5	2.6
22	36	2.5
23	22	1.1
24	12	1.6
25	16	2.0
26	4	1.1
27	37	1.5
28	14	0.7
29	4	1.0
30	22	0.7

than real, is listed in Table 1.3. It consists of thirty terms for two series x_t, y_t, with first terms $x_1 = -6$ and $y_1 = 40.9$. If one is making a forecast at time $n = 30$, looking ahead $h = 9$ steps, the information set will be all the information in the table. The forecast, however formed, will be $f_{30.9}$ and will be a number based on the information in the table. The main objectives of the text are deciding how this number should be formed and evaluated. Figure 1.3 shows the two series, the data in Table 1.3 plotted against time. Originally, one value for the y_t series, $y_2 = 5.6$, was seen to be quite different in magnitude than other values. Just from the visual evidence, this term would seem to be an outlier. When real data is being used, the reason for this unusual value will usually be clear. If this value is left in the data it could have a large but irrelevant effect on the forecasting model chosen and estimated. For the project, the outlier term is replaced by the average of its two neighbors, i.e., new $y_2 = \frac{1}{2}(0.9 + 0.7) = 0.8$. This value is used in all subsequent calculations. The x_t series is seen to take both positive and negative values and to generally lie around a constant. The sample mean is $\bar{x} = 2.0$ and the sample standard deviation is 24.14. For the y series, the sample mean is 0.04 and the standard deviation is 1.45.

QUESTIONS

1. List the major factors that you think will determine U.S. beef production in the next 20 years.
2. Produce point and 95% confidence interval forecasts of
   (a) how many films you will watch (other than on television) in the next year, and
   (b) how many cups of coffee you will drink in the next week.
3. Two methods of forecasting the number of companies going bankrupt in California per month produce the following errors:

				Month				
Method	1	2	3	4	5	6	7	8
(1)	6	11	−13	−14	19	−10	23	−31
(2)	12	−10	−28	−21	13	18	−16	−9

On this evidence, which method appears superior, using
(a) a squared error cost function and
(b) the cost function

$$C(e) = \begin{cases} e^2, & e \geq 0, \\ -4e, & e < 0? \end{cases}$$

2

Trend-Line Fitting
and Forecasting

The best qualification of a prophet is to have a good memory.

Marquis of Halifax

2.1 INTRODUCING TRENDS

Many aspects of society, and particularly the economy, when put into numerical form seem to have been steadily increasing throughout this century; population, prices, and number of crimes committed are three of the most widely discussed. A time series that appears to contain a smoothly increasing (or decreasing) component is said to contain a trend term. Some examples from the United States are shown in Table 2.1, in which figures for just a few selected years are given. There is no difficulty in finding many other examples from virtually any country in the world.

There are a number of major reasons for the existence of trends, including increases in population and the steady inflation observed in most countries. Because of this, many series are considered in "per capita" form to remove the effects of population increase and "in real" terms to allow for the price changes. Even then, many economic series and those measuring society at large still have clear trends, due to technological change and the resulting increase in standards of living. For example, in the U.S. the Gross National Product in constant (1972) dollars per capita rose from $4079 in 1960 to $5293 in 1970 and $6475 in 1980. Other trends are due to changes in attitudes or in the structure of the society, such as the declines in smoking, and percentage of the population who are married, or the increase in violent crime in the U.S. Many examples of actual estimates can be found in the annual statistical abstract of the United States and similar publications for other countries.

TABLE 2.1[a]

Year	Population (million)	Total horsepower (1000s)	No. of vehicles (1000s)	Autos per capita	Telephones per capita	Children aged Less than one Death rate per 1000
1890	63	NA[b]	NA[b]	—	3.6	—
1900	76	100	8	0.0001	17.6	162.4
1910	92	7714	312	0.0005	82	131.8
1920	106	280,000	9237	0.076	123	92.3
1930	123	1,420,000	26,749	0.187	163	69.0
1940	132	2,511,000	32,453	0.208	165	54.9
1950	151	4,403,000	49,161	0.267	281	33.0
1960	179	10,367,000	73,826	0.342	408	27.0
1970	203	19,325,000	108,375	0.435	584	21.4
1980	226	28,922,000	155,500	0.462	774	12.6
1983/4	236.6	31,338,000	163,800	0.535	N.A.[b]	~11.2
1985/6	241.5	32,529,000	170,237	0.546	N.A.[b]	~11.0

[a] Source: Statistical Abstract of the United States, U.S. Dept. of Commerce, U.S. Govt. Printing Office, Washington, D.C.
[b] NA: not available.

Although many important series appear to be trending from visual inspection of their plot against time, it is not at all easy to define trend. As an example of this difficulty, suppose that temperatures are recorded outside Nassau Hall at Princeton University on a spring day each five minutes from 5 A.M. until 3 P.M., giving a series of 120 values. Almost certainly the temperatures will have been steadily increasing over this period and so the data will appear to contain a trend. If this trend line is extended out beyond 3 P.M., very unfortunate temperatures will be reached by about midnight, but, of course, this does not happen. The apparent "trend" we saw in the data was just the upward swing of a daily cycle in temperature level. There is also an annual cycle in temperature in Princeton which could be misleading if a very long series of hourly reading were used, over the months of February to June, say. For the moment, these examples will be used just to point out difficulties in interpreting an apparent trend. Some further implications will be considered later.

Table 2.2 shows total U.S. personal consumption data for the period 1947–1984. These data are used throughout this chapter to provide examples of the forecasting techniques being considered. The "smoothed" series is explained later in this section. The data up to 1964 are to be used to fit broad curves and after 1964 to evaluate forecasts made using these curves.

TABLE 2.2[a]

Year	Total U.S. personal consumption (billions of 1958 dollars)	Smoothed data
1947	206.3	206.30
1948	210.8	209.45
1949	216.5	214.39
1950	230.5	225.67
1951	232.8	230.66
1952	239.4	236.78
1953	250.8	246.59
1954	255.7	252.97
1955	274.2	267.83
1956	281.4	277.33
1957	288.2	284.94
1958	290.1	288.55
1959	307.3	301.68
1960	316.1	311.77
1961	322.5	319.28
1962	338.4	332.66
1963	353.3	347.11
1964	373.7	365.72
1965	397.7	
1966	418.1	
1967	430.1	
1968	452.7	
1969	469.1	
1970	477.5	
1971	496.3	
1972	526.8	
1973	552.1	
1974	539.5	
1975		

[a] Source: Survey of Current Business, U.S. Dept. of Commerce, U.S. Govt. Printing Office, Washington, D.C., various issues.

Figure 2.1 shows these data plotted. Incidentally, it is always good practice to plot a time series before starting to analyze it so that any very special features can be noted, such as extraordinary values due to a strike or a particularly severe winter, say. That the series contains a trend appears clear, but there are also fluctuations about the smooth trend line. For a long time, the basic approach to time series analysis was to assume that the series are made up of three indentifiable components, a very smooth trend curve, a set of long swings, undulations, or cycles, plus a rather unimportant residual or "hash" consisting mainly of short fluctuations. As will be

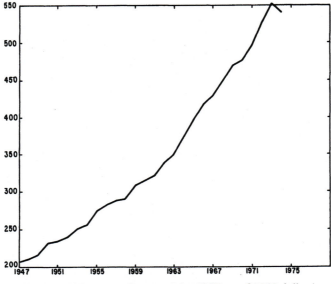

Fig. 2.1   U.S. personal consumption (billions of 1958 dollars).

clear later, this particular decomposition is no longer universally accepted. Figure 2.2 shows a constructed series made up of the three components. If a series is so composed, the relative importance of the three components depends largely on how far ahead one is forecasting. In the very short run, the trend and cycle components may have changed very little, so forecasts

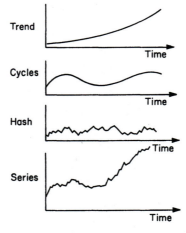

Fig. 2.2   Constructed series.

of the third component are the most important. However, when long-run forecasting, the trend term is usually dominant and the other two components are of relatively minor importance. In the middle run all three components could be important.

This chapter is concerned with methods of estimating the trend and then forecasting over the long run. The other two components are thus of lesser interest and it is usually worthwhile removing or at least reducing their importance before analyzing the trend. This is done by *smoothing* the series and this is best achieved by use of a *filter*, which is a linear transformation of the original series. A possible smoothing filter is to form a series y_t from the given series x_t by

$$y_t = \frac{1}{2m + 1} \sum_{j=-m}^{m} x_{t-j},$$

and this is called a (two-sided) moving average. However, as "future" x's are used to form y_t, in practice one loses data at each end of the series by use of such a filter. A better filter generates y_t from x_t by the interactive formula

$$y_1 = x_1, \qquad y_t = ky_{t-1} + (1 - k)x_t, \qquad t = 2, \ldots, n.$$

The larger the value of k, the greater the smoothing achieved. Typical appropriate values for k would be 0.7 for monthly data, 0.5 for quarterly data, and 0.3 for a series recorded annually. The smoothed personal consumption series, with $k = 0.3$, has been shown in Table 2.2.

It is important to note that if the series is smoothed, and then a forecast made of Y_{n+h} when at time $n, f_{n,h}^y$, then the corresponding forecast of X_{n+h} is given by

$$f_{n,h}^x = \frac{f_{n,h}^y - kf_{n,h-1}^y}{1 - k}.$$

It should be emphasized that the methods discussed in the next two sections do not necessarily provide good forecasts relative to methods discussed in later chapters. These trend-curve methods are occasionally useful and allow discussion of a number of important points about forecasting strategy and provide examples of some of the ideas introduced in Chapter 1.

2.2   CHOOSING AND ESTIMATING A CURVE

Suppose that a sales manager of some manufacturing company looks at the chart of sales over the last few years and sees a smooth curve of one of the shapes shown in Fig. 2.3. There are innumerable curves that might fit some of these shapes, but if one is interested in just simple curves involving only a few parameters, the following are good candidates:

(1)   the straight line $C(t) = a + bt$;
(2)   the exponential curve $C(t) = \exp(a + bt)$, so that $\log C(t) = a + bt$;
(3)   the parabolic curve $C(t) = a + bt + ct^2$;
(4)   the modified exponential curve $C(t) = a + br^t$;
(5)   the Gompertz curve given by $\log C(t) = a + br^t$, with $0 < r < 1$;
(6)   the logistic curve $C(t) = 1/(a + br^t)$, with $0 < r < 1$, so that $1/C(t) = a + br^t$.

Looking at the different sales curves, appropriate curves might be

(i)   Things going great
      exponential curve, with b positive,
      modified exponential, $r > 1$, $b > 0$,
      parabolic curve, b and c positive;
(ii) Things going well
      where the only curve appropriate is the straight line with $b > 0$;

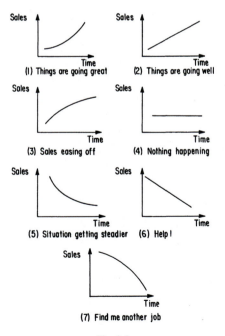

Fig. 2.3

(iii)   Sales easing off
        modified exponential, $r < 1$, $b > 0$,
        parabolic curve, c negative, b positive,
        Gompertz curve, $b > 0$,
        logistic curve, $b > 0$;
(iv)   Nothing happening
        straight line $C(t) = a$, so $b = 0$;
 (v)   Situation steadying
        modified exponential, b negative, $r > 1$
        parabolic curve, b negative, c positive,
        Gompertz curve, b negative,
        logistic curve, b negative;
(vi)   Steadily worse
        straight line, with $b < 0$; and
(vii)   Awful
        exponential curve, with b negative,
        modified exponential, with b negative,
        parabolic curve, with both b and c negative.

It is seen that in several cases a unique curve is not a possibility. When this occurs all the possible curves should be fitted and then a criterion applied to see which fits best, as will be illustrated. Two of the set of six curves introduced above may be unfamiliar to many readers, the Gompertz and logistic curves. Their use is a rather specialized one, as they tend to a limit, or asymptote, as t becomes large, this limit taking the value e^a for the Gompertz and $1/a$ for the logistic. They are thus only appropriate for variables for which there is a clear upper limit which will virtually be reached not too distant in the future, such as the percent of homes in the U.S. that have electrification. However, for many series, it is not clear if there is an upper limit. Consider the total number of automobiles per 1000 population in some developed country, for instance. If one has a clear-cut idea of what the upper limit will be, this should be used for e^a or a^{-1} rather than an estimate of these quantities. If the variable is not near any limit and the limit is estimated from the available data, some very strange forecasts of the eventual limit values can result.

Having chosen one or a few curves to fit to the data, the next stage is to estimate its parameters from the data. The curves used need not be one of those mentioned above if one has a preference for some other curve, but it should be remembered that the more complicated the curve, involving more parameters, the more difficult will be the estimation stage.

Because of the least-squares criterion suggested in Chapter 1 for choosing between forecasting methods, the obvious way to estimate the parameters in some curve $C(t)$ is to choose values for these parameters that minimizes

$$I = \sum_{t=1}^{n} (x_t - C(t))^2,$$

where x_t is the given or smoothed series, whichever is being used. If $C(t) = a + bt$, then some simple calculus and algebra gives as estimates

$$\hat{b} = \frac{\sum_{t=1}^{n} tx_t - \frac{1}{2}(n + 1)\sum_{t=1}^{n} x_t}{\frac{1}{12}n(n^2 - 1)}$$

and

$$\hat{a} = \frac{1}{n} \sum_{t=1}^{n} x_t - \frac{1}{2}(n + 1)\hat{b}.$$

These estimates ensure that the sum of squares of the distance between the line and the data points, as shown in Fig. 2.4, is made as small as possible.

For some of the curves, it is very difficult to find parameter estimates in this way, so when possible a transformed least-squares estimate is obtained instead. For example, the parameters of the exponential trend can be fitted by taking logarithms of both the data and trend curve, so that

$$\log C(t) = a + bt$$

is fitted to $\log x_t$, provided all data values are positive. Most computer centers will have least-squares curve fitting programs in their statistics package so the tedious task of actually doing the calculations oneself can be avoided.

However, even these days there are occasions when access to a computer is not possible, or is too costly, so an alternative, much simpler but suboptimum method of estimation will be described, known as the three-point method. As all of the curves considered above involve no more than three parameters, three points on the curves will determine exactly all other points. For the two-parameter curves, the straight line and the exponen-

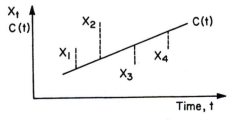

Fig. 2.4   Least-squares fit.

tial, two points are enough to completely determine the parameters and thus all other points. One could start by just choosing two or three actual data points and then making the curves go through these, but even after smoothing there can be values that lie off the trend curve, and if these were used in the three-point method very poor estimates could result. To reduce this problem, averages of adjacent points might be used. However, the most important points are clearly the very last few, as they probably contain the most information about the future, so it is suggested that later points be given greater weight than earlier ones, so that weighted averages are used. The actual formulas are as follows:

Suppose the available data are x_t, $t = 1, \ldots, n$, and that n is an odd integer. (If n is even, it is simplest to merely drop the earliest piece of data.) Denote by R, the weighted average of the first five terms, i.e.,

$$R = \tfrac{1}{15}(x_1 + 2x_2 + 3x_3 + 4x_4 + 5x_5);$$

denote by S the weighted average of the middle five terms, i.e.,

$$S = \tfrac{1}{15}(x_{d-2} + 2x_{d-1} + 3x_d + 4x_{d+1} + 5x_{d+2})$$

where $d = (n + 1)/2$ and as n is odd, d will be an integer; and further denote by T the weighted average of the last five terms, i.e.,

$$T = \tfrac{1}{15}(x_{n-4} + 2x_{n-3} + 3x_{n-2} + 4x_{n-1} + 5x_n).$$

The weighted sums are divided by 15 because this is the sum of the weights used.

To understand the method, consider the fitting of the straight line

$$C(t) = a + bt.$$

If the observed series lay exactly on this line, we would have

$$R = \tfrac{1}{15}[(a + b) + 2(a + 2b) + 3(a + 3b) + 4(a + 4b) + 5(a + 5b)],$$

so

$$R = a + \tfrac{11}{3}b$$

and

$$\begin{aligned} T = \tfrac{1}{15}([a + (n - 4)b] &+ 2[a + (n - 3)b] + 3[a + (n - 2)b] \\ &+ 4[a + (n - 1)b] + 5[a + nb]) \\ &= a + (n - \tfrac{4}{3})b. \end{aligned}$$

Solving for a and b, one has

$$b = \frac{T - R}{n - 5}, \qquad a = R - \frac{11}{3}b.$$

In practice, of course, the data will not exactly lie on the line but will vary about it, so the estimates of a and b are taken as

$$\hat{b} = \frac{T - R}{n - 5} \quad \text{and} \quad \hat{a} = R - \frac{11}{3}\hat{b}.$$

Suppose a straight line is fitted to the smoothed personal consumption data of Table 2.2 for the period 1948–1964, then $n = 17$, and

$$R = \tfrac{1}{15}(209.45 + 2 \times 214.39 + 3 \times 225.67 + 4 \times 230.66 + 5 \times 236.78)$$

$$= 228.12$$

and

$$T = \tfrac{1}{15}(311.77 + 2 \times 319.28 + 3 \times 332.66 + 4 \times 347.11 + 5 \times 365.72)$$

$$= 344.36,$$

so

$$\hat{b} = (344.36 - 228.12)/12 = 9.687$$

and

$$\hat{a} = 228.12 - \tfrac{11}{3}(9.687) = 192.6.$$

Thus, the fitted straight line trend is

$$C(t) = 192.6 + 9.687t,$$

with $t = 1$ in 1948.

In Table 2.3 all the fitted terms are shown and can be compared to the original data. The same method can be used for fitting the exponential curve, but using the logarithms of the data, the values of which are also shown in Table 2.3. Using the log data, one gets

$$R = 5.4291, \qquad T = 5.8403,$$

giving

$$\hat{a} = 5.3033, \qquad \hat{b} = 0.0343,$$

so that the trend curve is given by

$$\log C(t) = 5.3033 + 0.0343t.$$

The method of fitting the other curves is very similar, it being merely a matter of forming R, S, and T and then applying the formulas given in Table 2.4. However, if only a short series is available, say $n < 10$ if fitting a two-parameter, or $n < 15$ if fitting a three-parameter curve, slightly dif-

TABLE 2.3

Year	Data	t	Weights	Fitted straight line	Log (base e) Data	Log (base e) Weights	Fitted exponential curve
1948	209.45	1	1 ⎫	202.28	5.3444	1 ⎫	208.01
1949	214.39	2	2 ⎪ R	211.98	5.3677	2 ⎪ R	215.27
1950	225.67	3	3 ⎬ $= 228.12$	221.67	5.4190	3 ⎬ $= 5.4291$	222.78
1951	230.66	4	4 ⎪	231.35	5.4409	4 ⎪	230.56
1952	236.78	5	5 ⎭	241.04	5.4571	5 ⎭	238.60
1953	246.59	6		250.72	5.5077		246.93
1954	252.97	7	1 ⎫	260.41	5.5332		255.55
1955	267.83	8	2 ⎪ S	270.10	5.5903		264.46
1956	277.33	9	3 ⎬ $= 280.21$	279.78	5.6252		273.69
1957	284.94	10	4 ⎪	289.47	5.6522		283.24
1958	288.55	11	5 ⎭	299.16	5.6648		293.13
1959	301.68	12		308.85	5.7094		303.35
1960	311.77	13	1 ⎫	318.93	5.7424	1 ⎫	313.94
1961	319.28	14	2 ⎪ T	328.22	5.7662	2 ⎪ T	324.89
1962	332.66	15	3 ⎬ $= 344.36$	337.91	5.8072	3 ⎬ $= 5.9403$	336.23
1963	347.11	16	4 ⎪	347.59	5.8497	4 ⎪	347.96
1964	365.72	17	5 ⎭	357.28	5.9019	5 ⎭	360.11

ferent definitions of R, S, and T are used, that is, weighted averages over just three terms:

$$R = \tfrac{1}{6}(x_1 + 2x_2 + 3x_3),$$

$$S = \tfrac{1}{6}(x_{d-1} + 2x_d + 3x_{d+1}),$$

and

$$T = \tfrac{1}{6}(x_{n-2} + 2x_{n-1} + 3x_n)$$

where $d = (n + 1)/2$ as before.

The list of formulas to apply to fit the curves is given in Table 2.4.

Four different possible trend curves were fitted to the consumer expenditure data, the linear, exponential, parabolic, and modified exponential curves. The estimated parameters were found to be

(i)   linear[1]: $\hat{a} = 192.6$, $\hat{b} = 9.687$;
(ii) exponential: $\hat{a} = 5.3033$, $\hat{b} = 0.0343$;
(iii) parabolic: $\hat{a} = 201.96$, $\hat{b} = 6.449$, $\hat{c} = 0.1675$;
(iv) modified exponential: $\hat{a} = 3.131$, $\hat{b} = 197.790$, $\hat{r} = 1.0355$.

---

[1] If the linear function had been fitted by least squares, the coefficients would have been $\hat{a} = 191$, $\hat{b} = 9.69$, which are very similar to the two-point estimates.

TABLE 2.4

Formulas for Estimating Parameters Using the Three-Point Method

Ordinary series	Short series
(R, S, T weighted average of 5 terms)	(R, S, T weighted average of 3 terms)

(1) Straight line, $C(t) = a + bt$

$$\hat{b} = \frac{T - R}{n - 5} \qquad\qquad \hat{b} = \frac{T - R}{n - 3}$$

$$\hat{a} = R - \tfrac{4}{3}\hat{b} \qquad\qquad \hat{a} = R - \tfrac{1}{3}\hat{b}$$

(2) Exponential curve, $C(t) = \exp(a + bt)$

As for straight line, but using logarithms of data when forming R, S, and T.

(3) Parabolic curve, $C(t) = a + bt + ct^2$

$$\hat{c} = \frac{2(R + T - 2S)}{(n - 5)^2} \qquad\qquad \hat{c} = \frac{2(R + T - 2S)}{(n - 3)^2}$$

$$\hat{b} = \frac{T - R}{n - 5} - \frac{(3n + 7)}{3}\hat{c} \qquad\qquad \hat{b} = \frac{T - R}{n - 3} - \frac{(3n + 5)}{3}\hat{c}$$

$$\hat{a} = R - \tfrac{4}{3}\hat{b} - 15\hat{c} \qquad\qquad \hat{a} = R - \tfrac{1}{3}\hat{b} - 6\hat{c}$$

(4) Modified Exponential curve, $C(t) = a + br^t$

$$\log \hat{r} = \frac{2}{n - 5} \log \frac{T - S}{S - R} \qquad\qquad \log \hat{r} = \frac{2}{n - 3} \log \frac{T - S}{S - R}$$

$$\hat{a} = \frac{TR - S^2}{R + T - 2S} \qquad\qquad \hat{a} = \frac{TR - S^2}{R + T - 2S}$$

$$\hat{b} = \frac{k(S - R)^2}{R + T - 2S} \qquad\qquad \hat{b} = \frac{k(S - R)^2}{R + T - 2S}$$

where $k = 15/(\hat{r} + 2\hat{r}^2 + 3\hat{r}^3 + 4\hat{r}^4 + 5\hat{r}^5)$ where $k = 6/(\hat{r} + 2\hat{r}^2 + 3\hat{r}^3)$

(5) Gompertz curve, $\log C(t) = a + br^t$

Same as for modified exponential curve, but using logarithms of data when forming R, S, and T.

(6) Logistic curve, $1/C(t) = a + br^t$

Same as for modified exponential curve, but using the reciprocals of the data when forming R, S, and T.

Table 2.5 shows the original data, plus the fitted values of these four curves. The question remains, which curve fits best? Our criterion states that we should look at the average squared error, but this will not quite give a fair comparison since a curve involving three parameters has an

TABLE 2.5

t	Data	Straight line	Exponential	Modified exponential	Parabolic
1	209.45	202.23	208.01	207.94	208.58
2	214.39	211.98	215.27	215.21	215.53
3	225.67	221.67	222.78	222.74	222.81
4	230.66	231.35	230.56	230.54	230.44
5	236.78	241.04	238.60	238.61	238.39
6	246.59	250.72	246.93	246.97	246.68
7	252.97	260.41	255.55	255.63	255.31
8	267.83	270.10	264.46	264.59	264.27
9	277.33	279.78	273.69	273.87	273.57
10	284.94	289.47	283.24	283.48	283.20
11	288.55	299.16	293.13	293.44	293.17
12	301.68	308.85	303.35	303.74	303.47
13	311.77	318.53	313.94	314.41	314.10
14	319.28	328.22	324.89	325.46	325.08
15	332.66	337.91	336.28	336.91	336.38
16	347.11	347.59	347.96	348.76	348.02
17	365.72	357.28	360.11	361.03	360.00

advantage over one with just two, even if neither is the correct curve. The criterion used is designed to at least partly remove this possible bias:

$$\bar{S} = \frac{[\text{sum of squared errors (i.e., difference between data and curve)}]}{(n - m)}$$

where m is the number of parameters involved in the curve, so that $m = 2$ for the linear and exponential curves and $m = 3$ for the others.

The results for the four fitted curves of our example are given in the accompanying tabulation.

	m	$\bar{S}$
linear	2	39.0
exponential	2	10.3
parabolic	3	11.4
modified exponential	3	11.8

From the $\bar{S}$ value over the fitting period, it is clear that the straight line is the poorest approximation to the data but that there is virtually no reason to choose amongst the other three curves. In the circumstances, it is probably best to retain all three curves, make forecasts from them and average these values to get the eventual forecast. Within a few years, evidence will have accumulated on the relative abilities of the curves to actually forecast. The best curve can then be picked and its parameters reestimated and then used to forecast further ahead. The next section discusses how the forecasts are made and how well our curves actually did forecast.

2.3　FORECASTING USING TREND CURVES

To forecast for a particular year corresponding to $t = t_0$, using the curve $C(t)$, one simply calculates $C(t_0)$ and then corrects for the smoothing filter, if used, by applying the formula at the end of Section 2.1. Thus, for example, if the parabolic curve is being used,

$$C(t) = 201.96 + 6.449t + 0.167t^2.$$

Then to forecast for 1974, which corresponds to $t = 27$ as $1947 = 1$, one forms

$$C(27) = 201.96 + 6.449 \times 27 + 0.1675 \times (27)^2$$

$$= 498.19.$$

Similarly, the forecast for 1973 is

$$C(26) = 482.86.$$

Thus, the forecast for the original, unsmoothed series for 1974 is

$$f_{17,10} = \frac{498.19 - 0.3 \times 482.86}{1 - 0.3} = 504.76.$$

The whole set of forecasts for the original, unsmoothed series for the years 1965–1985 is shown in Table 2.6, together with the actual values where available. Are the forecasts good or bad? This question is virtually impossible to answer. All one *can* say is whether one technique appears superior to another, and at this point there is no other technique available for comparison. It is certainly to be expected that the forecasts will be made with error. In 1964 it would have been virtually impossible to forecast the occurrence of a strong depression in 1974–1975, for example. The exponential curves forecast U.S. consumer expenditure (in 1958 dollars) within 2% in 1975, and within 1% in 1982; which for many purposes would be considered to be a rather acceptable level of error for a forecast looking 18 years into the future. However, the forecasts for earlier years were less impressive, although errors were generally less than 7%. The occurrence of the depression of 1974–75 made the forecast for 1975 more respectable, and again the slowing of growth in the early 1980s was what made the 1982 forecast so good. Without the depressions, the

TABLE 2.6[a]

Year	t	Actual values	Linear	Exponential	Modified exponential	% Error	Parabolic
1965	18	397	371	378	379		377
1966	19	418	380	391	392		390
1967	20	430	390	405	406		403
1968	21	452	400	419	420		416
1969	22	469	409	434	435		430
1970	23	477	419	449	450		444
1971	24	496	429	465	466		459
1972	25	526	438	481	483		474
1973	26	552	448	498	500		489
1974	27	539	458	515	517		504
1975	28	554	467	534	536		520
1976	29	586	477	552	555		536
1977	30	615	487	572	574		553
1978	31	641	497	592	595	7	570
1979	32	659	506	613	616		587
1980	33	651	516	634	638	3	598
1981	34	664	526	657	600		622
1982	35	674	536	680	684	1.6	641
1983	36	706	546	704	708		659
1984	37	749	555	727	733		678
1985	38	774	565	752	748	3	689

[a] The conversion used of price with a $1982 base to a $1958 base is to multiply by 0.33.

forecasts would have continued to have been too low. It is clear from the table that the exponential and modified exponential forecasts are almost identical and both are superior to forecasts from the linear and parabolic models.

It is interesting to compare the successful exponential model with similar models formed in different ways. If the two point method is applied to the logarithms of the smoothed data set for the longer period 1947–1973, the new estimtes are $\hat{a} = 5.2951$ and $\hat{b} = 0.0366$, leading to a forecast of personal consumption of 727.7 in 1982, which is far too high. Thus, in this case using more recent data to fit the trend leads to a poorer forecast. This is not what one would usually expect and probably arises because of long swings around the basic exponential trend, which can throw off estimates achieved by the two or three point method. Using the least squares estimated exponential function based on the 1947 to 1964 data gives a forecast for 1982 of 785.5, again far too high. Thus, in this case the unsophisticated estimation produces the better forecasts, although again this is not what one would usually expect to occur. Overall, the example does suggest that trend curves do produce forecasts of some value for several years into the future, perhaps surprisingly so, given the basic lack of sophistication in model selection that is used.

To illustrate that exponential trend fitting is not always successful, an example is provided by Martino (1983, Chapter 5). Using U.S. electrical power production, in billions of kilowatt hours for the period 1945 to 1965, an exponential curve was fitted of the form

$$\log(r) = 2.214 + .0753t$$

where $t = 0$ in the year 1900. Forecasting from 1965 to 1970 gave a figure of 1780 compared to actual production of 1640, almost an 11% error. By the year 1980 the forecast was 3781 and the actual production was 2286. Clearly, the growth in electricity production in the period 1945 to 1965 was faster than in the later years.

The obvious problem with trend-curve fitting is the lack of any real theory underlying the forecasts, and this is true whatever method is used to estimate the parameters of curves. The set of curves considered is necessarily arbitrary, even if a wider set is used than those discussed in the previous section. The curve fitting process appears to be just "number crunching," and the method of forecasting consists of the blind hope that whatever mechanism generated the trend in the past will continue to work in the future. It is the main weakness of this approach that absolutely no attempt is made to understand this underlying mechanism.

The hope that things will continue in the future as they have in the past is clearly wrong on occasions. An example is provided by pollution levels in air and water in recent years. After years of increasing pollution in some locations, not only has the situation stabilized but the direction of trend has actually reversed. Air pollution levels in Pittsburgh and London are cases in point, as is the pollution content of some rivers such as the Thames in London, where some species of fish have recently been observed that have been hitherto absent throughout the twentieth century. There is a river in the eastern part of the United States that was so polluted that the oil and junk floating on its surface made it into an official fire hazard for a period, but it is now much improved. A second example of a change in trend appeared in a news item whilst this section was originally being prepared. By 1975, there were approximately a quarter of a million swimming pools in California, with sales of new pools running at about 12,000 a year. As virtually no existing pools were being removed, the total number was obviously trending upward. However, worries of a natural gas shortage led the state senate to pass a new law forbidding any new pool to be heated by gas, which is virtually the only practical way of doing it at this time. One would certainly expect the slope of the trend of total pools to be changed, at the very least. Whether this is a temporary change in the trend or a permanent one depends on the development of new technology to provide heat for pools not using natural gas. The question of whether the timing of such technological developments can be forecast will be discussed in Chapter 10.

A rather different example of the problems encountered when venturing outside one's normal range of experience comes from the situation faced by the sailors when they first left the Mediterranean Sea. For the first time they encountered substantial tides and initially had considerable difficulty in coping with this phenomenon. Any forecaster who extrapolates to an economy or society outside of previous experience has to be ready for similar difficulties.

It should be emphasized again that trend-curve forecasting cannot be recommended with complete confidence but can be a useful member of a parcel of alternative methods and does sometimes produce really worthwhile predictions.

The more important lessons of this chapter so far are derived from the approach taken to fitting and evaluating a technique. The basic steps in this approach are

(i)   the choice of a set of possible curves or models (the identification stage),

(ii) the estimate of the parameters of the model (the estimation stage), and

(iii) the use of a criterion to evaluate the relative goodness of fit of the models (the diagnostic checking stage).

A different example of the use of these stages will be provided by the techniques described in the next chapter.

2.4   TREND REMOVED BY DIFFERENCING

The fitting of trend curves is not the only method available for treating series apparently containing a trend. In the first section of this chapter a simple filter was introduced that removed the unsmooth components of a series leaving only the smooth or trend part. It is also possible to find filters that remove a trend, so that the remaining, relatively unsmooth parts can be forecast using methods to be outlined in the next two chapters and the original series then forecast by unraveling the filter. A simple example of how this is done comes from considering the effect of differencing a series. If the original series is x_t, the differenced series is

$$y_t = x_t - x_{t-1},$$

so that y_t is just the change in x_t. Suppose that x_t is just the straight line

$$x_t = a + bt.$$

Then

$$y_t = (a + bt) - (a + b(t-1)) = b,$$

so although x_t contains a trend, y_t does not. More generally, suppose that x_t consists of a linear trend plus some other, nontrending component x_t' having zero mean, so that

$$x_t = a + bt + x_t'.$$

Then

$$y_t = b + (x_t' - x_{t-1}').$$

If some method of forecasting the y_t is devised, producing forecasts $f_{n,h}^{(y)}$ in the notation of Chapter 1, then noting that

$$x_{n+h} = y_{n+h} + x_{n+h-1},$$

one obtains forecasts of x_{n+h} by

$$f_{n,1}^{(x)} = f_{n,1}^{(y)} + x_n,$$
$$f_{n,h}^{(x)} = f_{n,h}^{(y)} + f_{n,h-1}^{(x)}.$$

Provided that the mean of y_t, which is an estimate of b, is nonzero, the sequence of forecasts $f_{n,h}^{(x)}$ for $h = 1, 2, \ldots$ will contain a linear trend.

If the true trend curve is not linear, differencing the series once will not do a complete job of trend removal. There are various ways around this problem. Some trends are "locally linear," that is, can be well approximated over sections by straight lines, in which case differencing will remove most of the trend, but forecasting what remains may be complicated. If the trend is exponential, then by using the logarithm of the data the trend may be made linear and the differencing procedure applied. Finally, if the trend is parabolic in nature, it can be removed by differencing twice. This is seen by taking

$$x_t = a + bt + ct^2.$$

Then

$$\begin{aligned}
y_t &= x_t - x_{t-1} \\
&= a + bt + ct^2 - (a + b(t-1) + c(t-1)^2) \\
&= b + c(t^2 - (t^2 - 2t + 1)) \\
&= b + c + 2tc,
\end{aligned}$$

so that y_t now contains a linear trend which can be removed by differencing y_t.

The use of differencing series to remove trends has become popular again in recent years, after a couple of decades of neglect, and has been found to be effective for most economic data. This point is discussed further in Section 3.7.

2.5 IRREGULARLY RECORDED DATA

Virtually all of the data considered in this book are assumed to be recorded at virtually constant intervals of time, such as each day, week, month, or quarter. However, occasionally the only data available, or the most appropriate, are recorded at irregular intervals. One of the advantages of using least-square regression methods is that they can be used with this type of data, particularly with the simple curves. Consider, for example, the data given in Figure 2.5, which show those years from 1864 to 1975 when the men's mile run was finished in record time together with the world records. The times have reduced from the 4 minutes and 56 seconds by Charles Lawes in 1804 through to the 3:59.4 by Roger Bannister in 1954, and on to the 3:49.4 by John Walker in 1975. The names of the other temporary record holders can be found in the standard reference books. The plot of the data, shown in Fig. 2.5, suggests that a straight line would be an appropriate curve to fit. If the record years are denoted by x_j and the corresponding records by y_j, then the data consist of the pairs (x_j, y_j),

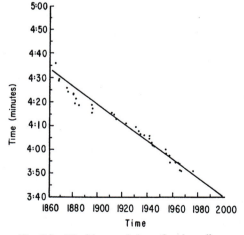

Fig. 2.5 World record times for the mile run.

$j = 1, \ldots, n$. In this case, if the x are recorded as the deviation in years from 1895 and the y's in minutes, then the relationship takes the form

$$y = a + bx + \text{error}.$$

Standard least-squares regression theory finds that a and b are obtained as the solutions to the following equations:

$$\sum_j y_j = na + b \sum_j x_j,$$

$$\sum_j x_j y_j = a \sum_j x_j + b \sum_j x_j^2.$$

In this case, Oakley and Baker (1977) estimated the straight line relationship to be

$$y = 4.33907564 - 0.00644959x.$$

The number of figures shown is far more than usually recorded; a more usual form might be

$$y = 4.339 - 0.0064x.$$

If the world record for the one-mile run continues to evolve at the same rate, then the record will be at almost exactly 3 minutes and 40 seconds by the year 2000, according to either of these equations.

The formula suggests that the record should be at 3 minutes 46 seconds in 1985. The actual record at that time was 3 minutes 46.31 seconds set by Steve Cram.

2.6   THE FORECASTING PROJECT

To summarize the procedure discussed in this chapter that may be applied to the series to be forecast in the project:

(i)   Look at the plot of the data against time and ask if it appears to contain a tendency to generally increase through time (or to generally decrease through time). If it does contain such tendencies then a curve-fitting technique can be used to form a forecast. (However, trend curves are most appropriate for long-run forecasting, whereas the project is an exercise in short-run forecasting. The use of forecasts based on trends in the project should be considered only as practice in the use of the techniques rather than serious forecasts.)

(ii)   From the shape of the plot, use Figure 2.3 and the tables around it to select one or two mathematical curves for fitting.

(iii)   If one has a suitable computer program, estimate the parameters of the curve (using least squares). Otherwise, use the three-point method discussed in the chapter. First change your data to an odd-numbered sample size by dropping the earliest data point if necessary. Then estimate R, S, T from the data and use the formula in Table 2.4 to estimate the parameters of the curves.

(iv)   Using the estimated parameter values, insert higher time t-values than occur in the sample into the curve to obtain forecasts.

For the data provided in Section 1.6, there does not appear to be any trend in the plot of x_t, and so a trend-fitting forecast is not appropriate. However, just for illustration, one could fit a linear trend to the x_t series. As $n = 30$, we chop the first term ($x_1 = -6$), giving a sample of size $n = 29$. (Strictly, this is not necessary when fitting a curve involving just two parameters, such as a straight line.)

$$R = \frac{19 + 2(-5) + 3 \times 10 + 4 \times 8 + 5(-19)}{1 + 2 + 3 + 4 + 5}$$

$$= -24/15 = -1.6$$

$$T = \frac{4 + 2 \times 37 + 3 \times 14 + 4 \times 4 + 5 \times 22}{15}$$

$$= 246/15 = 16.4$$

Fitting the straight line

$$C(t) = a + bt,$$

then from Table 2.4

$$\hat{b} = \frac{(6.4 - (-1.6))}{29 - 5}$$
$$= 0.75$$

and

$$\hat{a} = -1.6 - \frac{11}{3}(0.75)$$
$$= -4.35 \qquad .$$

The curve fitted is thus $C(t) = -4.35 + 0.75t$. $t = 1$ in the curve now corresponds to $t = 2$ in the data set, because the first term was dropped in the calculation. The forecast nine steps ahead is thus:

$$f_{30,9} = -4.35 + 0.75(29 + 9)$$

$$= 24.15 \qquad (1)$$

If a least squares estimate of the straight line is used (as discussed in the Appendix) the line fitted is

$$C(t) = -10.22 + 0.788t \qquad (t = -1.15)(t = 1.59).$$

Neither coefficient is statistically significantly different from zero according to the t-values. The time (t) in this case starts at the beginning of the sample. The nine-step forecast from it is thus:

$$f_{30,9} = -10.22 + 0.788(30 + 9)$$
$$= 20.51 \qquad\qquad (2)$$

However, as the data does not appear to contain a trend, neither of these forecasts can be taken seriously.

QUESTIONS

Data definitions and sources (Table 2.7):

- A   U.S. infant mortality rate (deaths in first year) per 1000 live births.
- B   U.S. per capita consumption of fishery products, pounds of edible meat,
- C   U.S. net production of electrical energy, in billions of kilowatt-hours,
- D   Price of silver, cents per fine ounce, New York.

For the period 1940–1970, the data are taken from *Historical Statistics of the United States, Colonial Times to 1970*. The more recent data are taken from the *Statistical Abstract of the United States, 1985*.

1. Using just the data from the sample period 1940–1965 (Table 2.7) identify and fit trend lines to each of the four series. Do not look at the postsample data when picking trend curves.
   Compare your forecasts for the period 1966–1984 with the actual postsample values. Do you consider the forecasts to have been successful? If no, suggest reasons.
   If instead of using annual data, you had used data for just the odd years (1941, 1943, etc.), would your curves have forecast 1983 significantly worse?

2. Consider the time series

t	1	2	3	4	5	6	7	8	9	10	11	12
x_t	−3	1	0	−1	3	5	6	8	5	11	8	12

TABLE 2.7

Sample Data

Year	Series A	B	C	D
1940	47.0	11.0	179	34
1941	45.3	11.2	208	34
1942	40.4	8.7	233	38
1943	40.3	7.9	267	44
1944	39.4	8.7	279	44
1945	38.3	9.9	271	51
1946	33.8	10.8	269	80
1947	32.2	10.3	307	71
1948	32.0	11.1	336	74
1949	31.3	10.9	345	71
1950	29.2	11.8	388	74
1951	28.4	11.2	433	89
1952	28.4	11.2	463	84
1953	27.8	11.4	514	85
1954	26.6	11.2	544	85
1955	26.4	10.5	629	89
1956	26.0	10.4	684	90
1957	26.3	10.2	716	90
1958	27.1	10.6	724	89
1959	26.4	10.9	797	91
1960	26.0	10.3	844	91
1961	25.3	10.7	881	92
1962	25.3	10.6	946	108
1963	25.2	10.7	1011	127
1964	24.8	10.5	1083	129
1965	24.7	10.9	1157	129

Postsample Data

Year	Series A	B	C	D
1966	23.7	10.9	1249	129
1967	22.4	10.6	1317	154
1968	21.8	11.0	1436	214
1969	20.9	11.2	1552	179
1970	20.0	11.8	1639	177
1971	19.1	11.9	1718	154
1972	18.5	12.4	1853	169
1973	17.7	12.9	1959	256
1974	16.7	12.2	1968	471
1975	16.1	12.2	2003	442
1976	15.2	12.9	2123	437
1977	14.1	12.7	2212	462
1978	13.8	13.4	2785	540
1979	13.1	13.0	2319	1109
1980	12.6	12.8	2286	2063
1981	11.9	12.9	2295	1052
1982	11.5	12.3	2241	795
1983	11.2	13.1	2310	1144
1984 (prelim.)	10.8	13.7	2416	814
1985 (prelim.)	NA	14.5	2469	614

Smooth, using the filter $y_t = 0.5y_{t-1} + 0.5x_t$, fit a straight line by the two-point method, and forecast a value of x_t for $t = 20$.

3. Suppose that you are given a puppy of a rare breed and with a rather unusual shape — low, thin, and long. By observing the puppy's growth during the first few weeks of your ownership, discuss how you would attempt to predict its eventual weight, height, and length.

4. The following table shows the men's world record pole vaults from 1957, when metal poles were introduced, to 1976. Fit a trend curve to these figures. (Only the records standing at the end of record-breaking years are shown.) How well does your curve forecast the value for 1987, when the record was 19 feet $9\frac{1}{4}$ inches?

	Record			Record	
Year	feet	inches	Year	feet	inches
1957	15	$8\frac{1}{4}$	1967	17	$7\frac{1}{4}$
1960	15	$9\frac{1}{4}$	1968	17	9
1961	15	$10\frac{1}{4}$	1969	17	$10\frac{1}{4}$
1962	16	2	1970	18	$\frac{1}{4}$
1963	17	$\frac{3}{4}$	1972	18	$5\frac{3}{4}$
1964	17	4	1975	18	$6\frac{1}{4}$
1966	17	$6\frac{1}{4}$	1976	18	$8\frac{1}{4}$

FURTHER READINGS

Armstrong, J. Scott (1978). *Long-Range Forecasting, from Crystal Ball to Computer*, New York: Wiley.
Wide-ranging discussion, with good, detailed examples.
Martino, J. P. (1983). *Technological Forecasting for Decision Making* (2nd Edition), New York: Amer. Elsevier.
Many excellent examples of trend curve fitting.
Oakley, C. O., and J. C. Baker (1977). "Least Squares and the 3.40 Minute Mile," *Mathematics Teacher* **70** (4), 322–324.

3

Forecasting from
Time Series Models

Some things are so unexpected that no one is prepared for them.
                    Leo Rosten in "Rome Wasn't Burned in a Day"

3.1 WHITE NOISE

Before consideration of how a time series is analyzed and forecast, it is necessary to be introduced to a few simple but important models, that is methods by which a series can be generated. The simplest possible model gives a *purely random series,* otherwise known as *white noise.* This second name comes from engineering and cannot properly be explained without entering the murky environment of a method of analysis known as spectral analysis, so no explanation will be attempted. A series is white noise if it has virtually no discernable structure or pattern to it. If such a series is denoted by ε_t, for all values of t, the formal definition is that this series is white noise if correlation$(\varepsilon_t, \varepsilon_s) = 0$, all $t \neq s$, and if also the mean, or expected value, of ε_t is a constant for all t. It is usual to take this constant to be zero, giving zero-mean white noise.

To appreciate this definition, it is perhaps best to consider some examples of purely random series.

(i)   Suppose you stand on the street corner and record the numbers on the license plates of passing cars. There is very little reason to suppose that there is any relationship between one number observed and the next.

(ii) A teacher asks everyone in his class to write down an integer from 0 to 9 inclusive. If the first twenty students, going across the first row, then the second row, and so forth, read out their numbers, will this help the teacher predict the number that would be read out next? Again, there is likely to be no pattern to the numbers. If the teacher thinks that each integer is equally likely to occur, then all he can predict is that there is a probability of 0.1 that the next number will be a 0, a 1, a 2, etc. The numbers read out by the first few students may suggest to the teacher that certain integers are more likely to occur than others, so he may change his prediction to a statement such as "there is a probability of 0.05 that the next number will be 0, of 0.07 that it will be 1, of 0.11 of it being 2, etc." In this case, the earlier data may be helpful in making his prediction statement, but it is important to note that he will be indifferent between any possible *order* in which these earlier numbers are given to him. A time series has a *structure*, strictly a temporal structure, if the order of the data not only matters but is of paramount importance. Examples will be given later.

(iii) The winning numbers on a state lottery ticket or the British premium bonds, if recorded monthly, make up a white noise series. Having the sequence of past winning numbers will in no way help you predict the next winning number.

(iv) A further example of a white noise series is the winning numbers in the numbers game. This game is, or was, played heavily in the lower income areas of the large eastern U.S. cities. You hand a slip of paper to a bookie with three integers on it, such as 275, plus your bet. If your number comes up, the organizers pay $600 for every $1 bet. The potential profit margin is huge, at about $400 for every $1,000 bet, which probably explains why the game is illegal and is said to be run by major criminal organizations whose names remind one of the Mediterranean. The rules of the game are simple, but how is the winning number to be chosen so that it cannot be "fixed?" The method used is to take the final three digits of the total amount of money bet at some specific horserace track that day, either in New York or Florida. This completely explains why this otherwise entirely useless statistic was historically printed by some New York newspapers.

Table 3.2 (Section 3.8) shows an example of a constructed white noise series. The main properties of these series are that

(i)   there is no correlation between terms, and
(ii) previous values do not help forecast future values.

This second statement needs amending if the white noise has nonzero mean of unknown size, as then the sample mean of the observed values can be used to predict this population mean. Note that the order in which the numbers are observed is of no consequence when forming the sample mean.

If a least-squares criterion is used, it can be shown that the best forecast of all future values of a white noise series is just equal to the series mean.

From a forecasting point of view, a white noise series is rather uninteresting, but it will later be shown to be a particularly important model when evaluating forecasts.

Exercises

1. Suggest two further examples of white noise series other than those mentioned in the text.
2. Do you think that any of the following provide examples of white noise series?
    (a) The number of companies going bankrupt in a month.
    (b) The daily changes in stock market prices.
    (c) The number of runs scored by a baseball team in a sequence of consecutive games (goals scored by a soccer team, points scored by a basketball team, or whatever).
    (d) The number of letters in succeeding words in a novel.
    (e) The number of letters in the names of succeeding months (January = 7, February = 7, March = 5, etc.).
    (f) The total number of telephone calls made in a day in some developed country.

3.2   MOVING AVERAGES

Most series observed in reality, particularly in economics, are much smoother than the white noise shown in Table 3.2. One method of forming smoother series is to use a moving average. If ε_t is a white noise series, a simple moving average is the series x_t generated by

$$x_t = \varepsilon_t + \beta \varepsilon_{t-1}, \tag{1}$$

although a better name would be weighted moving sum. If ε_t has mean zero, then so will x_t. A numerical example of x_t generated in this fashion, with $\beta = \frac{1}{2}$, is shown in Table 3.1A. A larger sample of this series is shown in Table 3.2. Although this particular moving average series could hardly be described as smooth, it is nevertheless smoother than the white noise series. It becomes somewhat smoother yet if β is near unity, but a negative

TABLE 3.1A

t	ε_t	$\frac{1}{2}\varepsilon_{t-1}$	x_t	t	ε_t	$\frac{1}{2}\varepsilon_{t-1}$	x_t
0	0.02	—	—	5	−0.04	−0.09	−0.13
1	−0.12	0.01	−0.11	6	0.00	−0.02	−0.02
2	0.20	−0.06	0.14	7	0.16	0.00	0.16
3	0.06	0.10	0.16	8	0.06	0.08	0.14
4	−0.18	0.03	−0.15				

value of β produces a series that is even less smooth than white noise, as a numerical example would show.

To examine the theoretical properties of this moving average series, values for the correlation between x_t and x_{t-j} are required, the so-called *autocorrelations* of the series, because the series x_t is checked to see if it is correlated with its own past. If two random variables X and Y are correlated, the formula used is

$$\text{corr}(X, Y) = \frac{\text{covariance}(X, Y)}{\sqrt{\text{variance}(X)\,\text{variance}(Y)}},$$

where, if X and Y both have zero mean, the terms used in the ratio are defined, using the expectation notation, by

$$\text{covariance}(X, Y) = E[XY]$$

and

$$\text{variance}(X) = E[X^2],$$

so

$$\text{variance}(Y) = E[Y^2].$$

However, it can be shown that for a moving average series $\text{variance}(x_{t-j}) = \text{variance}(x_t)$, so the autocorrelation formula becomes

$$\text{corr}(x_t, x_{t-j}) = \frac{E[x_t x_{t-j}]}{\text{var}(x_t)}.$$

Note that if x_t is white noise, then all of these autocorrelations are zero, provided $j \neq 0$. By substituting for x_t, x_{t-1} from the generating formula (1), it is seen that

$$E[x_t x_{t-1}] = E[(\varepsilon_t + \beta\varepsilon_{t-1})(\varepsilon_{t-1} + \beta\varepsilon_{t-2})]$$

$$= E[\varepsilon_t \varepsilon_{t-1}] + \beta E[\varepsilon_{t-1}^2] + \beta^2 E[\varepsilon_{t-1}\varepsilon_{t-2}] + \beta E[\varepsilon_t \varepsilon_{t-2}].$$

However, any term such as $E[\varepsilon_t\varepsilon_s]$, $t \neq s$, will be proportional to $\text{corr}(\varepsilon_t, \varepsilon_s)$, which is zero, so this formula simplifies to

$$E[x_t x_{t-1}] = \beta \, \text{var}(\varepsilon_t).$$

It follows that if β is positive, then adjacent terms of x_t will be positively correlated, so that an above average, i.e., positive, x_t will be inclined to be followed by a further above average value, and similarly, a below average term is likely to be followed by a below average value. For a white noise series, $\beta = 0$, an above average value is equally likely to be followed by an above average or a below average value, because of the zero correlation between adjacent terms in the series. If β is negative, then adjacent terms are negatively correlated, so an above average term is likely to be followed by a below average term, and so forth. It should thus be clear why the value of β determines the relative smoothness of the moving average series. These ideas are illustrated in Figure 3.1.

Now consider correlations between nonadjacent terms. To do this, one has to look at

$$E[x_t x_{t-j}] = E[(\varepsilon_t + \beta\varepsilon_{t-1})(\varepsilon_{t-j} + \beta\varepsilon_{t-j-1})],$$

but if the right-hand side is expanded, all the terms are of the form $E[\varepsilon_t\varepsilon_s]$, $t \neq s$, provided $j > 1$, and so

$$E[x_t x_{t-j}] = 0, \qquad j > 1,$$

i.e.,

$$\text{corr}(x_t, x_{t-j}) = 0, \qquad \text{all } j > 1$$

Thus, for the model (1), there is no correlation between the present value of x_t and all previous values apart from the most recent.

Suppose that you are told that a given series has been generated by model (1) and that also you are provided with the value of β, how would this information be used to forecast future values of the series? Further, suppose that the information set available to you is $I_n : x_{n-j}$, that is, just the

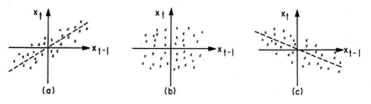

Fig. 3.1 MA(1) scatter plots. (a) $\beta > 0$, (b) $\beta = 0$ (white noise), and (c) $\beta < 0$.

past and present of the series to be forecast and consider the one-step forecast. At time n, you know from (1) that the next value of the x_t series will be generated by

$$x_{n+1} = \varepsilon_{n+1} + \beta\varepsilon_n.$$

Of these two terms, the first is not forecastable, with the information being used, as it is the next term of a white noise series, but the second term is known at time n. It should be clear that the optimum forecast of x_{n+1} is

$$f_{n,1} = \beta\varepsilon_n, \tag{2}$$

and this can be proved more formally. The one-step forecast error is

$$\begin{aligned}
e_{n,1} &= x_{n+1} - f_{n,1} \\
&= (\varepsilon_{n+1} + \beta\varepsilon_n) - \beta\varepsilon_n \\
&= \varepsilon_{n+1}. \tag{3}
\end{aligned}$$

Thus, it is convenient to write

$$\varepsilon_n = x_n - f_{n-1,1},$$

and so (2) becomes

$$f_{n,1} = \beta(x_n - f_{n-1,1}). \tag{4}$$

By using this formula, the whole sequence of one-step forecasts for different values of n can be generated, although there is a starting-up problem. If it is known that the mean of the series to be forecast is zero, it is usual to start up the sequence of forecasts by putting $f_{0,1} = 0$. To see how this works in practice, we look again at the figures in Table 3.1A, for which $\beta = \frac{1}{2}$. The column $x_t - f_{t-1,1}$ in Table 3.1B gives estimates of ε_t, the true values of

TABLE 3.1B

t	x_t	ε_t	$x_t - f_{t-1,1}$ (with $f_{0,1} = 0$)	$f_{t,1} = \frac{1}{2}(x_t - f_{t-1,1})$	x_{t+1}
0	—	0.02	—	0	—
1	−0.11	−0.12	−0.11	−0.055	0.14
2	0.14	0.20	0.195	0.0975	0.16
3	0.16	0.06	0.0625	0.03125	−0.15
4	−0.15	−0.18	−0.18125	−0.0906	−0.13
5	−0.13	−0.04	−0.0394	−0.0197	−0.02
6	−0.02	0.00	−0.0003	−0.00015	0.16
7	0.16	0.16	0.15985	0.0799	0.14
8	0.14	0.06	0.0601	0.03005	—

which are shown in the preceding column. It is seen that in this instance the two columns quickly become virtually identical. The number of figures after the decimal point carried in this table is much greater than can normally be justified but is necessary here to show the speed of convergence of the estimated ε_t terms to the actual values. It should also be noted that the optimum one-step forecast series $f_{t,1}$ does not closely match the terms being forecast, shown in the final column. This is because the error term, which is the unforecastable component of the value being forecast, is relatively important in this case. It is easily seen that

$$\text{var}(x_t) = E(x_t^2) = E[(\varepsilon_t + \beta\varepsilon_{t-1})^2]$$
$$= \text{var}(\varepsilon_t) + \beta^2\,\text{var}(\varepsilon_{t-1}) + 2\beta E[\varepsilon_t\varepsilon_{t-1}]$$
$$= (1 + \beta^2)\,\text{var}(\varepsilon_t).$$

A frequently used measure of the forecastability of a series is R^2, defined by

$$R^2 = 1 - \frac{\text{variance forecast error}}{\text{variance series being forecast}},$$

which in this case becomes

$$R^2 = 1 - \frac{\text{var}(\varepsilon_t)}{(1 + \beta^2)\,\text{var}(\varepsilon_t)} = \frac{\beta^2}{1 + \beta^2},$$

so, if $\beta = \frac{1}{2}$, $R^2 = 0.2$, which might be considered low. Some problems with the interpretation of R^2 will be discussed in Chapter 5.

A second example of moving average generation and the estimation of the innovations ε_t is shown in Table 3.1C.

TABLE 3.1C

(1)	(2)	(3)	(4)	(5)	(6)	(7)
t	ε_t	ε_{t-1}	$0.4\varepsilon_{t-1}$	x_t	$f_{t-1,1} = 0.4\hat{\varepsilon}_{t-1}$	$\hat{\varepsilon}_t = x_t - f_{t-1,1}$
0	8	—	—		—	—
1	−10	8	3.2	−6.8	0	−6.8
2	3	−10	4.0	−1.0	−2.7	1.7
3	7	3	1.2	8.2	0.7	7.5
4	−8	7	2.8	−5.2	3.0	−8.2
5	−5	−8	−3.2	−8.2	−3.3	−4.9
6	10	−5	−2.0	8.0	−2.0	10.0

The model is now

$$x_t = \varepsilon_t + 0.4\, \varepsilon_{t-1}.$$

The columns before the first vertical line give the components that build up to x_t, being the sum of columns (2) and (4). After the second vertical line, the calculations show how ε_t is estimated from knowledge of the true model plus an arbitrary starting point of $f_{t-1,1} = 0$. After six steps it is seen that $\hat{\varepsilon}_t$ converges to the true ε_t value.

Forecasting more than one step ahead proves to be particularly easy for series generated by model (1). At time n you know that x_{n+2}, for instance, will be generated by

$$x_{n+2} = \varepsilon_{n+2} + \beta\varepsilon_{n+1},$$

but both ε_{n+2} and ε_{n+1} are future terms in a white noise series and so are unforecastable. It follows that x_{n+2} is not forecastable, and the optimum forecast is just

$$f_{n,2} = 0,$$

and similarly,

$$f_{n,h} = 0, \qquad h > 1,$$

and $R^2 = 0$ in all these cases. These results should be expected from the observation that $\rho_h = \mathrm{corr}(x_t, x_{t-h}) = 0$ for $h \geq 2$.

A series generated by (1) is called a moving average of order 1, denoted by MA(1), because a single lag term appears on the right-hand side. The obvious generalization is a series generated by

$$x_t = \varepsilon_t + \beta_1\varepsilon_{t-1} + \beta_2\varepsilon_{t-2} + \cdots + \beta_q\varepsilon_{t-q}, \qquad (5)$$

where ε_t is again a zero-mean white noise series. This is called a moving average of order q and denoted MA(q). Using the same approach as with the simple MA(1) model, it is easy to show that

$$\mathrm{corr}(x_t, x_{t-j}) = 0, \qquad j > q,$$

and consequently that the optimum h-step forecast is

$$f_{n,h} = 0 \qquad \text{for} \quad h > q.$$

To consider the one-step forecast made at time n, put $t = n + 1$ in (5) to get

$$x_{n+1} = \varepsilon_{n+1} + [\beta_1\varepsilon_n + \beta_2\varepsilon_{n-1} + \cdots + \beta_q\varepsilon_{n-q+1}].$$

All the terms within the square brackets are known at time n and so these constitute the optimum one-step forecast,

$$f_{n,1} = \beta_1 \varepsilon_n + \beta_2 \varepsilon_{n-1} + \cdots + \beta_q \varepsilon_{n-q+1}, \tag{6}$$

and the one-step forecast error will again be

$$e_{n,1} = x_{n+1} - f_{n,1} = \varepsilon_{n+1}. \tag{7}$$

To actually form the optimum forecast, the values of past and present ε_t are required. These are not directly observed but can be estimated by using (7), so that

$$\hat{\varepsilon}_t = x_t - f_{t-1,1}. \tag{8}$$

After a starting up problem with the early terms these estimated values will usually closely approximate the true ε_t values.

A similar procedure is used to form $f_{n,j}$ for $j \leq q$: One writes down the expression for x_{n+j} and replaces every unknowable, future value of ε_t by zero and all the knowable values by the estimates from (8).

There are a number of ways that a moving average model might arise in the real world. Consider a small commodity market, say the Prickly Pear Commodity Exchange of Uganda, if such a thing existed. A commodity market is a place where buyers and sellers of a metal or an agricultural crop meet and trade. The current selling price might be thought to arise from the classical supply and demand arguments, but in practice there is great uncertainty about future supply by the miners or farmers, and so the users of the market have to maintain inventories of the good. The presence of uncertainty leads to the presence of speculators on the market, which sometimes complicates matters. However, the Uganda Prickly Pear market will probably not have attracted the attention of speculators and suppose that it is currently in equilibrium, so that everyone involved agrees on what should be the correct price at this time. If now some extra, unexpected piece of information reaches the market, for example, that a sudden tropical storm has wiped out half of the entire crop of prickly pears in Cuba or that a research doctor in Baltimore has found that rats regularly washed in prickly pear juice developed skin cancer, then this news item will very likely induce a change in price. If P_t is the price series, the next price might be determined by

$$P_{t+1} = P_t + \varepsilon_{t+1},$$

where ε_{t+1} is the effect on price of the unexpected news item. This may be written

$$y_{t+1} = \varepsilon_{t+1},$$

where y_t is the price change series. However, if the full impact of the news item is not immediately absorbed by the market, the price change on the next day might be formed by

$$y_{t+2} = \varepsilon_{t+2} + b\varepsilon_{t+1},$$

where ε_{t+2} is the effect of yet a further news item and $b\varepsilon_{t+1}$ reflects the reassessment of the earlier piece of news. If a sequence of unexpected news items keep affecting the price on the market and their complete impact takes several days to work out, the price change series will be well represented by a moving average model.

For a further example, consider a maternity hospital. Let ε_t be the number of new patients that arrive on day t and suppose that this is a white noise series, so that the number arriving one day is unrelated to the number coming the next day. Suppose that typically 10% stay just one day, 50% two days, 30% three days, and 10% four days. The number of patients leaving the hospital on day t, x_t, will then be given by

$$x_t = 0.1\varepsilon_{t-1} + 0.5\varepsilon_{t-2} + 0.3\varepsilon_{t-3} + 0.1\varepsilon_{t-4} + \eta_t,$$

where η_t is a white noise error term, because of random variations about the typical situation, so that $x_t \sim \text{MA}(4)$. Thus, one could predict how many patients will be leaving in one, two, three, or four days time but not in seven days time.

Exercises

1. $-0.50 \quad 0.40 -0.81 \quad 0.00 -0.24 -0.36 -0.39 \quad 0.79 \, 0.98 -0.17$
    $0.72 -0.45 \quad 0.52 -0.76 -0.18 -0.83 \quad 0.57 -0.86 \, 0.71 -0.72$

    are the first twenty terms of a white noise series ε_t, $t = 1, \ldots, 20$. Using these values, generate the MA(2) series x_t given by

    $$x_t = \tfrac{1}{3}(\varepsilon_t + \varepsilon_{t-1} + \varepsilon_{t-2})$$

    for $t = 3, \ldots, 20$. From the plots of ε_t and x_t against time, which do you consider to be the smoother in appearance?

2. You are told that the monthly change in sales of paperback books in a certain store obeys an MA(2) model of the form

    $$x_t = \varepsilon_t + 0.6\varepsilon_{t-1} + 0.3\varepsilon_{t-2}$$

    and are given the following recent values for x_t:$x_{20} = 180$, $x_{21} = -120$, $x_{22} = 90$, $x_{23} = 10$.
    (a) What forecast would you have made for x_{20} and x_{21} at time $t = 19$ if you had assumed $\varepsilon_{17} = -10$, $\varepsilon_{18} = 30$, $\varepsilon_{19} = 70$?
    (b) Using these same values for ε_{17}, ε_{18}, and ε_{19}, what do you forecast for x_{24}, x_{25}, x_{26}, and x_{27} at time $t = 23$?

3. Suppose that you are unsure whether a certain series has been generated by an MA(1) or an MA(2) model. How would the value of the

second autocorrelation coefficient ρ_2 help you choose between these alternative models?

4. Prove that the two series x_t and y_t, generated by

$$x_t = \varepsilon_t + 0.8\varepsilon_{t-1}$$

and

$$y_t = \eta_t + 1.25\eta_{t-1},$$

where ε_t, η_t are each zero-mean white noise series and $\text{var}(\varepsilon_t) = 1$, $\text{var}(\eta_t) = 0.64$, have identical variances and autocorrelation sequences ρ_k, $k = 0, 1, 2, \ldots$. Prove that if z_t is generated by

$$z_t = \theta_t + a\theta_{t-1} + b\theta_{t-2},$$

where θ_t is white noise, and if $b \neq 0$, then z_t cannot have the same autocorrelation sequence as x_t and y_t.

3.3 AUTOREGRESSIVE MODELS

An alternative way of producing a series with more structure than white noise is from an iterative generating equation of the form

$$x_t = \alpha x_{t-1} + \varepsilon_t \qquad (9)$$

where ε_t is zero-mean white noise. Given the sequence ε_t, $t = 1, 2, \ldots, n$ and a starting value x_0, the series x_t is formed by repeated application of (9). For example, with $\alpha = 0.5$, $x_0 = 0.16$, we have the values shown in Table 3.1D.

A relationship such as (9) is known as a difference equation and has a solution of the form

$$x_t = x_0\alpha^t + (\varepsilon_t + \alpha\varepsilon_{t-1} + \alpha^2\varepsilon_{t-2} + \cdots + \alpha^{t-1}\varepsilon_1). \qquad (10)$$

That this is a solution to (9) can be seen by writing (10) as

$$x_t = \alpha[x_0\alpha^{t-1} + (\varepsilon_{t-1} + \alpha\varepsilon_{t-2} + \alpha^2\varepsilon_{t-3} + \cdots + \alpha^{t-2}\varepsilon_1)] + \varepsilon_t$$

TABLE 3.1D

t	ε_t	$0.5x_{t-1}$	x_t	t	ε_t	$0.5x_{t-1}$	x_t
0	—	—	0.16	4	-0.18	0.075	-0.105
1	-0.12	0.08	-0.04	5	-0.04	-0.05	-0.09
2	0.20	-0.02	0.18	6	0.00	-0.045	-0.045
3	0.06	0.09	0.15				

and then noting that the expression in the square brackets is the same as (10) but with t replaced by $t - 1$. It can be proved that this is a complete solution to the difference equation.

The series ε_t is interpreted as a sequence of innovations or shocks to the system in the same way that news items affected the commodity market discussed at the end of the previous section. Without these shocks, x_t would equal just the first term in (10), which is a very smooth curve.

Suppose now that the generating mechanism for x_t did not start at time $t = 0$ but at $t = -N$. Then (10) becomes

$$x_t = x_{-N}\alpha^{t+N} + (\varepsilon_t + \alpha\varepsilon_{t-1} + \alpha^2\varepsilon_{t-2} + \cdots + \alpha^{t+N-1}\varepsilon_{-N+1}), \quad (11)$$

where x_{-N} is the starting value. This equation has two quite distinct interpretations depending on whether α lies inside the region from -1 to 1 or outside this region. If N is large and $-1 < \alpha < 1$, then the first term in (11) will be negligible and the weight given to a shock that occurred a long time ago, ε_{-N+1}, will also be extremely small. However, suppose $\alpha > 1$; then the first term in (11) will be large in magnitude and the weights given to distant shocks will be much greater than those given to more recent ones. This second situation is said to correspond to an *explosive model*, since the mean of the series, which is the first term in (11), explodes dramatically as t increases. This is also the case for the variance of x_t. These properties, together with the fact that innovations of the distant past are more important than recent ones, suggest that the model is of little use to approximate economic data and most other series met in practice. When $-1 < \alpha < 1$, the model produces a nonexplosive, or *stationary* series. A more rigorous definition of stationarity will be discussed in Section 3.5. The marginal case when $\alpha = 1$ gives a series that is not explosive but is not really stationary. The series produced by taking $\alpha = 1$ are called random walks and belong to a class that is particularly important in practice and will be dealt with in Section 3.7. For the rest of this section it will be assumed that $-1 < \alpha < 1$ and that N is very large, so that the solution to (9) is effectively

$$x_t = \sum_{j=0}^{\infty} \alpha^j \varepsilon_{t-j}. \quad (12)$$

It should be clear that if ε_t has zero mean, so will x_t. For later use, it should be noted that

$$E[x_t \varepsilon_{t+1}] = 0, \quad (13)$$

as all terms resulting from substituting for x_t from (12) are of the form $E[\varepsilon_s \varepsilon_{t+1}]$, $s < t + 1$, and are all zero as ε_t is white noise.

Squaring both sides of (12) and taking expectations gives

$$\text{var}(x_t) = E[x_t^2] = (1 + \alpha^2 + \alpha^4 + \alpha^6 + \cdots) \text{var}(\varepsilon_t) = \frac{\text{var}(\varepsilon_t)}{1 - \alpha^2} \quad (14)$$

using a well-known summation formula.[1]

The covariance between x_t and x_{t-1}, since this series has zero mean, is

$$\text{cov}(x_t, x_{t-1}) = E[x_t x_{t-1}]$$
$$= E[(\alpha x_{t-1} + \varepsilon_t)(x_{t-1})] \quad \text{[from (9)]}$$
$$= \alpha E[x_{t-1}^2] + E[\varepsilon_t x_{t-1}]$$
$$= \alpha \, \text{var}(x_t),$$

the second term vanishing because of (13). It thus follows that

$$\text{corr}(x_t, x_{t-1}) = \frac{\text{cov}(x_t, x_{t-1})}{\text{var}(x_t)} = \alpha. \quad (15)$$

To achieve this result, the equality of $\text{var}(x_t)$ and $\text{var}(x_{t-1})$ has to be used, which can be proved to be true if $-1 < \alpha < 1$ and the series started up a long time ago.

From (15) it is seen that

$$\text{corr}(x_t, x_{t-1}) > 0 \quad \text{if} \quad \alpha > 0,$$
$$< 0 \quad \text{if} \quad \alpha < 0,$$

so the degree of smoothness of the series is determined by the size of α, that is, most smooth for α near $+1$, very unsmooth for α near -1.

It is also easy to show that

$$\text{corr}(x_t, x_{t-k}) = \alpha^k \quad \text{for all } k,$$

but the proof will be omitted. As there is always some correlation between a value of the series and all future values, it should be expected that something can be forecast for all future time periods.

Forecasting from model (9) is easily achieved. First consider how the next value will be generated when at time n,

$$x_{n+1} = \alpha x_n + \varepsilon_{n+1}.$$

The first term is known, provided we are given a value for α, but the second term is not knowable from the information set $I_n : x_{n-j}, j \geq 0$. Thus the optimum forecast of x_{n+1} is clearly

$$f_{n,1} = \alpha x_n.$$

---

[1] If $|x| < 1$, then $\Sigma_{j=0}^{\infty} x^j = 1/(1 - x)$.

Now consider the value to occur at time $n + 2$, which will be formed by

$$x_{n+2} = \alpha x_{n+1} + \varepsilon_{n+2}.$$

The second term is not knowable and so should be replaced by its optimum forecast made at time n, which is just zero. The first term is not known, but it can be forecast when at time n, giving the two-step forecast

$$f_{n,2} = \alpha^2 x_n.$$

Similarly,

$$x_{n+3} = \alpha x_{n+2} + \varepsilon_{n+3}$$

and replacing x_{n+2} by its forecast $f_{n,2}$ one gets

$$f_{n,3} = \alpha^3 x_n,$$

and so forth, giving in general

$$f_{n,h} = \alpha^h x_n.$$

As α lies between -1 and $+1$, this will be very small for h large, suggesting that the series is always somewhat forecastable but that the effect of the present on the distant future is negligible in extent.

It is worth noting that the one-step forecast error is

$$e_{n,1} = x_{n+1} - f_{n,1} = x_{n+1} - \alpha x_n = \varepsilon_{n+1},$$

so that the sequence of one-step errors is a white noise.

Throughout this section it has been assumed that x_t has zero mean. If this is not so, the mean should be added to the forecasts and x_n replaced by $(x_n - \text{mean})$ in the analysis and the models.

Autoregressive models can arise in various ways. For example, let x_t equal this month's number of employed in a city. Suppose that typically the proportion of last month's unemployed that get jobs within the month is $1 - \alpha$, but that a further number ε_t enter the unemployed and that ε_t is a white noise. It follows that x_t will be given by Eq. (9). This is not necessarily a realistic model for unemployment.

As a second example, consider a tank that contains M units of a mixture of two liquid chemicals, A and B. Let Z_t be the concentration level of A at start of week t, so that

$$Z_t = \frac{\text{total amount of A in tank, week } t}{\text{total amount of chemicals in tank } (= M)}.$$

During each week one unit of the mixture is removed from the tank for use and at the end of each week the tank is topped up from a set of one-unit barrels. Let the concentration level of A in the barrel used in week t be ε_t, a white noise series. Note that $\varepsilon_t \geq 0$, so it is not a zero-mean white noise. The amount of A in the tank at the beginning of week t is MZ_t, and so at the end of the week the amount of A in the tank is $(M-1)Z_t$. To refill, an amount ε_{t+1} of A is added to the tank, so that the amount of A at the start of week $t+1$ will be

$$(M-1)Z_t + \varepsilon_{t+1}$$

and the concentration level is now

$$Z_{t+1} = \frac{M-1}{M} Z_t + \frac{\varepsilon_{t+1}}{M}.$$

These two examples both lead to models similar to (9), which generate series called *autoregressive of order 1*, as just x_t with a single lag occurs on the right-hand side. This is denoted $x_t \sim \mathrm{AR}(1)$. An obvious generalization is a series generated by

$$x_t = \alpha_1 x_{t-1} + \alpha_2 x_{t-2} + \alpha_3 x_{t-3} + \cdots + \alpha_p x_{t-p} + \varepsilon_t$$

and called an autoregressive series of order p, denoted $\mathrm{AR}(p)$. In this case, p starting values are required, $x_{-j}, j = 0, 1, \ldots, p-1$, and then together with the white noise series ε_t the values of x_t are calculated iteratively.

If this model arises and its coefficients are known, it is again easy to use to form forecasts. x_{n+1} will be generated by

$$x_{n+1} = (\alpha_1 x_n + \cdots + \alpha_p x_{n-p+1}) + \varepsilon_{n+1},$$

the last term of which is not knowable at time n, so the optimum forecast is

$$f_{n,1} = \alpha_1 x_n + \cdots + \alpha_p x_{n-p+1}.$$

Similarly, x_{n+2} will be generated by

$$x_{n+2} = \alpha_1 x_{n+1} + (\alpha_2 x_n + \cdots + \alpha_p x_{n-p+2}) + \varepsilon_{n+2}.$$

The last term is not knowable, the term in parentheses is entirely known at time n, and the first term is forecasted by $\alpha_1 f_{n,1}$, so that

$$f_{n,2} = \alpha_1 f_{n,1} + (\alpha_2 x_n + \cdots + \alpha_p x_{n-p+2}).$$

It is obvious how further forecasts are formed: One simply writes down the generating mechanism for the value to be forecast, with everything that is known part of the forecast and everything that is not known replaced by *its* optimum forecast.

As an example, suppose x_t is generated by

$$x_t = 0.5 x_{t-1} + 0.2 x_{t-2} + \varepsilon_t$$

and that

$$x_n = 50, \qquad x_{n-1} = 40;$$

then

$$f_{n,1} = 0.5 \times 50 + 0.2 \times 40 = 33,$$

$$f_{n,2} = 0.5 \times 33 + 0.2 \times 50 = 26.5,$$

$$f_{n,3} = 0.5 \times 26.5 + 0.2 \times 33 = 19.85,$$

$$f_{n,4} = 0.5 \times 19.85 + 0.2 \times 26.5 = 15.225,$$

$$f_{n,5} = 0.5 \times 15.225 + 0.2 \times 19.85 = 11.58,$$

$$\vdots$$

The time series properties of the AR(p) process are quite difficult to determine, but it can be shown that they greatly depend on the largest root of the equation

$$Z^p = \alpha_1 Z^{p-1} + \alpha_2 Z^{p-2} + \cdots + \alpha_{p-1} Z + \alpha_p.$$

Let θ be this largest root and denote by $|\theta|$ the absolute size of this root, so that a positive value is taken if θ is negative and the modulus if θ is a complex root. Theory states that if $|\theta| < 1$, then x_t will not be an explosive series, but if $|\theta| > 1$, it will be explosive. Further, $\text{corr}(x_t, x_{t-k})$ is well approximated for k not small by $A\theta^k$ if θ real and positive or will approximately lie in the region $\pm A|\theta|^k$ otherwise, where A is some constant. This helps determine the shape of the plot of this correlation against k, which is a particularly useful diagram and will be discussed in Section 3.6.

Exercises

1. If you are told that the number of accidents in a factory in month t obeys an AR(1) model of the form

$$x_t = 10 + 0.7x_{t-1} + \varepsilon_t,$$

where ε_t is zero-mean white noise, and that $x_{19} = 20$, $x_{20} = 24$, $x_{21} = 16$, what forecasts would you make
   (a) for x_{22}, x_{23}, and x_{24} at time $t = 21$?
   (b) for x_{23} and x_{24} at time $t = 20$?
2. A company economist believes that a rival firm's quarterly advertising expenditures obey the AR(3) model

$$x_t = 0.2x_{t-1} + 0.6x_{t-2} - 0.3x_{t-3} + \varepsilon_t.$$

If the values for the last three quarters are $x_{10} = 180$, $x_{11} = 140$, and $x_{12} = 200$, forecast expenditures for the next three quarters, $t = 13$, 14, and 15.

3. A time series is constructed on a computer by an AR(1) model. You are told that the series has zero mean, that the second autocorrelation is $\rho_2 = 0.64$, and that $x_{50} = 10$. Forecast x_{51} and x_{52}. Why would knowing the value of ρ_3 help forecast x_{51} but not x_{52}?

4. If a series x_t is generated by

$$x_t = 0.8x_{t-1} + \varepsilon_t,$$

where ε_t is zero-mean white noise with variance 25, find the variances of the one-, two-, and three-step forecast errors, i.e., var($e_{n,h}$), $h = 1, 2$, and 3.

3.4 MIXED AUTOREGRESSIVE-MOVING AVERAGE MODELS

A much wider class of models can be produced by mixing an autoregressive and a moving average, so that x_t is generated by

$$x_t = \alpha_1 x_{t-1} + \alpha_2 x_{t-2} + \cdots + \alpha_p x_{t-p} + y_t, \tag{16}$$

where y_t is a moving average of order q,

$$y_t = \varepsilon_t + b_1 \varepsilon_{t-1} + b_2 \varepsilon_{t-2} + \cdots + b_q \varepsilon_{t-q}.$$

This is a mixed autoregressive-moving average model of order p, q, denoted ARMA(p, q). A specific example is the ARMA(1, 1) generating process

$$x_t = 0.5x_{t-1} + \varepsilon_t + 0.3\varepsilon_{t-1},$$

so that given a starting value for x_0 and the white noise sequence ε_t, x_t is formed iteratively.

Forecasting is straightforward by just using the rules given in the previous two sections, so that in the ARMA(1, 1) example, x_{n+1} is formed by

$$x_{n+1} = 0.5x_n + \varepsilon_{n+1} + 0.3\varepsilon_n.$$

Then

$$f_{n,1} = 0.5x_n + 0.3\varepsilon_n = 0.5x_n + 0.3(x_n - f_{n-1,1})$$

by noting that the one-step forecast error is

$$e_{n,1} = \varepsilon_{n+1},$$

so

$$\varepsilon_n = e_{n-1,1} = x_n - f_{n-1,1}.$$

Further, x_{n+2} is given by

$$x_{n+2} = 0.5x_{n+1} + \varepsilon_{n+2} + 0.3\varepsilon_{n+1}.$$

Both of the last two terms are best forecast by their mean values, which are taken as zero, so

$$f_{n,2} = 0.5f_{n,1},$$

and so forth.

The condition that the process generated by (16) be nonexplosive is exactly the same as that for the general autoregressive process, as discussed in the previous section.

Although these mixed models appear complicated and their statistical properties are difficult to derive, they are of real importance in practice. One reason for this is that there are good theoretical reasons for believing that mixed models are the most likely to be found in the real world, particularly in economics and business. This statement follows from the following theorem, which is stated without proof. If

$$x_t \sim \text{ARMA}(p_1, q_1), \qquad y_t \sim \text{ARMA}(p_2, q_2),$$

x_t, y_t are independent series, and

$$z_t = x_t + y_t,$$

then typically

$$z_t \sim \text{ARMA}(P, Q),$$

where

$$P = p_1 + p_2,$$

$$Q = p_1 + q_2 \quad \text{or} \quad p_2 + q_1, \quad \text{whichever is larger.}$$

It is possible to invent situations where P and Q are less than the values shown here, but these situations are unlikely to occur in practice. To show the relevance of this theorem, suppose that a company makes two products sold to quite independent markets and that the two sales value per month series are x_t and y_t. The total value of sales for the company is then

$$z_t = x_t + y_t.$$

If x_t and y_t are both AR(1) series, but with different parameters, then z_t will be ARMA(2, 1). The condition of independence between x_t and y_t can be relaxed in realistic ways and the general form of the model still hold. As many series in economics and business are *aggregates,* the theorem implies that if each component obeys a simple AR model, then the sum of these components will be ARMA. Equally, if some components are AR and others MA, again their sum is a mixed process. The only case where an ARMA model does not arise is when all the components are moving averages.

Suppose now that some "true" economic series obeys an AR(p) model but that this series can only be observed with a measure error, which might be assumed to be white noise (MA(0)) series. Then the observed series will be ARMA(p, p) according to the above theorem. As virtually all economic and business series contain observation errors, the observed series is seen likely to be ARMA.

As many series are aggregates of components measured with error, the practical importance of ARMA models should be clear.

3.5 STATIONARITY AND INVERTIBILITY[2]

It has been shown in the last few sections that if a time series model is given, it is easily used to form forecasts. However, in practice a model is not given and one just starts with a set of data from which a model has to be derived. The first question to ask is, which model to choose to fit to the data. Should it be a moving average, an autoregressive, a mixed model, or something else? To assist with this decision a number of statistical tools can prove useful, but before these can be introduced and their interpretation discussed, a number of fundamental ideas need to be considered.

Suppose that x_t is a time series with zero mean, so that $E[x_t] = 0$, for all t. Define $\mu_{t,k}$ by

$$\mu_{t,k} = \text{cov}(x_t, x_{t-k}) \equiv E[x_t x_{t-k}].$$

In general, this autocovariance will depend both on the time of observation t and also on k, the distance in time between the two variables being considered, x_t and x_{t-k}. However, a particularly useful class of time series models, known as *stationary* models, arise from assuming that $\mu_{t,k}$ does not depend on t, so that

$$\text{cov}(x_t, x_{t-k}) = \mu_k.$$

This means that the extent to which two terms in the time series are related depends only on the time interval between them and not on time itself.

---

[2] This section is rather technical. A complete understanding of its contents is not necessary for what follows.

Essentially, this means that the generating function for the series does not itself change through time. Thus, for example, if x_t were generated by the equation

$$x_t = \varepsilon_t + b(t)\varepsilon_{t-1}$$

and the parameter $b(t)$ alters with time, then the series would not be stationary. It should be noted that one implication of the definition of stationarity is that the variance of the series, which is μ_0, also is time invariant. The definition of stationarity just given assumes that the series has zero mean, but this assumption can be replaced with no difficulty by one that takes the mean to be a constant for all time.

There are many ways in which a series encountered in the real world can be nonstationary, but the most important is that where the mean or level of the series is not a constant. This situation, known as *trend in mean*, was considered in Chapter 2. If a suitable trend curve can be found or if trend in mean can be effectively removed by differencing the series, then this particular form of nonstationarity can be removed. It is also quite common to meet series whose variability is changing through time, called a *trend in variance*. Such series can often be made stationary, or more nearly so, by considering the logarithms of the series values, which usually transfer the trend in variance to one in mean. More complicated types of nonstationarity can also occur but require techniques of such complexity and sophistication to handle them that they are not considered here.

Most series met in economics and business are probably nonstationary but can be made sufficiently near to stationarity for purposes of forecasting by removal of trend in mean by curve fitting or differencing, possible after taking logarithms, as discussed in Chapter 2. Why is the assumption of stationarity, or of achieved stationarity, such an important one? The main reason is the existence of a remarkable theorem.

Wold's Theorem. Any stationary series can be considered to be the sum of two parts, a self-deterministic component and a moving average of possibly infinite order.

It will be recalled that a self-deterministic series is one that can be forecast perfectly, that is, without error, from its own past. It is now widely accepted that virtually all series arising in business and economics do not contain a self-deterministic component, except possibly a seasonal part, which is discussed later in Section 4.1. If this is so, then a nonseasonal series can always be represented by a MA(∞) model. In practice, this does not get us very far, except for the strong belief that all actual MA(∞) models that arise in practice can be very well approximated by either a MA(q), AR(p), or ARMA(p', q') models with at least one of these models having a modest number of parameters, so that one of q, p, or $p' + q'$ will not be large. If this is accepted, it now means that, given stationarity, the models considered above are sufficient to represent any series and so no further models need to be considered.[3]

It was shown in Section 3.3 that an AR(1) model could always be "solved" to provide an equivalent MA(∞) model and any AR(p) can be similarly represented. A condition was also given to ensure that the moving average form was nonexplosive, the stationarity condition. If the AR(p) model obeys this condition, then it will generate a stationary series. Precisely the same condition applied to the autoregressive part of an ARMA(p, q) model will also ensure both stationarity and the correspondance of this mixed model to a nonexplosive MA(∞) model.

It can easily be shown that all moving average models of finite order are stationary. However, there is an alternative condition that has to apply to a moving average model to make it useful for forecasting purposes, known as *invertibility*. Consider the MA(1) model

$$x_t = \varepsilon_t + b\varepsilon_{t-1}, \tag{17}$$

which can be considered as a difference equation for the ε_t series and has solution

$$\varepsilon_t = x_t - bx_{t-1} + b^2 x_{t-2} - b^3 x_{t-3} + \cdots + (-b)^k x_{t-k} + \cdots, \tag{18}$$

as can be checked by substituting this expression and the corresponding one for ε_{t-1} into (17). It should be noted that in practice we only directly observe the x_t series and the ε_t's can only be estimated by an equation such as (18). Clearly, if b is larger than, or equal to, unity in magnitude, the weights given to more and more distant x_t values will increase in size, and again an explosive solution results, meaning that current ε_t cannot be estimated from past x_t. If a nonexplosive solution such as (18) is found, the moving average is said to be invertible. For the MA(1) model, the condition for invertibility is just that b is less than unity in magnitude, i.e., $b < 1$, ignoring the sign of b. For the MA(q) model,

$$x_t = \varepsilon_t + b_1 \varepsilon_{t-1} + \cdots + b_q \varepsilon_{t-q},$$

where the invertibility condition is that the root with the largest magnitude of the equation

$$Z^q + b_1 Z^{q-1} + \cdots + b_q = 0$$

---

[3] This is not strictly true. What is really being said is that no other *linear* models need be considered. Discussion of nonlinear models takes us into too deep water for a text of this level.

should have magnitude less than 1. A theorem concerning invertibility is mentioned in Section 3.7.

3.6   THE CORRELOGRAM AND PARTIAL CORRELOGRAM

Suppose that you are considering fitting either an AR(1) or a MA(1) model to some data. In practice, of course, it would be rare to consider only these two models, as other alternatives would also need to be considered, but to provide an example this pair will do. Which model should be chosen? A diagram that may well prove helpful in making this choice is the plot of the autocorrelations

$$\rho_k = \mathrm{corr}(x_t, x_{t-k})$$

or their estimates

$$r_k = \frac{\sum_{t-k+1}^{n} (x_t - \bar{x})(x_{t-k} - \bar{x})}{\sum_{t-1}^{n} (x_t - \bar{x})^2}, \qquad \text{where} \quad \bar{x} = \frac{1}{n} \sum_{t-1}^{n} x_t,$$

against k. The first of these plots is known as the *theoretical correlogram* and the second is the *estimated correlogram*.

It was shown in Sections 3.2 and 3.3 that the AR(1) model

$$x_t = ax_{t-1} + \varepsilon_t$$

has

$$\rho_k = a^k, \qquad k = 0, 1, 2, \ldots,$$

and the MA(1) model

$$x_t = \varepsilon_t + b\varepsilon_{t-1}$$

has

$$\rho_1 = \frac{b}{1 + b^2}, \qquad \rho_k = 0, \quad k = 2, 3, \ldots.$$

Figures 3.5 and 3.6 (Section 3.8) show the theoretical and estimated correlograms for the AR(1) model with $a = 0.5$ and for the MA(1) model with $b = 0.5$, with the estimated curves based on a generated series of length $n = 200$. The plots are seen to be quite different in shape, although the difference is naturally rather less clear cut for the estimated correlogram. Returning now to the problem of choosing between an AR(1) or an MA(1) model, if the data are used to form a correlogram and if the resulting diagram is similar in shape to one of these in Figure 3.5 or 3.6, the appropriate model can be selected and fitted. This process of selecting what seems to be an appropriate model has been called the *identification* stage in model building.

The estimated correlogram is an important tool in identification, because the theoretical correlogram takes distinctive shapes for AR(p) and MA(q) models. The AR(p) model has autocorrelations ρ_k which, for large enough k, are approximated by

$$\rho_k = A\lambda^k,$$

where λ is some constant less than 1 in magnitude, although it can be negative, and A is a positive constant also less than 1. This means that for large enough k, particularly $k \geq p$, the correlogram will either decline steadily or will be bounded by a pair of declining curves, as shown in Fig. 3.2. For the MA(q) model, the theoretical correlogram has a particularly distinctive shape, being zero for all $k > q$ but having no clear shape for $k \leq q$. An example is shown in Fig. 3.3.

It is clear that, in theory at least, the correlogram should enable one to both identify between an AR(p) and an MA(q) model, and an expert will be able to make a good guess at p or q. In practice, the decisions are not always so easily made, so a second diagram should also be considered, known as the *partial correlogram*.

To appreciate this second curve, consideration has to be given to the estimation of the parameters of an autoregressive model for a zero-mean series. First note that for the AR(1) model

$$x_t = a_{11}x_{t-1} + \varepsilon_t$$

we have

$$\rho_1 = a_{11},$$

and so an estimate of a_{11} is just r_1, the estimate of ρ_1. For the AR(2) model

$$x_t = a_{21}x_{t-1} + a_{22}x_{t-2} + \varepsilon_t$$

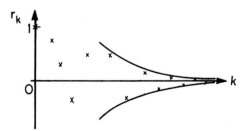

Fig. 3.2 Correlogram for AR(p).

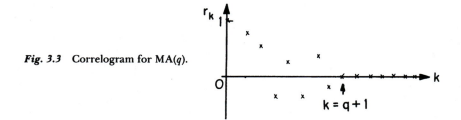

Fig. 3.3 Correlogram for MA(q).

it can be shown (by multiplying through by x_{t-1}, x_{t-2} and taking expectations) that the following two equations hold:

$$\rho_1 = a_{21} + a_{22}\rho_1$$

and

$$\rho_2 = a_{21}\rho_1 + a_{22}.$$

By replacing ρ_1 and ρ_2 by their estimates, r_1 and r_2, these equations can be solved to give estimates for a_{21} and a_{22}. Similarly, for the AR(3) model

$$x_t = a_{31}x_{t-1} + a_{32}x_{t-2} + a_{33}x_{t-3} + \varepsilon_t$$

the following three equations hold:

$$\rho_1 = a_{31} + a_{32}\rho_1 + a_{33}\rho_2,$$

$$\rho_2 = a_{31}\rho_1 + a_{32} + a_{33}\rho_1,$$

$$\rho_3 = a_{31} + \rho_2 + a_{32}\rho_1 + a_{33}.$$

Once more, replacing the ρ's by their estimates, the equations can be solved to give estimates of the a_{3j}'s, $j = 1, 2, 3$. In general, the AR(p) model

$$x_t = a_{p1}x_{t-1} + a_{p2}x_{t-2} + \cdots + a_{pj}x_{t-j} + \cdots + a_{pp}x_{t-p}$$

gives rise to equations

$$\rho_s = a_{p1}\rho_{s-1} + a_{p2}\rho_{s-2} + \cdots + a_{pj}\rho_{s-j} + \cdots + a_{pp}\rho_{s-p},$$

noting that $\rho_{-m} = \rho_m$ by definition. These equations are called the *Walker–Yule equations* and are used to provide estimates for the a_{pj}'s by replacing ρ's by r's and solving. Suppose we want to fit an autoregressive model, but are not sure of what order to use; then we could first fit a first-order model, then a second-order one, then a third-order, and so forth. Denote by $\hat{a}_{kk}$ the estimate of the coefficient of x_{t-k} when a kth-order autoregressive is fitted; then the plot of $\hat{a}_{kk}$ against k is called the *partial correlogram*. The name derives from the interpretation that $\hat{a}_{kk}$ is the estimated correlation between x_t and x_{t-k}, after the effects of all intermediate x's on this correlation are taken out. If the true model is AR(p), then it is clear that the true value of a_{kk} is zero for $k > p$. For example, if $p = 2$, then fitting a third-order model should give a zero coefficient to x_{t-3} as this term does not enter into the model. Thus, the theoretical shape of the partial correlogram for an AR(p) model is distinctive, being exactly the same as that for the correlogram (not partial) for an MA(p) model. Interestingly enough, the theoretical shape of the partial correlogram for an MA(q) model is exactly the same as the correlogram for an AR(q) model.

To summarize the rules for identification:

(i) If the correlogram "cuts off" after some point, say $k = q$, then the appropriate model is MA(q).

(ii) If the partial correlogram "cuts off" after some point, say $k = p$, then the appropriate model is AR(p).

(iii) If neither diagram cuts off at some point, but does decline towards zero in some steady fashion, the appropriate model is ARMA(p', q') for some p', q'.

There is thus seen to be a chance of identifying the appropriate model and even of providing an initial guess at the orders of the models in some cases. The rules are illustrated in simplified form in Fig. 3.2–3.4.

To become an expert in these rules and a few others to be discussed below requires a great deal of experience in data analysis. They outline a process that can only be acquired by considering many examples and learning from one's mistakes. It has been said to be so difficult that it should never be tried for the first time. This is perhaps a little too pessimistic and it is hoped that this section will at least give a feel for the kind of evidence that expert model builders use when deciding on a model.

An appendix to this chapter reviews the AR(1) and MA(1) models.

3.7 THE BOX–JENKINS APPROACH TO MODEL BUILDING

A specific approach to model building has been proposed by Box and Jenkins (1970) and has proved to be very useful. To ease discussion, it will

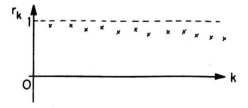

Fig. 3.4 Correlogram that requires differencing.

initially be assumed that the series considered has no seasonal component. This assumption is eased in Section 4.1. There are three stages to be used in model building:

(i)   *identification*, which is the choice of one or of just a few models that seem appropriate for further consideration,

(ii) *estimation*, in which the parameters of the models are estimated from the data, and

(iii) *diagnostic checking*, which involves applying various tests to see if the model(s) selected and estimated do really fit the data adequately, or if further models should be considered.

Let us consider these three stages in turn.

3.7.1   Identification

If the series being considered is stationary, one tries to use the correlogram and the partial correlogram to choose an appropriate model, as discussed in the previous section. With some practice, it is not too difficult to convince oneself that at most a couple of models are likely. If a single model cannot be selected at this point, then all of the alternative models should be retained. It is common for anyone considering identification for the first time to choose too high orders for his models, so that either p, q, or $p' + q'$ are about 5 or more rather than 1, 2, or 3. It is generally thought to be good policy to at least start with simple, low-order models and then move to higher-order ones only if the diagnostic stage suggests that this is necessary. This preference for simple models over more complicated ones, called *parsimonious parametrization* by Box and Jenkins, is based not on a belief that the world is necessarily simple but on the more pragmatic reason that a model with few parameters will be more satisfactorily estimated than one having many parameters. In what follows, if two models appear to fit the data equally well, the one with the fewest parameters will always be preferred. A specific example of the use of the identification procedure is given in the following section.

In practice, few series met with in business or economics appear to be stationary, but rather most contain either trends or long swings. This is particularly true when the series is a *level*, such as price, unemployment, or production, rather than a *rate* of change or return. To make such series amenable to the use of our identification procedure, Box and Jenkins strongly advocate differencing the data. To check whether or not differencing is required, the correlogram of the raw data is calculated and plotted. If this plot declines rather slowly, then differencing is indicated. In theory, a series that needs to be differenced to produce a stationary series has autocorrelations near unity for all lags, but in practice, as estimated autocorrelations are used based on a finite sample, the correlogram might look like Fig. 3.4. If, after differencing, the correlogram *still* has this shape, the series should be differenced once more, although it is rather rare for economic series to need to be differenced more than once. It is also rare for levels to require differencing less than once. Suppose that the series is differenced d times before an interpretable correlogram of the kind discussed in the previous section is achieved and that the resulting series is identified to be ARMA(p', q'). The original series is then said to be an integrated mixed autoregressive-moving average series, denoted ARIMA(p', d, q').

3.7.2 Estimation

In the sections above dealing with the moving average and autoregressive models, expressions were derived for autocorrelations given the coefficients of the models. For example, the first autocorrelation ρ_1 is given by

$$\rho_1 = a \tag{19}$$

for the AR(1) model

$$x_t = ax_{t-1} + \varepsilon_t \tag{20}$$

and by

$$\rho_1 = \frac{b}{1 + b^2} \tag{21}$$

for the MA(1) model

$$x_t = \varepsilon_t + b\varepsilon_{t-1}, \tag{22}$$

where ε_t is white noise in each case. The estimation of parameters is achieved by reversing this process — given the autocorrelations, equations are obtained that can be solved for the parameters. Of course, in practice the actual autocorrelations for the models are not known but can be estimated from the available data, ρ_k being estimated by

$$r_k = \frac{\sum_{t=1}^{n-k} (x_t - \bar{x})(x_{t+k} - \bar{x})}{\sum_{t=1}^{n} (x_t - \bar{x})^2}.$$

If n is reasonably large, greater than 30 say, quite acceptable estimates are achieved for k not too big. Thus, for example, from (19) the estimate of a is

$$\hat{a} = r_1$$

and from (21) estimates of b are

$$\hat{b} = \frac{1 \pm \sqrt{1 - 4r_1^2}}{2r_1}. \tag{23}$$

It is interesting to note that for a MA(1) model $\rho_1 \leq \frac{1}{2}$, so, in theory at least, $\hat{b}$ should be real. It is also clear from (23) that two alternative estimates of $\hat{b}$ occur, but it can be shown that only *one* of these corresponds to an invertible moving average model, as discussed in Section 3.6. As for forecasting purposes, it is essential to have an invertible moving average, and so the value of b that gives an invertible model is always strongly preferred. A more general theorem is available when estimating the coefficients of an MA(q) model. Using the equations for $\rho_1, \rho_2, \ldots, \rho_q$ and replacing these quantities by their estimates $r_1, r_2, \ldots, r_q$ one gets q nonlinear equations for the coefficients $b_1, b_2, \ldots, b_q$ of the MA(q) model. There are many possible solutions for these parameters but *only one* solution set gives an invertible model. The computer programs available for solving the equations will always provide this invertible form. For low-order models, it is not too difficult to obtain estimates of parameters, but as orders increase the process soon becomes too complicated for analytical solutions and a computer program becomes necessary.

Once a model has been estimated, it can be taken to be a true model and forecasts formed in the manner discussed in earlier sections of this chapter. However, before using these forecasts, it is important to check that the model achieved is a satisfactory one. This is done by use of diagnostic checks.

3.7.3 Diagnostic Checking

The best way to investigate if a model is fitting the data satisfactorily is to see how well it performs outside of the sample period. That is, one set of data is used to identify and estimate a model and a later set is used to check how good the model is. However, frequently the amount of data available is insufficient for this approach to be used, so that models are identified, estimated, and diagnostically checked over the same data set. The usual test is to fit a model, estimate the residuals from it, form the correlogram of these residuals, and then see if this correlogram suggests that the residuals are a white noise as they should be. If the residuals had been formed from post-sample data, this would be a useful test, but when the sample is used for all purposes this test is rather weak and lacking in power. The best available approach seems to be to fit a slightly higher-order model and then to see if the extra parameters are significantly different from zero.

For instance, if the model fitted is ARMA(1, 1), then the test involves fitting ARMA(2, 1) and ARMA(1, 2) models and then looking carefully at the coefficients of the extra terms. Details of how this should be done can be found in more specialized texts, such as those by Box and Jenkins (1970), Nelson (1973), and Granger and Newbold (1977).

Some numerical examples of the techniques discussed in Sections 3.6 and 3.7 are presented in the following section.

3.8 NUMERICAL EXAMPLES

In this section the correlograms and partial correlograms for six series are discussed. Five of these series were generated on a computer by the models discussed earlier in this chapter and the sixth series consists of real economic data. The six series are

E. white noise, with zero mean and a variance of 1;

F. MA(1) $x_t = \varepsilon_t + b\varepsilon_{t-1}$, with $b = 0.5$, ε_t white noise;

G. AR(1), $x_t = ax_{t-1} + \varepsilon_t$, with $a = 0.5$;

H. AR(2), $x_t = 0.7x_{t-1} + 0.2x_{t-2} + \varepsilon_t$;

J. ARIMA(0, 1, 1), $x_t - x_{t-1} = \varepsilon_t + 0.6\varepsilon_{t-1}$, so that differenced x_t is MA(1);

K. U.S. Index of Industrial Production, monthly data from January 1948 to October 1974, so that there are $n = 322$ terms.

The generated series were constructed for $t = 1 - 200$ for $E - G$ and for $t = 1 - 300$ for series H and J, and the last 50 terms are shown in Table 3.2, together with the last 50 terms of series K.

As we look at the data listings in Table 3.2 some of the series are seen to be smooth, varying little from one term to the next, particularly series $H - K$, whereas others vary greatly, including frequent changes in sign, particularly series E, with series F and G being intermediate.

Table 3.3 shows the estimated correlograms and partial correlograms derived from the full series. The theoretical values for the correlations of series E are all zero, as it is a white noise series, and the estimated values are seen to be generally small in absolute value. However, a question arises in deciding what is "small." It is well known in statistical theory that if a population parameter has true value zero, then estimates of this parameter from a sample of finite size will be near zero but are unlikely to take exactly the value zero. The standard deviation of these estimates about the true parameter value is known as the standard error, and one would generally expect most of these estimates to be in the region from $-2 \times$ (standard error) to $+2 \times$ (standard error). In the present context, if the true corre-

TABLE 3.2

Fifty Terms of Sample Series[a]

k	E	F	G	H	J	K
0	0.50	—	—	—	—	—
1	−0.41	−0.16	2.29	−3.79	26.15	106.3
2	1.46	1.26	0.32	−4.47	26.37	103.7
3	1.91	2.64	−1.53	−4.94	25.00	102.8
4	0.88	1.84	−0.59	−4.56	24.78	104.9
5	−0.54	−0.10	0.91	−2.16	24.71	105.5
6	−0.44	−0.71	−0.06	−3.49	25.16	106.0
7	0.47	0.25	−1.97	−3.27	24.17	106.0
8	0.22	0.45	0.14	−2.63	22.37	106.5
9	0.68	0.78	−0.44	−1.47	21.09	107.4
10	0.27	0.61	0.19	−1.56	19.69	107.4
11	1.07	1.21	0.60	−0.85	16.99	106.7
12	−1.08	−0.55	0.18	−1.82	14.93	105.6
13	0.42	−0.12	1.29	−0.37	13.26	107.1
14	1.39	1.60	0.25	−0.37	11.56	106.8
15	0.54	1.23	−1.48	−0.71	11.11	107.4
16	−2.66	−2.39	−1.11	−0.11	10.72	108.1
17	0.65	−0.68	−1.90	1.05	9.66	108.7
18	−3.34	−3.02	−0.57	−2.52	9.85	110.0
19	−1.55	−3.22	−2.05	−2.40	10.97	111.6
20	−0.90	−1.68	−2.56	−0.39	8.39	132.2
21	1.57	1.12	−0.89	−0.58	6.58	113.8
22	−0.07	0.72	0.38	0.92	5.30	114.4
23	0.13	0.10	0.22	0.49	5.33	115.1
24	1.90	2.00	0.41	1.32	5.87	116.3
25	−1.05	−0.10	1.66	0.89	6.08	117.6
26	−1.98	−2.50	−0.02	1.90	6.43	119.2
27	−0.05	−1.04	0.64	1.40	7.89	120.2
28	−2.04	−2.07	1.01	1.01	8.59	121.1
29	−0.52	−1.54	−0.33	1.62	7.82	122.2
30	0.95	0.69	0.26	1.41	7.14	123.4
31	−0.40	0.08	3.61	−1.05	7.35	123.7
32	1.04	0.84	2.58	−1.15	6.74	124.1
33	−0.32	0.21	0.32	−0.65	7.57	124.9
34	0.16	0.00	0.27	−1.34	7.61	125.6
35	−0.01	0.07	2.29	−0.86	6.56	126.7
36	−1.58	−1.58	1.11	0.50	8.03	126.5
37	−0.44	−1.23	0.39	−1.10	10.24	126.8
38	1.46	1.24	−1.12	−1.05	10.91	127.6
39	−0.03	0.70	−0.44	−1.28	10.21	127.5
40	−0.35	−0.36	0.60	−1.94	9.35	126.5
41	1.17	1.00	0.14	−2.30	8.07	125.4
42	−1.86	−1.27	−0.36	−3.51	6.86	124.6
43	0.50	−0.43	0.79	−1.49	6.41	124.7
44	−0.58	−0.33	1.72	−2.22	7.40	124.9
45	0.78	0.49	1.93	−2.43	8.71	125.7
46	0.71	1.10	0.29	−2.23	8.86	125.8
47	−0.50	−0.15	−0.95	−0.82	9.05	125.5
48	0.57	0.32	−0.73	−0.24	7.76	125.2
49	−0.46	−0.17	−0.64	0.08	7.36	125.6
50	0.47	0.24	1.19	0.68	7.77	124.9

[a] *Note:* As the numbers shown are the last 50 terms, they are at times $n − 50 + k$, where n is the sample size and k is shown in the first column.

TABLE 3.3

Estimated Correlograms and Partial Correlograms[a]

	Lag												Standard error
	1	2	3	4	5	6	7	8	9	10	11	12	
Series E													
Correlation	0.13	−0.05	0.00	−0.01	0.08	0.04	−0.02	0.01	−0.05	−0.08	−0.02	0.06	0.07
Partial Corr.	0.13	−0.08	0.02	−0.02	0.09	0.01	−0.01	0.02	−0.05	−0.07	−0.01	0.07	0.07
Series F													
Correlation	0.42	0.03	−0.03	−0.12	−0.15	−0.11	−0.06	0.02	0.05	0.07	0.02	−0.10	0.07
Partial Corr.	0.42	−0.18	0.04	−0.14	−0.05	−0.05	−0.01	0.04	−0.00	0.04	−0.06	−0.09	0.07
Series G													
Correlation	0.58	0.35	0.21	0.13	0.02	−0.03	0.05	0.04	0.08	0.05	−0.08	−0.06	0.07
Partial Corr.	0.58	0.03	−0.01	0.01	−0.09	−0.03	−0.03	0.08	0.04	0.01	−0.12	0.01	0.07
Series H													
Correlation Levels	0.90	0.84	0.78	0.71	0.66	0.61	0.57	0.53	0.49	0.45	0.42	0.37	0.06
Differences	−0.23	0.03	−0.01	−0.01	−0.08	0.03	−0.04	−0.01	0.03	−0.06	0.08	−0.03	0.06
Partial Corr. Levels	0.90	0.19	−0.01	−0.03	−0.02	0.06	−0.02	0.01	−0.00	−0.04	0.03	−0.09	0.06
Differences	−0.23	−0.02	−0.00	−0.02	−0.10	−0.01	−0.04	−0.03	0.02	−0.06	0.06	−0.01	0.06
Series J													
Correlation Levels	0.98	0.95	0.92	0.89	0.86	0.84	0.81	0.78	0.75	0.72	0.69	0.66	0.06
Differences	0.42	−0.01	0.04	0.07	0.02	−0.08	−0.08	0.05	0.13	0.02	−0.06	0.03	0.06
Partial Corr. Levels	0.98	−0.21	0.07	0.01	−0.05	−0.03	0.03	0.01	−0.10	−0.06	−0.01	0.01	0.06
Differences	0.42	−0.06	−0.04	−0.10	0.01	−0.03	0.05	0.03	0.02	−0.08	−0.03	−0.07	0.06
Series K													
Correlation Levels	0.99	0.98	0.97	0.96	0.95	0.94	0.93	0.92	0.91	0.90	0.89	0.88	0.06
Differences	0.40	0.21	0.15	0.11	0.03	0.06	0.07	0.04	0.07	0.05	−0.03	−0.19	0.06
Partial Corr. Levels	0.99	−0.04	−0.02	−0.02	−0.01	−0.01	−0.00	−0.01	−0.02	−0.02	−0.03	−0.02	0.06
Differences	0.40	0.06	0.06	0.02	−0.04	0.05	0.03	−0.01	0.05	−0.01	−0.08	−0.20	0.06

[a] *Note*: Throughout this table and section "correlation" is used for "autocorrelation" for convenience.

lation is zero, it is usual to expect that its estimate should be in the region $\pm 2/\sqrt{n}$, where n is the sample size. Thus, for series $E-G$ n is 200 and $2/\sqrt{n} = 0.14$, so estimates should lie in the region from -0.14 to 0.14. Other standard errors, using this same formula, are shown in Table 3.3, although it should be pointed out that the formula is, at best, rather approximate.

The correlations for series E are all seen to be in the region ± 0.14, although that for lag 1 is only just in this region. Thus, the estimates agree with the true zero values. In this instance, the partial correlations are of no interest as all the required information, which tells about how the series should be identified, is in the correlations.

For an MA(1) series, such as F, all autocorrelations are zero except for that at lag 1, and the estimated correlations are seen to have exactly this pattern. Thus, an MA(1) model is easily identified. The MA(1) model

$$x_t = \varepsilon_t + b\varepsilon_{t-1}$$

has first autocorrelation equal to $b/(1 + b^2)$. The estimated autocorrelation with lag 1 is 0.42, and this formula gives an estimate for b of 0.565, which compares well with the true value of 0.5 used to actually generate the series. Apart from the correlation at lag 1, all of the others are small and in the region ± 0.14, or at least very nearly so. The value of -0.15 at lag 5 is just outside this region but is not really large enough to alter the identification of an MA(1) model, which is simple compared to an alternative model, such as MA(5). Once more, the partial correlogram is not relevant as it is not needed for model identification.

Series G is AR(1) and the theoretical value of its autocorrelation of lag k is $(0.5)^k$, so that the theoretical sequence is 0.5, 0.25, 0.125, 0.0625, and the rest very small (Fig. 3.5). The estimated values (Fig. 3.6) follow this pattern fairly well, although by no means exactly. The partial correlations are particularly designed to help identify autoregressive models. For an AR(1) model, the partial autocorrelations should be small except for lag 1 and the estimated values show exactly this pattern, so the correct model is easily identified. The coefficient of an AR(1) model is estimated by the autocorrelation of lag 1, which in this case is 0.58, and this value compares well with the true parameter value of 0.5.

Series H is AR(2) of form

$$x_t = 0.7x_{t-1} + 0.2x_{t-2} + \varepsilon_t. \tag{24}$$

The correlogram for the series, denoted by "levels" in Table 3.3, is seen to be smooth and to decline rather slowly as lag increases. From the rules given earlier in this chapter, autocorrelation values suggest that the differ-

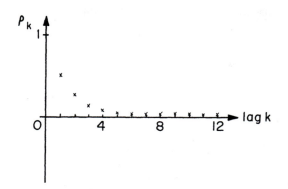

Fig. 3.5 Theoretical correlogram AR(1) series G.

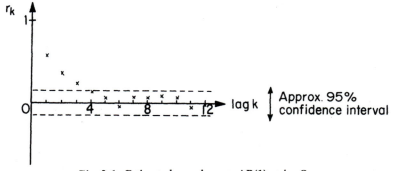

Fig. 3.6 Estimated correlogram AR(1) series G.

enced series be considered. Suppose we do that and look at the correlogram and partial correlation of the differences, which are also shown in Table 3.3. Both of these sets of numbers have a significant value at lag 1 and small values at all of the other lags shown. This suggests that the difference series could either be AR(1) or MA(1).[4] Suppose that the first of these is chosen; then the identified and estimated model would be

$$x_t - x_{t-1} = -0.23(x_{t-1} - x_{t-2}) + \varepsilon_t, \qquad (25)$$

as the first autocorrelation of the differenced series is -0.23. Rearranging

---

[4] It is easy to show that the AR(1) model $x_t = ax_{t-1} + \varepsilon_t$ and the MA(1) model $x_t = \varepsilon_t + a\varepsilon_{t-1}$ have correlograms and partial correlograms very similar in appearance if a is fairly small, say 0.3 or less.

the terms in this expression gives

$$x_t = 0.77x_{t-1} + 0.23x_{t-2} + \varepsilon_t, \tag{26}$$

which is seen to be quite similar to the true model of series H. Alternatively, one could say that the correlogram dies out sufficiently fast for differencing not to be required. If we now look at the partial correlogram for levels, the first two values look significant, being outside the range ± 0.12, and all other values are small, suggesting identification of an AR(2) model, which would be correct.

If we try to estimate the AR(2) model

$$x_t = a_{21}x_{t-1} + a_{22}x_{t-2} + \varepsilon_t, \tag{27}$$

it will be recalled that the partial autocorrelation with lag 2 is an estimate of a_{22}, so that this estimate is 0.19, which is very near the true value of 0.2. It will also be recalled from Section 3.6 that, if r_k is the kth autocorrelation, then for the AR(2) model one has the equation

$$r_1 - a_{21} - a_{22}r_1 = 0.$$

Using $r_1 = 0.90$, from Table 3.3, and the estimate of a_{22} just achieved, one finds the estimate of a_{21} to be 0.73, which is again near the true value of 0.7. Thus, the alternative identified and estimated model is

$$x_t = 0.73x_{t-1} + 0.19x_{t-2} + \varepsilon_t. \tag{28}$$

With the information given in Table 3.3 for series H, it is difficult to decide which of the two models (26) or (28) should be preferred. In practice, it quite frequently happens that one cannot satisfactorily decide between two alternative models. It will generally be true to say that for short-term forecasting, say one or two steps, it will make little difference which model is selected, but for longer-term horizons the models could produce substantially different forecasts. For example, the one-step forecasts are 0.512 using (28) and 0.542 using (26), the two-step forecasts are 0.503 using (28) and 0.574 from (26), but the ten-step forecasts are 0.24 by (28) and 0.68 by (26). There are a number of ways of deciding which model one prefers, if a choice is necessary, but the safest way is to choose the model that forecasts the better out of sample, using medium or long-term forecasts.

Turning now to series J, this is a series that does need differencing, and the correlogram for levels shows this quite clearly as it is both smooth and declines very slowly. The fact that the first autocorrelation of 0.98 is so near 1 confirms that differencing is required. Looking at the correlogram for the differenced series, only the first value is of any real significance, suggesting that MA(1) should be identified, as is correct. Recalling series

F, the estimated model for the differenced series has parameter 0.545, i.e.,

$$x_t - x_{t-1} = \varepsilon_t + 0.545\varepsilon_t,$$

whereas the true parameter value is 0.6. Thus, the identification and estimation appear to be satisfactory.

Data from real economic series, such as series K, the index of production, do not always allow such easy identification. The smoothness of the correlogram and the very high value for the first autocorrelation certainly suggest that the differenced series should be examined. The correlogram of the differences, taking values 0.40, 0.21, 0.15, 0.11 for the first four lags, declines as one would expect an AR model to do. The partial correlogram has a clearly significant value at lag 1 but other values are generally small, so that an AR(1) model for the differenced series is identified. The estimated model is

$$x_t - x_{t-1} = 0.4(x_{t-1} - x_{t-2}) + \varepsilon_t,$$

and no other model is suggested by the values in the table. There is, however, a significant value of -0.19 for the lag 12 autocorrelation of the differenced series. The data used have been seasonally adjusted, that is, a seasonal component has been removed by a technique similar to those discussed in the next chapter. It is quite frequently observed that the purely automatic techniques extract too much, in a sense, and so impose a negative autocorrelation at lag 12 with monthly data. For most forecasting purposes this problem adds little time structure and does not require a more complicated model to be constructed, as such a model would produce forecasts very little different from those of the simpler model.

To summarize, for each series the data should be plotted against time, the correlogram and partial correlogram should be estimated and plotted, and the approximate 95% confidence intervals at $2/\sqrt{n}$ should be added to these plots. If the correlogram suggests that differencing is appropriate, as in examples J, H, and K, then the above process should be repeated again using the differenced data. Just occasionally a further differencing is required, but this is quite rare with economic data. Finally, an attempt should be made to identify a model. Quite often, the diagrams are not easy to interpret, and two or more models could appear to be appropriate. The first rule is to choose the simplest model — that is, the one with the fewest parameters — so that if the choice is between an MA(3) or an AR(2), one picks the latter. The second rule is to ignore, at least initially, any marginally "significant" autocorrelations or partial autocorrelations at lags that are large or difficult to interpret. If these effects are real they may have little relevance for forecasting or will possibly be picked up at the diagnostic checking stage.

There can still occur occasions when more than one model is identified, as happened in example H above. It is usually true when this happens that either model provides similar short run forecasts, and these models are designed just to help with short run forecasting. The models may give quite different longer run forecasts.

A difficulty frequently met in identification is between an AR(1) or an MA(1) model. The differenced data in example J shows the problem; the correlogram is that of an MA(1) process, the partial correlogram of an AR(1), as the first terms are significant but no others. In this instance an identification can be made using the following reasoning: if the model were AR(1), then it has the form

$$\Delta x_t = 0.42 \, \Delta x_{t-1} + \varepsilon_t$$

where $0.42 = \hat{a}_{11}$. For this model, the autocorrelation between Δx_t and Δx_{t-2} should be $(0.42)^2 = 0.177$, which would be significant in the correlogram. As r_2 is not significant, the identification is that an MA(1) is more appropriate.

However, if x_t is an AR(1)

$$x_t = \alpha x_{t-1} + \varepsilon_t$$

and α is quite small, say 0.25, then it can be well approximated by an MA(1) model, as

$$x_t = \varepsilon_t + \alpha \varepsilon_{t-1} + \alpha^2 \varepsilon_{t-2} + \alpha^3 \varepsilon_{t-3} + \cdots$$

and $\alpha^2 = .06$ and α^3 etc. are even smaller. Thus, ignoring the small terms gives the approximation

$$x_t = \varepsilon_t + \alpha \varepsilon_{t-1}.$$

For purely pragmatic reasons, if the choice is between an AR(1) or an MA(1), both with small coefficients, then it is preferable to select the AR(1) model. Both will give very similar forecasts, but these are easiest to form using the AR(1) model.

3.9   THE PROJECT

The first decision required for the methods discussed in this chapter concerns any trend in mean that your data may contain. If there is a distinct trend, it should be removed by the methods discussed in Chapter 2, either by subtracting an estimated trend curve $\hat{C}(t)$ or by differencing, whichever is thought to be the most appropriate. Thus, if $\tilde{x}_t =$ is the original data, form new data $x_t' = \tilde{x}_t - \hat{C}(t)$, $t = 1, \ldots, n$ or $\Delta \tilde{x}_t = \tilde{x}_t - \tilde{x}_{t-1}$, which should be free of trends. For the data used in the example project, given in

Chapter 1, no trend was observed and no transformation is used so that $\tilde{x}_t = x'_t$.

If the new series has a nonzero average (or mean) value, this should be estimated and removed. Thus, one forms

$$\bar{x}' = 1/n \sum_{t=1}^{n} x'_t$$

and then a zero-mean data set

$$x_t = x'_t - \bar{x}'.$$

For the example project, the new zero-mean data is shown in Table 3.4

TABLE 3.4

Data for Example Project with Means Removed

Time	New x_t	New y_t
1	−8	0.86
2	17	0.76
3	−7	0.66
4	8	−0.64
5	6	−2.44
6	−21	−2.04
7	44	−3.64
8	−31	−3.44
9	−69	−1.84
10	−35	−1.84
11	18	−0.14
12	13	−0.44
13	−5	−0.24
14	16	−0.14
15	−14	−1.74
16	−39	−1.84
17	−20	−0.04
18	−22	0.16
19	−7	−0.44
20	4	0.86
21	3	2.56
22	34	2.46
23	20	1.06
24	10	1.56
25	14	1.96
26	2	1.06
27	35	1.46
28	12	0.66
29	2	0.96
30	20	0.66

which is the original data of Table 1.3 with $\bar{x}' = 2.0$ and $\bar{y}' = 0.04$ subtracted from the x and y series respectively.

The major tools for building the models introduced in this chapter are the correlogram and the partial correlogram. The correlogram is based on the estimated autocorrelations which are given by

$$r_k = \left(\sum_{t=k+1}^{n} x_t x_{t-k} \right) \bigg/ \sum_{t=1}^{n} x_t^2$$

(remembering that x_t has a zero average). These values are plotted against k, and the resulting shape is evaluated using the rules in 3.7.1. In particular, if the values of r_k are all near one, this may suggest that the series should be differenced before an autoregressive or moving average model is fitted.

The second basic tool is the partial correlogram which involves fitting AR(k) models to the data for $k = 1, 2, 3, \ldots$ and then extracting the estimated coefficient of the longest lagged x, denoted $\hat{a}_{kk}$ in Section 3.6. These values are then plotted against k.

Table 3.5 shows the values for the correlogram and partial correlogram using both the x and the y data in the example project. Values of r_k, a_{kk} are estimated only up to $k = 5$, as the data series is rather short and estimates of these quantities for higher values of k would be likely to be unreliable.

With $n = 30$ observations, the 95% confidence intervals are approximately $\pm 2/\sqrt{30} = \pm 0.365$ so that no values of r_k or a_{kk} are clearly significant for the x series. An AR(1) or MA(1) model may just be appropriate, i.e.,

$$x_t = \alpha x_{t-1} + \varepsilon_t$$

TABLE 3.5

x_t series

k	1	2	3	4	5
autocorrelations r_k	.28	−.02	.06	−.09	−.02
partial autocorrelation a_{kk}	.28	−.12	.12	−.17	.08

y_t series

k	1	2	3	4	5
r_k	.81	.61	.47	.27	.12
a_{kk}	.81	−.11	.04	−.32	−.02

or

$$x_t = \varepsilon_t + \beta \varepsilon_{t-1}$$

where ε_t is white noise.

An estimate for α is r_1 according to Section 3.7.2.

$$\text{i.e., } \hat{\alpha} = 0.28$$

For this model, the residual has standard deviation $= 22.25$.

For the MA(1) model, β is estimated by solving

$$r_1 = \frac{\beta}{1 + \beta^2}$$

i.e., $\beta = 3.26$ or 0.31 and then selecting the value in the range -1 to 1, i.e., $\hat{\beta} = 0.31$.

Using the AR(1) model, the h-step forecast is $(0.28)^h x_{30}$, so the nine-step forecast is $(0.28)^9 \times 22$, but this is a very small number and thus is effectively zero. Similarly, using the MA(1) model the nine-step forecast is zero (the mean of the adjusted series), as moving average models can only produce nonzero forecasts a few steps out. If one returns to the original series, by putting back the mean of 2, it follows that the nine-step forecasts of the x series are just 2 from these models.

For later use, the y series also has to be modelled. The autocorrelations show a lot more structure for this series with the first three being significantly different from zero and also the first partial autocorrelation. The two models identified from these values are MA(3) or AR(1), and the latter is both the more parsimonious and easier to use. Thus, the model selected for the y series is

$$y_t = \alpha y_{t-1} + \text{white noise}$$

and the estimate of α is

$$\hat{\alpha} \equiv r_1 = 0.81.$$

The residual has variance 0.72 and thus standard deviation 0.85. Note that the eight- and nine-step forecasts for y are

$$f^y_{30,8} = (.81)^8 \times y_{30}$$
$$= .185$$

and

$$f^y_{30,9} = (.81)^9 \times y_{30}$$
$$= .150$$
.

QUESTIONS

1. The following are 20 values from a white noise series ε_t, $t = 1, \ldots,$
   20: $-7.5, -7.1, -4.7, 5.0, -8.9, -7.9, -8.9, 5.1, 6.9, -3.5, -1.4,$
   $-7.6, -3.3, 1.4, -4.2, -4.6, -8.5, 3.5, 0.0, 7.0.$
   Form the two series x_t and y_t by

   $$x_t = 0.9x_{t-1} + \varepsilon_t \quad \text{and} \quad y_t = \varepsilon_t + 0.9\varepsilon_{t-1},$$

   for $t = 2, \ldots, 20$, assuming $x_1 = 2$. Plot ε_t, x_t, and y_t against t. By examining the theoretical values of ρ_1, the first autocorrelation, discuss which model should produce the smoothest series.

2. Show that for the MA(1) model $x_t = \varepsilon_t + b\varepsilon_{t-1}$, $\rho_1 = b/(1 + b^2)$, and hence $\rho_1 \leq \frac{1}{2}$.

3. During a severe drought in Southern California there was a worry that exceptionally low rainfall years were inclined to occur in groups. Annual total rainfall data was gathered for San Diego for 100 years. The estimated autocorrelations for this series were

   $$r_1 = -0.50, \quad r_2 = 0.14, \quad r_3 = 0.12, \quad r_4 = 0.20, \quad \text{and} \quad r_5 = 0.06.$$

   How would you interpret these figures? How would the interpretation be different if $r_1 = -0.05$?

4. Suppose the recent observed values of the series Z_t are

t	1	2	3	4	5
Z_t	-2	0	6	4	16.

   A statistician suggests that Z_t is generated *either* by

   $$Z_t = 0.5Z_{t-1} + \varepsilon_t$$

   or by

   $$Z_t = \eta_t + 0.5\eta_{t-1},$$

   where ε_t and η_t are taken to be white noise series with zero means. Provide forecasts for Z_6 and Z_7 using both models, assuming $\eta_0 = 0$. Discuss (nonnumerically, nonmathematically) how you might decide which was the better model for forecasting purposes by repeating the above exercise for many values of t.

5. Suppose that a long sample of x_t gives the following estimates of autocorrelations (i.e., of $\text{corr}(x_t, x_{t-k}) = \rho_k$):

k	0	1	2	3	4	5	6
Estimate of ρ_k	1	0.3448	0.002	0.001	-0.001	0	0.

Suggest a possible model for x_t. Supposing that your one-step forecast error made at time $t = 5$ in forecasting x_6 was -0.36 and $x_7 = 1$, forecast x_8.

6. A statistician claims to have fitted both an MA(1) model and an AR(1) model to some annual factory accident data with a mean removed, denoted x_t. The two models he provides are

$$x_t = \varepsilon_t + 0.5\varepsilon_{t-1} \quad \text{and} \quad x_t = x_{t-1} + \varepsilon_t,$$

where ε_t is supposed to represent white noise. Why might you be surprised that he is unable to distinguish between these two models? Given the following observations from the x_t series

t	1	2	3	4	5	6	7	8
x_t	-4	0	-1	5	-1	-4	3	2,

form one- and two-step forecasts during each of the years $t = 1$ to $t = 6$ using both of the models, and compare the relative forecasting abilities of the models. (Assume $\varepsilon_0 = 0$.)

7. If x_t is generated by

$$x_t = \varepsilon_t + 0.3\varepsilon_{t-1} + 0.4\varepsilon_{t-2},$$

where ε_t is zero-mean white noise with variance 2, prove $\text{var}(x_t) = 2.5$ and has first autocorrelation $\rho_1 = 0.336$. If $e_{n,2}$ is the two-step forecast error using the optimum forecast based on this model, find the variance of $e_{n,2}$.

8. Suppose you observe the time series

t	0	1	2	3	4	5	6	7	8	9	10
x_t	-6	4	6	-2	2	0	-4	4	2	-4	-2.

Statistician A states that he believes the series to be generated by the AR(1) model

$$x_t = 0.5x_{t-1} + \varepsilon_t,$$

but statistician B believes the true model is

$$x_t = \varepsilon_t + 0.5\varepsilon_{t-1},$$

where ε_t is zero-mean white noise in each case. Given that $\varepsilon_0 = 4$, find the one-step optimum forecasts $f_{n,1}$ for each n from 0 to 9 from both alternative models. Given your results, which model do you prefer and comment briefly on its quality.

9. (more difficult) The series x_t and y_t obey the MA(1) models

$$x_t = \varepsilon_t + 0.4\varepsilon_{t-1} \quad \text{and} \quad y_t = e_t + 0.8e_{t-1},$$

where ε_t, e_t are independent, zero-mean white noises. z_t is the sum of x_t and y_t, so that

$$z_t = x_t + y_t.$$

If the variance of x_t is 2.32, that of y_t is 4.92 and, of course, the variance of z_t is the sum of these, i.e., 7.24, show that z_t obeys the model

$$z_t = \eta_t + 0.60\eta_{t-1},$$

where η_t is white noise.

If you forecast z_{n+1}, using the information set $I_n : z_{n-j}, j \geq 0$, what is the variance of the forecast error? If now you forecast z_{n+1}, using the information set $I'_n : x_{n-j}, y_{n-j}, j \geq 0$, what will be the forecast error variance? Intuitively, why should you expect the second of these variances to be smaller than the first?

10. Explain why the mixed ARMA model can be expected to arise frequently in practice.

11. The following table shows a series generated by the model

$$x_t = \varepsilon_t + 0.4\varepsilon_{t-1}$$

and also the method of estimating the ε_t series if one is just given the observable x_ts and knowledge of the form of the model. Thus, one uses

$$f_{n,1} = 0.4\varepsilon_n$$

so that

$$\varepsilon_n = x_n - f_{n-1,1}.$$

There is a numerical mistake in the table. Find it and correct the rest of the table.

t	ε_t	ε_{t-1}	$0.4\varepsilon_{t-1}$	x_t	$f_{t-1,1}$ $= 0.4\hat{\varepsilon}_{t-1}$	$\hat{\varepsilon}_t = x_t - f_{t-1,1}$
0	8	—	—	—		
1	-10	8	3.2	-6.8	0	-6.8
2	3	-10	-4.0	-1.0	-2.7	1.7
3	7	3	1.2	8.2	0.7	7.5
4	-8	7	2.8	-5.2	3.0	-8.2
5	-5	-8	-3.2	-8.2	-3.3	-6.9
6	10	-5	-2.0	8.0	-2.76	10.76
7	0	10	4.0	4.0	4.3	-0.3

12. If $x_t \sim \mathrm{AR}(1)$, is $E[x_t \varepsilon_{t+2}] = 0$? If $x_t \sim \mathrm{AR}(2)$, is $E[x_t \varepsilon_{t+1}] = 0$?

13. Consider the two models

$$x_t = \varepsilon_t + b\varepsilon_{t-2}$$

$$y_t = ay_{t-2} + e_t$$

where ε_t, e_t are white noises with zero mean. Do you think that ρ_1 (first autocorrelation) and a_{11} (first partial autocorrelation) are zero for these models?

FURTHER READINGS

Box, G. E. P., and G. M. Jenkins (1970). *Time Series Analysis, Forecasting and Control*, San Francisco: Holden Day.
   The original account of ARIMA modeling, very detailed and with plenty of examples.
Granger, C. W. J., and P. Newbold (1986). *Forecasting Economic Time Series* second edition, Chapters 1 and 3, New York: Academic Press.
Nelson, C. R. (1973). *Applied Time Series Analysis for Managerial Forecasting*, San Francisco: Holden Day.
   An account of ARIMA modeling more elementary than Box and Jenkins's.

APPENDIX: REVIEW OF TWO SIMPLE MODELS

There is a fundamental distinction in statistical theory between a population and a sample. In time series analysis, population translates into a generating mechanism that completely determines the manner in which the series is generated. The available data, $x_t, t = 1, \ldots, n$, is the sample from which one attempts to determine what the generating mechanism is that has produced this particular data. Two simple examples of generating mechanisms are

(i) the autoregressive of order one (AR(1)), in which x_t is generated by

$$x_t = ax_{t-1} + \varepsilon_t, \ |a| < 1$$

where ε_t is a white noise series, and

(ii) the moving average of order one (MA(1)) in which x_t is generated by

$$x_t = \varepsilon_t + b\varepsilon_{t-1}, \ |b| < 1.$$

These are two mechanisms that are simple and have practical importance. Provided ε_t has zero mean, so will x_t for both mechanisms. From statistical theory it is possible to prove a number of population properties for series generated by these mechanisms. In particular,

	AR(1)	MA(1)
var x_t	$\dfrac{\text{var } \varepsilon}{1 - a^2}$	$(1 + b^2)\,\text{var } \varepsilon$
$\rho_k = \text{corr } (x_t, x_{t-k})$ $\quad k = 1, 2 \ldots$	a^k	$\dfrac{b}{1 + b^2}$ for $k = 1$ $\quad 0 \qquad$ for $k = 2, 3, \ldots$
$f_{n,h}$ (optimum h-step forecast)	$a^h x_n$	$b\varepsilon_n,\, h = 1$ $\quad 0,\, h > 1$

It is seen that the AR(1) provides forecasts for various horizons, although $f_{n,L} \to 0$ as L gets large, but the MA(1) provides only an interesting one-step forecast.

If one is given some data, $x_t,\ t = 1, \ldots , n$, how would one decide whether either of these models is appropriate? An obvious approach is to check whether the date has properties predicted by the models. The ρ_k values can be estimated by the r_k using the formula given at the start of section 3.4. As the r_k are estimates based on a finite sample, they will only be approximates to the actual underlying ρ_k values. Plotting r_k against k creates the correlogram, and its shape can be compared to the theoretical ρ_k values for MA(1) and AR(1) models to see whether either of these models are *identified* as being likely generating models for the data. To help interpret the correlogram, it is important to form the 95% confidence interval of $\pm 2/\sqrt{n}$ to emphasize those r_k values that appear to be significantly different from zero.

A second diagram that is helpful is the partial correlogram in which a sequence of AR models are fitted to the data of increasing order. So, a_{kk} is the coefficient on x_{t-k} when an AR(k) model is fitted. Clearly, if the true mechanism is AR(1) then all a_{kk} will be zero except for $k = 1$. The a_{kk} sequence can be estimated using the methods discussed in section 3.4, plotted against k, and interpreted with an approximate 95% confidence of $\pm 2/\sqrt{n}$, as before.

If either model is identified as a likely mechanism, the next step is to estimate the parameter involved. For the AR(1) model, a is estimated by r_1, and for the MA(1), b is estimated by solving the equation

$$r_1 = \frac{b}{1 + b^2}$$

and selecting the value that is between -1 and 1.

Forecasts are then formed using the formula given above so that for the

AR(1) they are formed by

$$f_{n,h} = \hat{a}^h x_n$$

$$= r_1^h x_n$$

The one-step forecast for the MA(1) model is

$$f_{n,1} = \hat{b}\varepsilon_n$$

where ε_n has to be estimated from the observed data. An iterative procedure is to use

$$\varepsilon_n = x_n - f_{n-1,1}$$

and to start the forecasting process with

$$f_{0,1} = 0.$$

Throughout, it has been assumed that the data has mean zero. If this is not so, the mean should be estimated and subtracted from the data before model analysis is attempted. The forecasts above will be for this "mean-removed" series. To forecast the original series, the mean should be added back. Thus, if the original x_t has mean m, estimated by

$$\hat{m} = \frac{1}{n} \sum_{t=1}^{n} x_t,$$

let $y_t = x_t - \hat{m}$, and suppose that y_t is AR(1) with coefficient 0.4, and then the two-step forecast of y_{n+2} is $(0.4)^2 y_n$, and that of x_{n+2} is $\hat{m} + (0.4)^2 y_n$.

CHAPTER

4

Further Aspects of
Time Series Forecasting

An unsophisticated forecaster uses statistics as a drunken man uses lamp-posts
—for support rather than for illumination.

after Andrew Lang

4.1 CYCLES AND THE SEASONAL COMPONENT

When statisticians first turned their attention to time series to any appreciable extent, in the late nineteenth century, it was immediately obvious that most series were too smooth to be white noise, so an appropriate class of models was sought to explain this smoothness. It so happened that most of the rather limited number of series that were then available and of any worthwhile length contained cyclical components. These are parts of the series that consist of some shape that is continually repeated with little variation in a periodic and fairly regular fashion. An example was the monthly price of wheat, which would generally be lowest directly after the harvest, because of a plentiful supply, but would then be inclined to increase as the available supply was reduced until the next harvest started the cycle off again. Agricultural prices provided many of the time series then available and they all contained this twelve-month, or seasonal, cycle. Other series that were analyzed that contained, or appeared to contain, cycles were the varying light intensity of a pair of rotating stars, annual death rates, and a sunspot series. The mortality data contained long swings of fairly constant deviation because some disease would sweep the country causing high deaths and would be inclined to leave the young and healthy as survivors, who could fend off the effects of other possible epidemics until they also became older and vulnerable, when a new disease would appear and raise the death rate once again. The sunspot series arises from

93

the fact that if one looks at the surface of the sun, it will usually contain dark spots, which are areas of relative coolness. It seems that every eleven years or so the sun suffers a serious case of acne and the proportion of the sun's disk that is covered by the spots increases dramatically. Since the mid-eighteenth century, an observatory in Switzerland has been recording monthly a measure of the number of sunspots, for reasons of their own and presumably at considerable risk to the astronomer's eyesight, thus providing one of the longest, but least useful, time series available for analysis. The fact that the sunspot measure reaches a peak roughly every eleven years, for reasons that are still not completely understood, leads to a cycle in the data. An appropriate model for all of these series might seem to be

$$x_t = A \cos(\omega t + \theta) + \varepsilon_t, \tag{1}$$

where ε_t is a white noise series and the first term is a purely periodic component with amplitude A and frequency ω (corresponding to period $2\pi/\omega$), and θ is the phase value. When such models were fitted to the series, a worthwhile fit was usually obtained, but the estimated residuals were frequently observed to still be too smooth to be white noise. As previously the smoothness had been attributed to the presence of a cycle, it was natural to extend model (1) to include several cosine, cyclical terms, of possibly unknown periods. Some very sophisticated techniques were developed to identify these cyclical components, but by the 1930s analysts were becoming dissatisfied with models involving cycles. The ARMA models, discussed in the previous chapter, were therefore developed. These were found to provide satisfactory explanations of the fluctuations in most series and to involve fewer parameters than the numerous cycles that previous techniques were "finding." With the important exception of the seasonal cycle, most academic time series analysts now strongly discount the usefulness of searches for cycles in most economic and business series. This view is not universally held, as is shown by the existence of groups such as The Society for the Investigation of Recurring Events or journals such as *Cycles*. It is possible that occasionally a true cycle is to be found in some data, for whatever reason, and if this occurs, it is essential to identify this cycle and use it to help forecast future values of the series. Such cycles are more likely to be found in physical series such as found in oceanography, geophisics, or chemical engineering rather than in economics or business series.

The one very clear exception to these remarks is the seasonal, or annual, cycle which is found very frequently in economic data. Examples of series containing strong seasonal components are those concerned with production, sales, inventories, personal income and expenditure, government receipts and expenditures, profits, unemployment rates, imports, and exports. Thus, for example, unemployment figures are highest during the winter months, when construction workers may be laid off, most vacation resorts are shut down and many high school and college graduates may still be looking for their first full-time job. The main causes of the seasonal swings are the timing of public holidays, such as Christmas and Easter, of school vacations, and of the payment of company dividends, the choice of when a tax year or accounting period ends, and of course, the effects of weather. Figure 4.3 (Section 4.5) shows an example of a seasonal series.

There are many ways of dealing with the seasonal component of an economic series, but they all basically aim to produce a series that appears to be nonseasonal. This can either be done directly by filtering,[1] or indirectly by estimating the seasonal component and then subtracting this estimate from the series. However, some of the proposed methods of seasonal adjustment are not really suitable in a forecasting framework as they are designed only to remove a seasonal component from a set of historical data and, in doing this, some of the most recent pieces of data are lost. As these pieces of data are the most important when forecasting, such methods are inappropriate.

The seasonal problem would not be difficult if the seasonal component consisted of a regular shape that reoccurred regularly every 12 months. If this were so, then a twelve-month difference would totally remove the component. That is, if

$$x_t = S(t) + z_t,$$

where x_t is the observed series, $S(t)$ is a perfectly regular seasonal component such that $S(t) = S(t - 12)$ and z_t is the remaining, nonseasonal component, then

$$y_t^{(12)} = x_t - x_{t-12}$$
$$= S(t) - S(t - 12) + z_t - z_{t-12}$$
$$= z_t - z_{t-12},$$

and $y_t^{(12)}$ has no seasonal component. However a consequence of this procedure is that if a time series model is fitted to the differenced series, such as an AR(p) or ARMA(p', q'), the orders of these models, p or $p' + q'$, will probably be very large. Box and Jenkins have extended their model-building approach, as described in the previous chapter, to include seasonal series. The method is based on the use of a twelve-month difference and the fitting of particular high-order models to the resulting series, but the

---

[1] If a series y_t is formed from another series x_t by a formula of the form $y_t = \Sigma_j d_j x_{t-j}$, then y_t is said to be a filtered version of x_t. Thus, a moving average is a filtered white noise.

details are too complicated for this text. The method has been successfully applied to series that do not have a constant seasonal pattern but rather slowly evolve through time. Once the full seasonal model has been achieved, forecasts are made from it in exactly the same way as from the models discussed in the previous chapter. Thus, for example, if y_t is the twelve-month difference

$$y_t = x_t - x_{t-12}$$

and the model fitted to y_t is

$$y_t = 0.6y_{t-1} + 0.2y_{t-12} + 0.3y_{t-13} + \varepsilon_t,$$

then, using the rules outlined in Chapter 3, the one-step forecasts will be

$$f_{n,1}^{(y)} = 0.6y_n + 0.2y_{n-11} + 0.3y_{n-12},$$

$$f_{n,1}^{(x)} = f_{n,1}^{(y)} + x_{n-11},$$

$$f_{n,2}^{(y)} = 0.6f_{n,1}^{(y)} + 0.2y_{n-10} + 0.3y_{n-11},$$

$$f_{n,2}^{(x)} = f_{n,2}^{(y)} + x_{n-10},$$

$$\vdots$$

An alternative, and rather easier approach, is to first estimate the seasonal component. A convenient way of doing this is to put the available data into tabular form as shown in Table 4.1, where the data x_t are assumed to be recorded monthly, with the first value x_1 occurring in a January and the most recent observation in a December. Thus, all January values are found in the first column, all the February values in the second column, and so forth. One way of estimating the seasonal is to form the average of each column, $\bar{x}_J, \bar{x}_F, \ldots, \bar{x}_D$. A plot of these averages against the months shows the estimated seasonal pattern, as in Fig. 4.1.

To illustrate the results of this method in practice, Table 4.2 shows average U.S. sales of various supermarket and drug store items for pairs of

TABLE 4.1

Jan.	Feb.	March	$\cdots$	Nov.	Dec.
x_1	x_2	x_3		x_{11}	x_{12}
x_{13}	x_{14}	x_{15}		x_{23}	x_{24}
x_{25}	x_{26}	x_{27}		x_{35}	x_{36}
$\vdots$	$\vdots$	$\vdots$		$\vdots$	$\vdots$
x_{n-11}	x_{n-10}	x_{n-9}		x_{n-1}	x_n
$\bar{x}_J$	$\bar{x}_F$	$\bar{x}_M$		$\bar{x}_N$	$\bar{x}_D$

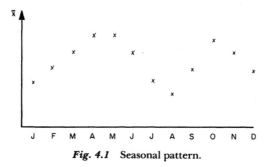

Fig. 4.1 Seasonal pattern.

months. The figures have been adjusted so that the bimonthly average is 100. DJ denotes December and January, FM February and March, and so forth.

The causes of seasonal sales fluctuating due to temperature is obvious, but the swings in acne remedy sales are less clear cut. Provided several year's data is available and the seasonal component changes little from year to year, this estimate will be a good one. To remove the seasonal component from the data, the values in each column have the column average subtracted from them, so that the resulting series y_t is given by

$$y_1 = x_1 - \bar{x}_J, \qquad y_2 = x_2 - \bar{x}_F, \qquad y_3 = x_3 - \bar{x}_M, \qquad \text{etc.}$$

Suppose a time-series model, such as an autoregressive model, is then fitted to the y_t values and forecasts of future y values are constructed. Forecasts of the x's are made by adding the appropriate month average to these y forecasts. Thus, for example, if x_t is recorded in a December, then

TABLE 4.2

Seasonal Sales[a]

	DJ	FM	AM	JJ	AS	ON
Cake mix	89	100	110	94	94	105
Carbonated soft drinks	92	87	99	117	114	91
Frozen dinners	100	107	106	91	90	106
Canned dog food	101	96	98	99	102	104
Acne remedies	98	94	89	100	119	104
Deodorants	87	96	106	110	108	93
Throat lozenges	143	115	73	58	86	124

[a] Figures taken from *The Nielsen Researcher*, No. 1 (1976).

the forecasts for the subsequent January, February, and March values are

$$f_{n,1}^{(x)} = f_{n,1}^{(y)} + \bar{x}_J, \qquad f_{n,2}^{(x)} = f_{n,2}^{(y)} + \bar{x}_F, \qquad f_{n,3}^{(x)} = f_{n,3}^{(y)} + \bar{x}_M, \qquad \text{etc.}$$

If the seasonal pattern is changing through time, but in a slow fashion, the procedure just outlined will not be appropriate, as the monthly averages include data values which include a seasonal shape that no longer occurs. To get around this problem, the monthly averages could be taken over just a few recent years, say the last 5 years. As new data become available, the most distant value is replaced by the new one when forming the average. An alternative method of estimating a changing seasonal is to form

(current January average) $= \alpha$(Previous January average)

$+ (1 - \alpha)$(most recent January figure),

where α is some parameter to be chosen by the analyst. A typical value for α would be 0.7, a value larger than this is appropriate if the seasonal is thought to change very little, and a smaller value for α should be used if the seasonal cycle is thought to be changing rapidly. This iterative procedure is started by taking the first monthly average equal to the first monthly value of x_t.

To illustrate the first of these methods of estimating a changing seasonal pattern and using it for forecasting, consider the data shown in Table 4.3A.

Although there is no evidence of a changing seasonal shape, suppose that averages over the last five years are used. In January of year 5, the most recent five January figures are 18, 19, 22, 20, and 18, with an average of 19.4, so the seasonally adjusted figure is $18 - 19.4 = -1.4$. In January of year 6, the most recent January figures are 19, 22, 20, 18, and 21, with average 20, so the adjusted figure is $21 - 20 = 1$. The other averages are shown in Table 4.3A and the adjusted values for years 5 and 6 are in Table 4.3B.

TABLE 4.3A

Original Data (x_t)

		Year	Jan.	Feb.	March	Nov.	Dec.
First average period	Second average period	1	18	15	10	10	20
		2	19	16	11	14	19
		3	22	18	9	12	20
		4	20	17	12	14	22
		5	18	18	11	15	18
		6	21	16	12	13	16
5th year average			19.4	16.8	10.6	14.4	19.8
6th year average			20	17	11	14	19

TABLE 4.3B

Adjusted Data, Recent Years (y_t)

Year	Jan.	Feb.	March	$\cdots$	Nov.	Dec.
5	-1.4	1.2	0.4		0.6	-1.8
6	1	-1	1		-1	-3

Suppose now that for the whole set of adjusted data an AR(1) model is found to be appropriate, of the form

$$y_t = 0.7y_{t-1} + \varepsilon_t.$$

The forecasts of y_t for January and February of year 7 are then

$$f_{n,1}^{(y)} = 0.7(-3) = -2.1, \qquad f_{n,2}^{(y)} = (0.7)^2(-3) = -1.47,$$

with the forecasts made in December of year 6 using the rules for forecasting an AR(1) model given in Chapter 3. The corresponding forecasts for the original x_t series are

January of year 7

$$f_{n,1}^{(x)} = -2.1 + 20 = 18.9, \qquad f_{n,2}^{(x)} = -1.47 + 17 = 15.53.$$

The method of seasonal adjustment used by the U.S. government is based on the five-year average method just outlined, although a number of further sophistications are added. The current method used by the U.S. Department of Commerce is known officially as the "X-11 variant of the census method II seasonal adjustment program," but is usually called just X-11. Not only does it allow for the possibility of there being a changing seasonal shape, but the effect of untypical figures, or outliers, is automatically allowed for, as is the variation in the number of working days or trading days from one month to another.[2] An example of the use of X-11 will be found in Section 4.5.

The methods of seasonal adjustment described in this section and virtually all of those used by governments are autoadjustment methods; that is, the values of a series are used to adjust this series. More advanced methods would ask what is causing the seasonal variation and use values, from the causal series, such as temperature, in the adjustment process. These techniques are much more costly as more sophisticated analysis is required and frequently insufficient data is available for the causal vari-

---

[2] A complete description of X-11 may be found in Technical Paper No. 15, "The X-11 variant . . . ," published by the U.S. Dept. of Commerce, Bureau of the Census in 1967.

ables. Problems with modeling interrelationships among series will be discussed in Chapter 5.

The question of how to best deal with a seasonal element in a series is one of the oldest, most difficult and most studied aspects of analyzing an economic time series. Very sophisticated approaches are possible and attitudes towards the question are still developing. It should be noted that most of the macroeconomic series that contain a seasonal are published by government statistical offices in a seasonally adjusted component form. The adjusted series usually are free of a seasonal component, but the adjustment procedure can occasionally induce other undesirable properties in the series which make model building more difficult. When available, most forecasters prefer to work with unadjusted series.

Exercise

Using the above figures and model for the adjusted series y_t, show that forecasts of x_t for January and February of year 6 made in December of year 5 are 18.14 and 15.92 respectively.

4.2   LOW-COST TIME SERIES FORECASTING METHODS

The whole process of analyzing a time series, from worrying about trends and seasonal patterns to identifying, estimating, and diagnostic checking a time series model, is likely to be a lengthy and costly one. The main costs involved are for the use of complicated computer programs plus that of the time of a, one hopes, competent statistician who has to look at various diagrams and draw on his experience to make essential decisions. If this is all done properly, then the available information in the information set being used, the past and present of the series to be forecast, is efficiently squeezed out and a relatively successful forecasting formula is attained, at least in the short run. However, there exist forecasting situations where either the required expertise is not available to use this approach or the cost of the whole procedure is too great. A small firm, for example, may want to forecast sales for several brands in each of ten sales areas.

An obvious way of reducing costs is to use a technique that provides forecasts without the necessity of employing an expensive specialized statistician. It is not difficult to decide whether or not to use a differenced series to remove or reduce a trend, and also to use a simple seasonal adjustment method such as those outlined in the previous section. In fact, these aspects of the analysis can be completely automated by using a computer program provided with suitable criteria to apply if decisions have to be made. The complete identification of models is more difficult to automate, but various methods have been devised to choose and fit autoregressive models which are capable of producing good, if not completely optimum forecasts. One of these methods, known as stepwise autoregressive series, proceeds as follows (assuming x_t does not need differencing and has no seasonal component):

(i) All models of the form

$$x_t = \alpha_{1k} x_{t-k} + \varepsilon_t^{(1)}$$

are fitted for $k = 1, 2, \ldots, K$, and choose the one that fits best, so that $\text{var}(\varepsilon_t^{(1)})$ is a minimum.

(ii) Fit all models of the form

$$x_t = \alpha_{2j} x_{t-j} + \alpha_{2m} x_{t-m} + \varepsilon_t^{(2)},$$

$j, m = $ all $1, 2, \ldots, K$ and choose the one that fits best.

(iii) Fit all models of the form

$$x_t = \alpha_{3r} x_{t-r} + \alpha_{3s} x_{t-s} + \alpha_{3q} x_{t-q} + \varepsilon_t^{(3)}$$

and choose the best, etc.

Thus, in the first stage the best equation involving a single lagged x_t is found (the lag need not be 1), in the next stage, the best equation involving a pair of lagged x's is found (the lags need not necessarily include that used in the first stage, but will usually do so), and so forth. A criterion can be given which tells the computer to stop when the addition of further variables does not significantly improve the fit of the equation. The result is an autoregressive series of possibly a high order but with many zero coefficients such as

$$x_t = 0.4x_{t-3} + 0.1x_{t-5} + 0.2x_{t-8} + \varepsilon_t.$$

Many computers have programs available to form such a stepwise autoregressive model, and once the model is obtained, forecasts are made from it in the usual way. Although such a method is often quite successful, it is still fairly sophisticated and costly to find the model and to form forecasts from it. On some occasions, even lower cost methods of forecasting are required.

Consider, for example, a company that manufactures very complicated pieces of machinery, such as an aeroengine. Each engine may contain 100,000 separate and distinct parts. To allow for servicing and repairs of the engines, the company will have to keep spares of each of the parts in at least one place in the world, and maybe in several places. If an insufficient inventory of parts is maintained, customers who have purchased the engines may find that these expensive pieces of machinery are remaining idle

for long periods, whilst special parts are manufactured, which could lead
to them buying alternate makes of engines sometime in the future. However, the manufacturing company will find it very expensive tying up large
amounts of capital in over-large inventories of spare parts. Inventory
theory provides fairly simple formulas to be applied by the company to
help decide how many spares of each part to keep available, but these
formulas require forecasts of demand for each part over some prescribed
time period, say the next three months. The company could certainly
monitor demand for each part for a period but is unlikely to be willing, or
able, to analyze each of the resulting 100,000 time series and find or use
sophisticated forecasting techniques for each. What is required is a really
low cost method that does have *some* forecasting ability.

A number of simple so-called *adaptive* or exponentially weighted moving average methods (EWMA) methods have been developed specifically
for such situations. They are based on quite a different philosophy about
what is the most important aspect of a time series than those encountered
so far. Suppose that the series to be forecast x_t fluctuates around some
unknown mean m. Then if an estimate of m can be obtained, denoted by $\hat{m}$,
a not totally hopeless forecast for all future values of the series would be $\hat{m}$,
i.e., $f_{n,h} = \hat{m}$, all $h \geq 1$. Now suppose that occasionally some unknown outside influence changes the value of m, so that before the influence x_t
fluctuates about m_1 but after it x_t lies around a different value m_2. A
technique is required to estimate the *current* mean, or level value, for the
series and the forecast is made that all future values will be equal to this
current mean. Figure 4.2 shows the underlying idea.

Denote the current mean by $\bar{x}_t$; then one method of estimating this
quantity is by the iterative equation

$$\bar{x}_t = \alpha x_t + (1 - \alpha)\bar{x}_{t-1},\tag{2}$$

where α is a parameter in the region $0-1$, and the sequence $\bar{x}_t$ is started by

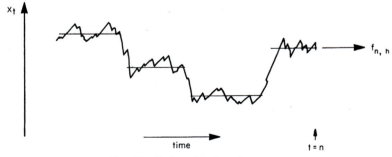

Fig. 4.2 Series with changing mean.

taking $\bar{x}_1 = x_1$. By continual substitution, it is found that (2) may be written

$$\bar{x}_t = \alpha x_t + \alpha(1 - \alpha)x_{t-1} + \alpha(1 - \alpha)^2 x_{t-2} + \alpha(1 - \alpha)^3 x_{t-3} + \cdots, \quad (3)$$

so that apart from the α that is in all of the terms $\bar{x}_t$ is seen to give weight 1 to the current x_t, $(1 - \alpha)$ to the previous x_t, $(1 - \alpha)^2$ to the x_t before that, and so forth. Because $1 - \alpha$ lies between 0 and 1, $\bar{x}_t$ is seen to give less weight to more distant x_t values. The big advantage in forming (2) to estimate $\bar{x}_t$ rather than (3) is its considerable simplicity, particularly when run on a computer, as only the values α, $\bar{x}_{t-1}$, and x_t need be stored in the computer's memory. The quantity α is called the smoothing constant. It can either be estimated from past data, although at considerable computing cost, or a value can simply be guessed at, depending on how variable the series is about a mean and how often one believes the current mean value really changes. If the mean level is thought to change value frequently, a value of α near one is appropriate, but if the series is volatile about a fairly constant mean, a value of α near zero is better. A simple rule that has been suggested is to take α equal to one of 0.7, 0.5, or 0.3 on purely subjective grounds. Once $\bar{x}_n$ is obtained, all forecasts are put equal to this value, i.e.,

$$f_{n,h} = \bar{x}_n.$$

The simplicity and underlying philosophy of this approach is appealing, and it is much used in industry, possibly also because of its low cost of operation. In practice, the forecasts produced are usually far from optimal but are generally by no means valueless. In terms of cost effectiveness, such methods have much to recommend them.

It is fairly natural to ask if they can be improved to a worthwhile extent whilst retaining their main characteristics. Many improvements have been suggested, particularly to take into account observable trends or seasonality. For example, it has been suggested that the main features of a time series can be captured by considering a linear trend, with changing parameter values, plus a changing seasonal series. To estimate all of the components, the following three equations are used:

$$\bar{x}_t = \alpha(x_t - S_{t-12}) + (1 - \alpha)(\bar{x}_{t-1} + T_{t-1}),$$
$$T_t = \beta(\bar{x}_t - x_{t-1}) + (1 - \beta)T_{t-1},$$
$$S_t = \gamma(x_t - \bar{x}_t) + (1 - \gamma)S_{t-12},$$

where $\bar{x}_t$ represents the current level for the series, T_t is the current slope of the straight-line trend and S_t is the current estimate of the seasonal, assuming monthly data. Then

$$f_{n,h} = \bar{x}_n + hT_n + S_{n+h-12},$$

for $h = 1, 2, \ldots, 12$. For h between 13 and 24, the last term is replaced by S_{n+h-24}, and so forth. If the parameters α, β, and γ are merely selected by the forecaster rather than estimated from the data, the forecasting procedure is purely automatic and makes little demands on a computer or its memory. In this case some simplicity is lost but not too much and doubtless rather better forecasts can result. Other, more sophisticated, generalizations have also been suggested, but most become too complicated for the technique still to be characterized as low cost, so the only clear-cut gain over the modeling techniques described in the previous chapter is lost. As will be seen in Chapter 8 these low-cost techniques do have a role to play in a forecasting strategy.

4.3   WHICH METHOD TO USE

In this and the previous chapter three quite different time series methods of forecasting have been discussed based on:

(i)   the ARIMA or Box–Jenkins modeling procedure, which typically requires a number of critical decisions to be made at the identification stage by a well-trained statistician,

(ii)   the stepwise autoregressive model, and

(iii)   the adaptive or EWMA models.

Once any of these models have been determined, the production of forecasts is usually quite easy. Given an actual forecasting situation, which method should be used? The decision has to depend on how much time and money one is able to spend, on how important it is to get as good a forecast as possible and on how much data is available. The last two methods listed above are typically cheaper, use less data, and produce rather poorer forecasts than the first method. If one has virtually no data, then the adaptive method is the only one available, the stepwise autoregressive method can be used with 30 or more pieces of data, whereas it is recommended that Box–Jenkins modeling be not attempted unless 60 or so data points are available. The ARIMA modeling methods are expensive because of the necessary intervention of a (probably) highly paid statistician at the identification decision-making stage, but as automatic modeling procedures, by which a computer makes decisions by applying various comprehensive criteria, become more widely available this particular expense will decline. There will still be a relatively considerable computing cost for ARIMA models compared to adaptive.

The question of how to measure the relative quality of the methods is discussed in Chapter 8, where the possibility of obtaining improved forecasts by combining different methods is also mentioned.

4.4 PROPERTIES OF OPTIMUM FORECASTS

Whenever an optimum forecast is produced from a proper information set,[3] the resulting forecast errors are found to have certain useful properties. The most important of these properties are the following:

(i)   The h-step forecast errors $e_{n,h}$, when plotted against n, obey an MA($h-1$) model. In particular, the one-step errors $e_{n,1}$ will be white noise. The relevance of this latter result is that if the errors produced by some forecasting procedure are not white noise, then it is not an optimum procedure. This should be clear, as if the $e_{n,1}$ are not white noise, then they will be at least partially forecastable from past errors. Thus the original forecasts can be improved by adding to them these forecasts of the errors.

(ii) The variance of $e_{n,h}$, when plotted against h, will generally be a increasing curve, and, as h gets large enough, this value gets close to the variance of x_t, the series being forecast. An alternative way of stating this property is that generally the further ahead one forecasts, the less well one does. Also, if one tries to forecast very far ahead, the information set ceases to contain anything of relevance, so that for n fixed and increasing h, $f_{n,h}$ tends to the mean of x_t, and $e_{n,h}$ and x_{n+h} have equal variances. The forecast errors occur because of the occurence of unforeseeable events. The further ahead one forecasts the more opportunity there is for such events to occur and to accumulate, which is why the variance of the errors increases as h increases.

The proof of these results will be given just for the information set I_n: $x_{n-j}, j \geq 0$, but they do hold true for larger information sets containing the past and present of x_t and of other series. If x_t is a stationary series with zero mean and no deterministic or perfectly forecastable components, such as a linear trend or a pure cycle, then according to Wold's theorem, it can always be represented by a moving average model of the form

$$x_t = \sum_{j=0}^{m} c_j \varepsilon_{t-j}, \qquad c_0 = 1,$$

where m may be infinite. In particular, any ARMA(p, q) model can be so represented. Assume that the c_j values are known; then x_{n+h} will be generated by

$$x_{n+h} = \sum_{j=0}^{h-1} c_j \varepsilon_{n+h-j} + \sum_{j=h}^{m} c_j \varepsilon_{n+h-j}.$$

[3] That is, an information containing all past values of the series being forecast plus those of any other variables used to make the forecast.

All of the components in the second of these terms are potentially knowable at time n, and so this second component can be equated with $f_{n,h}$. (In practice, with only a finite amount of data, this will only be true approximately, but generally such details can be safely ignored.) Thus, the h-step error will be

$$e_{n,h} = \sum_{j=0}^{h-1} c_j \varepsilon_{n+h-j}$$

and in particular, the one-step error is just ε_{n+1}. It is immediately obvious that $e_{n,h}$ is MA($h-1$) and has variance

$$\mathrm{var}(e_{n,h}) = \left(\sum_{j=0}^{h-1} c_j^2 \right) \sigma_\varepsilon^2,$$

so that, for example,

$$\mathrm{var}(e_{n,h}) - \mathrm{var}(e_{n,h-1}) = c_{h-1}^2 \sigma_\varepsilon^2,$$

which cannot be negative. It follows that the sequence of these variances will generally increase as h increases.

A further use for these results is to provide confidence intervals around the point forecasts $f_{n,h}$. If the residuals are normally distributed or nearly so, the approximate 95% confidence forecast interval is $f_{n,h} \pm \sqrt{\mathrm{var}(e_{n,h})}$, where $\mathrm{var}(e_{n,h})$ is given above. To evaluate this quantity the c_j values are required. There are various ways of finding these values, but one of the easiest is just to substitute for x_t into an ARMA model and get iterative equations for the c_j's. For example, suppose one has the AR(2) model

$$x_t - a_1 x_{t-1} - a_2 x_{t-2} = \varepsilon_t,$$

which becomes

$$\sum_{j=0}^{m} c_j \varepsilon_{t-j} - a_1 \sum_{j=0}^{m} c_j \varepsilon_{t-1-j} - a_2 \sum_{j=0}^{m} c_j \varepsilon_{t-2-j} = \varepsilon_t.$$

Gathering up terms, this gives

$$(c_0 - 1)\varepsilon_t + (c_1 - a_1 c_0)\varepsilon_{t-1} + (c_2 - a_1 c_1 - a_2 c_0)\varepsilon_{t-2}$$
$$+ (c_3 - a_1 c_2 - a_2 c_1)\varepsilon_{t-3} + \cdots = 0.$$

This equation must hold true for any set of ε_t values, and for this to be true, every coefficient must be identically zero. Remembering that $c_0 = 1$, this gives

$$c_1 = a_1, \qquad c_2 = a_1 c_1 + a_2, \qquad c_3 = a_1 c_2 + a_2 c_1, \qquad \text{etc.}$$

These equations are easily solved iteratively. A similar procedure can be used for any ARMA(p, q) model, although for large p the sequence of equations can become quite complicated. The only other quantity required to form var($e_{n,h}$) is σ_ε^2, which can be estimated as the variance of the residuals from the fitted ARMA model. The resulting confidence bands will be rather approximate and experience suggests that they are often optimistically narrow.

All of the methods and results in this section also apply to series generated by ARIMA models, but are better applied to the data after differencing.

To give a specific example of the preceding theory, suppose that an ARMA(1, 1) model has been fitted to some data of the form

$$x_t - 0.6x_{t-1} = \varepsilon_t + 0.3\varepsilon_{t-1}, \qquad \hat{\sigma}_\varepsilon^2 = 0.42.$$

Substituting

$$x_t = \sum_{j=0}^{m} c_j \varepsilon_{t-j}, \qquad c_0 = 1,$$

and similarly for x_{t-1} into the model and gathering terms gives

$$(c_0 - 1)\varepsilon_t + (c_1 - 0.6c_0 - 0.3)\varepsilon_{t-1} + (c_2 - 0.6c_1)\varepsilon_{t-2}$$
$$+ (c_3 - 0.6c_2)\varepsilon_{t-3} + \cdots = 0,$$

so that

$$c_1 = 0.9,$$
$$c_2 = 0.6c_1 = 0.54,$$
$$c_3 = 0.6c_2 = 0.324,$$
$$c_4 = 0.6c_3 = 0.194,$$
$$c_5 = 0.6c_4 = 0.117,$$
$$\vdots$$

Then using the theory,

$$e_{n,1} = \varepsilon_{n+1},$$
$$e_{n,2} = \varepsilon_{n+2} + 0.9\varepsilon_{n+1},$$
$$e_{n,3} = \varepsilon_{n+4} + 0.9\varepsilon_{n+3} + 0.54\varepsilon_{n+2} + 0.324\varepsilon_{n+3},$$
$$\vdots$$

and

$$\text{var}(e_{n,1}) = \sigma_\varepsilon^2 = 0.42,$$

$$\text{var}(e_{n,2}) = \sigma_\varepsilon^2(1 + (0.9)^2) = 0.76,$$

$$\text{var}(e_{n,3}) = \sigma_\varepsilon^2(1 + (0.9)^2 + (0.54)^2) = 0.88,$$

$$\text{var}(e_{n,4}) = \sigma_\varepsilon^2(1 + (0.9)^2 + (0.54)^2 + (0.324)^2) = 0.927,$$

$$\text{var}(e_{n,5}) = \text{var}(e_{n,4}) + \sigma_\varepsilon^2(0.194)^2 = 0.942,$$

$$\text{var}(e_{n,6}) = \text{var}(e_{n,5}) + \sigma_\varepsilon^2(0.117)^2 = 0.948,$$

$$\vdots$$

From the form of the model, it can be shown that the theoretical variance of x_t is 0.952.

For this model, the optimum forecasts are

$$f_{n,1} = 0.6x_n + 0.3(x_n - f_{n-1,1}), \quad \text{and} \quad f_{n,h} = (0.6)^{h-1}x_{n,1}, \quad h > 1.$$

Thus, if $x_t = 10, f_{n-1,1} = 8$, the approximate 95% confidence intervals are (using 2 in place of the correct 1.96)

$$h = 1: \quad 6.6 \ \pm 2\sqrt{0.42}, \quad \text{i.e.,} \quad 5.30 \text{ to } 7.90,$$

$$h = 2: \quad 3.6 \ \pm 2\sqrt{0.76}, \quad \text{i.e.,} \quad 2.22 \text{ to } 5.70,$$

$$h = 3: \quad 2.16 \pm 2\sqrt{0.88}, \quad \text{i.e.,} \quad 0.50 \text{ to } 4.46,$$

$$h = 4: \quad 1.23 \pm 2\sqrt{0.927}, \quad \text{i.e.,} \ -0.50 \text{ to } 3.35,$$

$$h = 5: \quad 0.74 \pm 2\sqrt{0.942}, \quad \text{i.e.,} \ -1.09 \text{ to } 2.79,$$

$$\vdots$$

4.5   NUMERICAL EXAMPLE OF SEASONAL SERIES

Tables 4.4 and 4.5 show the value of retail sales in the United States, in millions of dollars, for the period 1953–1964, both the original series and also the series seasonally adjusted by the simplest version of X-11, as discussed in Section 4.1. These series are plotted in Figs. 4.3 and 4.4. As can be seen both from Fig. 4.3 and also from the monthly means, the original data contain a clear-cut seasonal variation, with lows in January and February and a high in December. The adjusted data is seen to contain little or no seasonal pattern.

TABLE 4.4

U.S. Total Retail Sales in Millions of Dollars, Original Series

Year	Jan.	Feb.	Mar.	Apr.	May	Jun.	Jul.	Aug.	Sep.	Oct.	Nov.	Dec.	Total
1953	12903	12198	13711	14115	14520	14442	14250	14045	13952	14819	13828	16314	169097
1954	12213	11948	13576	14025	14116	14533	14259	13771	14012	14538	14401	17738	169130
1955	13147	12642	14609	15450	15333	15600	15261	15481	15765	15685	15751	19124	183848
1956	13727	13551	15527	15074	16109	16579	15382	16187	15582	16130	16493	19380	189721
1957	14741	14058	15945	16285	17205	17114	16864	17490	16373	16949	17133	19844	200001
1958	15286	13783	15464	16362	17364	16603	16596	17000	16326	17360	17039	21174	200357
1959	16225	14961	16967	17821	18600	18708	18332	18054	17570	19095	17635	21454	215422
1960	16312	15829	17632	18973	18548	18918	18066	18153	17848	18648	18385	22153	219465
1961	15803	15071	17714	17618	18532	18907	17922	18325	18158	18761	19224	22881	218916
1962	17007	16042	19193	19097	20226	20254	19138	19920	18863	20576	20911	24127	235354
1963	18261	17087	19653	20518	21228	20737	20540	21018	19267	21528	21494	25104	246435
1964	19154	18758	20502	21186	22508	22242	22145	21778	21313	22605	21720	27719	261630
Avg.	15398	14661	16708	17210	17857	17886	17396	17602	17086	18058	17834	21418	

TABLE 4.5

U.S. Total Retail Sales in Millions of Dollars, Seasonally Adjusted Series

Year	Jan.	Feb.	Mar.	Apr.	May	Jun.	Jul.	Aug.	Sep.	Oct.	Nov.	Dec.	Total
1953	14582	14212	13997	14101	14306	13974	14121	14003	14095	14609	13869	13414	169284
1954	13802	13921	13859	14011	13908	14062	14179	13709	14195	14355	14371	14596	168969
1955	14816	14724	14917	15492	15068	15098	15234	15373	16020	15507	15588	15792	183631
1956	15392	15802	15890	15192	15733	16025	15400	16028	15922	15950	16252	16070	189656
1957	16363	16446	16418	16471	16681	16557	16851	17316	16790	16706	16891	16488	199976
1958	16878	16189	15997	16530	16770	16035	16581	16874	16793	17038	16877	17519	200081
1959	17896	17644	17572	17941	18011	18060	18329	18003	18042	18659	17442	17692	215291
1960	18072	18733	18185	19061	18024	18241	18213	18144	18323	18168	18065	18229	219459
1961	17549	17903	18215	17680	18015	18281	18161	18288	18679	18236	18724	18905	218636
1962	18880	19072	19749	19181	19560	19665	19459	19796	19520	19960	20250	20014	235106
1963	20220	20300	20293	20602	20436	20237	20849	20815	20014	20856	20770	20900	246291
1964	21179	22247	21231	21284	21608	21758	22479	21568	22139	21899	20988	23077	261457
Avg.	17136	17266	17193	17295	17343	17333	17488	17493	17544	17662	17507	17725	

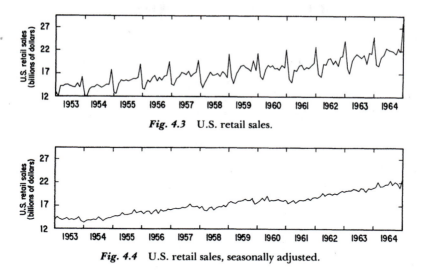

Fig. 4.3   U.S. retail sales.

Fig. 4.4   U.S. retail sales, seasonally adjusted.

Exercises

With this data, why do you think it is better to use a method that uses monthly averages over five years rather than over the full twelve-year period? Is there any evidence that the seasonal has changed in *shape*, rather than merely in *level?*

Denote $\bar{x}_T$ as the average monthly value for the year T (so that with the above data $\bar{x}_{1953} = 169097/12 = 14091$) and consider the following seasonal adjustment procedure:

(Adjusted January figure for year $T + 1$) = (original January figure for $T + 1$) − (original January figure for year $T − \bar{x}_T$),

and similarly for other months. Thus, January 1954 adjusted = $12213 − (12903 − 14091) = 13401$. Compare the adjusted figures using this method for year 1954 and 1964 with those from the X-11 method. Do you think this method of adjustment may have any advantages or disadvantages compared to X-11 and discuss its relationship with the twelve-month differencing method.

Use the low-cost forecasting methods discussed in Section 4.2 to forecast both the original and the adjusted retail sales figures for 1963 and 1964, the forecasts to be made in December 1962.

4.6   THE PROJECT

If the variable being forecast in the project contains a clear seasonal, it is important to take this into account when forming forecasts. Variables such as sales of consumer goods or relating to the vacation or construction industries or unemployment rates may be expected to contain seasonal components, whereas most price, interest, and exchange rate series do not. The first step of the analysis is to look at the plot of the project data, assuming that it extends over several years. If the data contains an important seasonal component, it should be obvious from the plot. If the seasonal is not clear in the plot, it may not be important enough to model when considering simple forecasting techniques. If a seasonal is present, a straightforward way of dealing with it is to form the annual difference $x_t - x_{t-52}$ (assuming weekly data), that is, the value in week t of this year with the value for the corresponding week last year subtracted from it. The resulting difference can then be used in the modelling techniques discussed in Chapter 3. The forecasting model will then produce forecasts of the annual difference such as

$$g_{n,1} = \text{forecast of } (x_{n+1} - x_{n+1-52})$$

so that

$$\text{forecast of } x_{n+1} = g_{n,1} + x_{n-51}$$

and so forth for larger horizons.

The data used in the example project was constructed and contains no seasonal.

The adaptive, EMWA, low-cost method of forecasting introduced in equation (2) of Section 4.2, can be used with any series. If the original data contained a seasonal and/or a trend and these have been removed, then this low-cost method can be used to predict what is left. However, it may be easier just to put the original data into the adaptive formula at the end of Section 4.2 involving $\bar{x}_t$, T_t, and S_t.

Using the data in the example project, just the last ten terms in Table 1.2 will provide a very easily formed forecast. It is not necessary to remove the mean. However, by now in the actual project more weekly data will have become available, and it is very important that it be utilized in the forecasts. Suppose that four more weeks' data has become available. The fourteen terms used in forming the forecast are shown in Table 4.6 together with $\bar{x}_t$ given by

$$\bar{x}_t = \alpha x_t + (1 - \alpha)\bar{x}_{t-1}$$

starting with $\bar{x}_{21} = x_{21} = 5$ and taking $\alpha = 0.7$.
Thus,

$$\bar{x}_{22} = 0.7 \times 36 + 0.3 \times 5 \quad = 26.7$$

$$\bar{x}_{23} = 0.7 \times 22 + 0.3 \times 26.7 = 23.4$$

TABLE 4.6

t	x_t	$\bar{x}_t$
21	5	5
22	36	26.7
23	22	23.4
24	12	15.4
25	16	15.8
26	4	7.5
27	37	28.2
28	14	18.3
29	4	8.3
30	22	17.9
31	8	11.0
32	−6	−0.9
33	−2	−1.7
34	4	2.3

The other topic of relevance for the project that is discussed in Chapter 4 is the formation of confidence intervals around the point forecast. If a simple AR or MA model has been selected in Chapter 3, suppose that the residuals of this model have variance S^2. The model now has to be transformed into a (possibly large order) moving average model.

$$x_t = \Sigma c_j \varepsilon_{t-j},$$

as described in Section 4.4. If the model chosen for the project is AR(1) or AR(2), as will usually be the case (once trend and seasonal components have been removed), this will be fairly simple. If a higher order AR model is used, the task will be much less simple. The h-step 95% confidence interval is then

$$\pm 1.96 \left[\sum_{j=0}^{h-1} c_j^2 \right]^{1/2}.$$

If there is very little forecastability for the series, as with the x_t series in the example project, and h is fairly large, such as $h = 9$ for the project, then this interval will be approximately

$$\pm 1.96 \, S_x$$

where S_x^2 is the sample variance of the series being forecast.

The y series in the example project makes a more interesting illustration. The model selected for this series is

$$y_t = \alpha y_{t-1} + \varepsilon_t$$

with $\alpha = 0.81$ and $S^2 = 0.72$, and from the results in Chapter 3, this is equivalent to

$$y_t = \varepsilon_t + \alpha\varepsilon_{t-1} + \alpha^2\varepsilon_{t-2} + \alpha^3\varepsilon_{t-3} + \cdots$$

so that $c_0 = 1$, $c_1 = \alpha$, $c_2 = \alpha^2$, $c_3 = \alpha^2$, etc.

The h-step 95% confidence intervals are thus

$$\pm 1.96 \times 0.85 \left[\sum_{k=0}^{h-1} \alpha^{2k}\right]^{1/2} = 1.66 \left[\frac{1 - \alpha^{2h}}{1 - \alpha^2}\right]^{1/2} \quad \text{with } \alpha = 0.81,$$

using the useful formula

$$\sum_{j=0}^{P} x^j = \frac{1 - x^{P+1}}{1 - x} \quad \text{if } |x| < 1.$$

Thus the h-step 95% confidence intervals are the h-step forecast plus and minus the following values:

h	value
1	1.66
2	2.14
3	2.40
4	2.55
5	2.65
6	2.71
7	2.76
8	2.79
9	2.80
10	2.81

QUESTIONS

1. A firm records sales over a quarter. It finds that an appropriate model seems to be

    Sales in tth quarter $= $ (seasonal) $+ y_t$.

    The average quarterly values over the last six years are

	Average
1st quarter	136
2nd quarter	271
3rd quarter	482
4th quarter	193

The estimated autocorrelations for the y values over the same period are observed to be

k	0	1	2	3	4	5	6	7
ρ_k	1	0.8	0.66	0.50	0.40	0.33	0.25	0.20

and the average y over the period is zero.

The company statistician suggests that an appropriate model for the y's is

$$y_t = 0.8y_{t-1} + \varepsilon_t,$$

where ε_t is zero-mean white noise. Do you agree with his suggestion (giving reason)?

Given that sales in the 4th quarter in 1974 are 213, forecast sales for each of the four quarters in 1975.

A director asks for a forecast of total sales in 1975. What forecast would you give?

2. For the quarterly, nonseasonal series x_t, whose first five values are

t	1	2	3	4	5
x_t	10	-5	15	10	-10,

forecast x_t for $t = 6$ and 7 using a simple, low-cost forecasting method.

3. If I_n is some information set that includes the past and present of the series to be forecast x_t and $f_{n,1}$ is the optimum forecast based on I_n, resulting in the error series $e_{n,1}$, why would you expect $e_{n,1}$ to be white noise?

4. An industrial forecaster decides to use the following low-cost model for predicting quarterly sales (x_t):

$$\bar{x}_t = \alpha(x_t - S_{t-4}) + (1 - \alpha)\bar{x}_{t-1}, \qquad S_t = \gamma(x_t - x_{t-4}) + (1 - \gamma)S_{t-4},$$

where $\bar{x}_t$ estimates the current level of the sales series and S_t estimates the seasonal component (with S_{1+4k} occurring in the first quarter, S_{2+4k} in the second quarter, etc., as $k = 0, 1, 2, \ldots$). The sales figures in 1974 and 1975 were

Quarter	1	2	3	4
1974	20	18	16	20
1975	24	20	18	22

the values of S_t in 1974 were

Quarter	1	2	3	4
S_t	8	0	-4	4

and the value of $\bar{x}_t$ for the final quarter of 1974 was 16. If $\alpha = 0.5$, $\gamma = 0.5$, forecast sales for all four quarters of 1976 and 1977. Briefly discuss why this is unlikely to be an optimum forecast.

5. (i) Discuss the use of inexpensive (adaptive) methods of forecasting, including their advantages and disadvantages.

   (ii) Three different models are being used to forecast the series x_t. They are

   (a) adaptive model,

   $$\bar{x}_t = 0.7\bar{x}_{t-1} + 0.3x_t;$$

   (b) AR(1),

   $$x_t = 0.5x_{t-1} + \varepsilon_t + 20;$$

   (c) MA(1),

   $$x_t = e_t + 0.6e_{t-1} + 50;$$

   where e_t and ε_t are taken to be zero-mean white noise. At time $t = 20$, the forecasts made by these models for x_{21} are (a) 80, (b) 110, and (c) 90. At time $t = 21$, what forecasts of x_{22} and x_{23} do these models produce given that $x_{21} = 100$?

6. (i) Briefly discuss why ARMA models might well be expected to arise in practice when analyzing a single time series.

   (ii) A statistician working for the Central Bank in a small South American country wants to forecast money supply for the country. He only has monthly data of the seasonally adjusted series from July 1965 to February 1976 ready for the computer and figures for March and April 1976 in print. He wants to fit a simple time series model and is uncertain about whether to use an MA(1) or an AR(1) model. How would you advise him to decide on a model?

   He puts the computer-available data onto his computer and obtains an estimate of 0.5 for ρ_1, the first-order serial correlation coefficient and 100 for the mean of the series. However, the machine loses the data whilst performing this calculation. The two remaining values for his series are 126 and 84 for March and April 1976 respectively.

   Using the available information and both of the two simple models, obtain alternative forecasts for money supply in May and June 1976.

7. In general, would you expect the plot of $f_{n,h}$ to look similar in shape to x_{n+h} as h increases and with n fixed? If no, say why.

8. An electrical utility company thinks that there is a weekly variation in the total daily demand for electricity. Figures, in some appropriate unit, for the first week of each of the last seven months were

Month	Sat.	Sun.	Mon.	Tues.	Wed.	Thurs.	Fri.
1	4	9	8	7	8	10	6
2	8	6	6	10	6	8	4
3	6	5	10	8	10	4	9
4	5	4	4	6	5	6	3
5	7	7	9	11	7	7	5
6	2	3	5	5	9	5	7
7	3	8	7	9	11	9	8

Forecast daily sales for the next month. If you were now told that the data for the first week of month 6 was disturbed by a very violent storm bringing down power lines and disrupting service, how, if at all, would your forecast vary? Do your forecasts take into account the fact that electricity demand varies seasonally?

9. If x_t is AR(1) of the form

$$x_t = \alpha x_{t-1} + \varepsilon_t, \quad 0 < \alpha < 1,$$

ε_t is zero-mean white noise and you use optimum forecasts one and two steps ahead, find the variances of the errors made, and prove that the two-step error variance is necessarily the larger of the two. State what time series models these series of errors obey.

10. The number of working man-days lost due to strikes, S_t, are recorded quarterly by a large company. The average quarterly values over the five years 1970–1974 and 1971–1975 are

Quarter	1	2	3	4
Average 1970–1974	83	96	41	102
Average 1971–1975	80	91	40	94

and the actual values observed in 1974 and 1975 were:

Quarter	1	2	3	4
Values 1974	85	100	44	105
Values 1975	76	84	39	90

The company statistician observes that if the most recently available five-year quarterly averages are subtracted from the actual series, the resulting residuals x_t obey the moving average model $x_t = \varepsilon_t + 0.5\varepsilon_{t-1}$. Using this procedure, the forecast of the actual series for the first quarter 1975 made in the fourth quarter of 1974 was 70. The statistician also notes that if the annual differences are formed, $y_t = S_t - S_{t-4}$, the resulting series obeys the AR(2) model

$$y_t = 0.6y_{t-1} + 0.2y_{t-2} + e_t.$$

Assuming that both ε_t and e_t are zero-mean white noises, forecast the values of S_t throughout 1976 using the alternative procedures.

FURTHER READINGS

Gilchrist, W. (1976). *Statistical Forecasting*, London: Wiley.
  Sound detailed survey of several statistical forecasting methods.
Granger, C. W. J., and P. Newhold (1986). *Forecasting Economic Time Series*, second edition, Chapters 4 and 5, New York: Academic Press.

CHAPTER 5

Regression Methods
and Econometric Models

An economist is an expert who will know tomorrow why the things he predicted yesterday didn't happen today.

Evan Esar

5.1 RELATING VARIABLES

In the previous three chapters forecasts have been made by relating a variable to its own past, so that if a forecast is required of x_{n+h}, the information set considered is I_n: x_{n-j}, $j \geq 0$. It is now time to move to wider information sets, such as

$$I_n: x_{n-j}, y_{n-j}, z_{n-j}, \qquad j \geq 0,$$

so that the forecast of x_{n+h} will be based on the past and present values not only of x_t but also of other series y_t and z_t. For example, a forecast of future unemployment could be based on past and present unemployment and also past and present production figures.

A linear relationship between a pair of random variables of the form

$$X = a + bY + \text{error} \tag{1}$$

is known as a regression of X on Y. The formulation and estimation of regression relationships is a major topic in classical statistics and a complete account can be found in any statistics text. The parameters a and b are estimated using a least-squares criteria, as explained briefly in Chapter 2. The estimation technique is easily extended to the more complicated multiple regression case, where

$$X = a + bY + cZ + dW + \cdots + \text{error}, \tag{2}$$

119

although use of a computer is necessary to form these estimates. The variable being explained is called the dependent variable and the variables on the right-hand side of the equation are called the independent or explanatory variables. The main difficulty in forming such models, and then using them to forecast, is to decide what set of independent variables to use. Questions such as whether or not lagged values of the dependent variable should be included amongst the explanatory variables and what other economic time series are appropriate are very important and can make a considerable difference to the forecasting performance of the model.

In the next section, a particular example is considered in some detail to illustrate the difficulties in forming an appropriate forecasting model. The third section in this chapter then returns to discussion of the general case.

5.2   CAUSAL MODELS: AN EXAMPLE

Suppose that one is interested in forecasting the dividend that some corporation is going to declare next month. If the sequence of previous annual dividends is denoted by D_t, the methods of earlier chapters would involve building a model from this sequence and then using it to forecast. However, anyone at all versed in economics may well think that it would be worthwhile expanding the information set by trying to explain dividends in terms of company earnings, otherwise known as after-tax profits. It might be argued that the money paid out to shareholders in the form of dividends has to come from the earnings, denoted by E_t, and so it becomes appropriate to consider a relationship of the form

$$D_t = a + bE_t + e_t, \tag{3}$$

where in this and other equations to follow e_t just represents some residual or "error" series with indeterminate properties. The coefficients a and b are chosen from the available data to give the "best" fit possible, using the classical least-squares regression technique. Suppose that a and b have been estimated and so can be taken as being known and that a forecast of D_{n+1} at time n is required. Equation (3) then gives

$$D_{n+1} = a + bE_{n+1} + e_{n+1}, \tag{4}$$

and so is immediately seen to be of little direct use for forecasting, as the future value of one variable has simply been expressed in terms of the future value of some other variable. An equation such as (3) can be called an *explanatory model*. These models can be used for forecasting purposes in two different ways. The first is to use them to provide *conditional forecasts*, that is, to forecast the value of D_{n+1} given some specific value for E_{n+1}. For example, the company management may have announced earlier an expected earnings figure for the year and formula (4) may be used to forecast dividends conditional on the assumption that the expected earnings figure turns out to be the correct one. The formula can be used to provide a whole table of forecasts for D_{n+1} for different E_{n+1} values, using

$$\text{forecast of } D_{n+1} = a + bE_{n+1},\qquad (5)$$

although, as will be explained later, this may not be the optimal forecasting use of the model, as the forecastability of the error term is being ignored. If one has some prior set of beliefs about possible earnings figures, such as

$$E_{n+1} = 1000 \quad \text{with probability} \quad 0.2$$
$$= 1100 \quad \text{with probability} \quad 0.3$$
$$= 1250 \quad \text{with probability} \quad 0.2$$
$$= 1350 \quad \text{with probability} \quad 0.2$$
$$= 1500 \quad \text{with probability} \quad 0.1,$$

then these beliefs can be transformed into a distribution for forecast dividends. For example, if $a = 100$, $b = 0.1$, direct substitution into (5) gives

$$D_{n+1} = 200 \quad \text{with probability} \quad 0.2$$
$$= 210 \quad \text{with probability} \quad 0.3$$
$$= 225 \quad \text{with probability} \quad 0.2$$
$$= 235 \quad \text{with probability} \quad 0.2$$
$$= 250 \quad \text{with probability} \quad 0.1.$$

Conditional forecasting may also be relevant for control purposes, as will be explained later.

Explanatory models can also be used to provide forecasts of the variable being explained by linking it with forecasts of the explanatory variables. For example, a financial analyst who is familiar with the company and also other firms in the same industry may provide a forecast for earnings which could be converted into a forecast for dividends by using (4) in the form

$$\text{forecast of } D_{n+1} = a + b(\text{forecast of } E_{n+1}).\qquad (6)$$

Any forecast for earnings can be used here, but obviously the better the forecast for earnings the better that for dividends. A remarkably simple but widely applicable and successful model is available for company earnings, of the form

$$E_t = m + E_{t-1} + \varepsilon_t,\qquad (7)$$

where ε_t is white noise. A variable generated by such a model is said to be a random walk with drift, and this property of company earnings has been described as "higgledy-piggledy growth." Accepting (7) as true and putting $t = n + 1$ gives a good forecast of earnings,

$$\text{forecast of } E_{n+1} = m + E_n, \tag{8}$$

and substituting into (6) gives

$$\text{forecast of } D_{n+1} = a + b(m + E_n). \tag{9}$$

Note that this forecast is strictly derived from the pair of relationships (4) and (7), but it could equally well have been reached by simply regressing D_{n+1} on E_n, that is, by considering a model of the form

$$D_t = \alpha + \beta E_{t-1} + e'_t. \tag{10}$$

However, using the pair of relationships might be thought preferable since more use is then made of an economic theory, however naive. A model of the form (10) may be called a forecasting relationship, as it relates a variable to past values of some other variables.

The economic basis of the original model (3) relating current dividends to current earnings is a very simple-minded one. In practice, the dividend payment in any particular year need not come out of current earnings, but could come from reserves or from borrowed capital, although such a policy could not continue indefinitely. Management often appears to place a great deal of emphasis on stability of dividends, apparently believing that shareholders greatly appreciate this, and so empirical studies of actual dividend data find that a better explanatory model is

$$D_t = c + dD_{t-1} + fE_t + e_t. \tag{11}$$

A positive value of d is almost inevitably found, and this ensures that the dividend sequence is less variable than if d took the value zero. Combining (11) with the higgledy-piggledly earnings growth model gives the improved forecasting relationship

$$D_t = c' + dD_{t-1} + fE_{t-1} + e'_t. \tag{12}$$

For any particular company the coefficients c', d, and f could be estimated by the standard least-squares multiple regression procedure using past observed dividends and earnings figures, which are readily available in the financial literature for most large firms. The usual estimation procedures allow the coefficients of the model to take any values so that the model fits as well as possible. However, on occasion one might have a strong belief about the value that a coefficient should take, and if this belief is expressed in the form of a constraint, then a constrained least-squares estimating procedure is needed. For example, one might require that d in (12) be positive. Computer programs are available on most machines that allow one to find estimates for the parameters that achieve the best possible fit, in terms of the lowest sum of squared errors, whilst obeying any constraints placed on the parameters. If the belief is correct, then generally a superior model, in terms of its forecasting ability, is achieved. What kind of belief should one have about the coefficient f in (12)? One could certainly argue that management's aim is to please shareholders and so the larger earnings, the more dividends they will pay, implying f should be positive. This belief could be imposed on the estimation procedure and a forecasting model obtained. However, if the belief is incorrect, the model so achieved will be inferior to one with no constraint on the sign of the coefficient f. That this belief could be wrong is suggested by the observation that fairly frequently a decline in earnings is accompanied by an increase in dividend. Why should this be? It seems to follow from an idea that the intrinsic value of a share, which might be equated with its price on the stock exchange, can be expressed by

$$P_t = gE_t + hD_t + e_t,\qquad(13)$$

where P_t is the current price and e_t is some error series. If management believes that shareholders are more concerned with capital gains than with dividends, as may well be true due to inequalities in the tax rates, then a method of stabilizing prices if earnings should fall is to raise dividends simultaneously. It is thus seen that our earlier theory of how management should interrelate earnings and dividends may be wrong, and so any constraint placed on a forecasting model based on this theory may lead to a model that is incorrect.

Sometimes it seems as though one of the main preoccupations of upper-middle-class Americans is the prediction of stock market prices. If it were correct, Eq. (13) would seem to provide a method of predicting these prices, as substituting from (12) and (7) gives a forecasting model of the form

$$P_t = k + pE_{t-1} + qD_{t-1} + e_t'.\qquad(14)$$

In fact, a popular method of share price prediction, known as the fundamentalist method, is based on this relationship or its generalization by adding further explanatory variables to the right-hand side. Unfortunately, considerable empirical testing has found no evidence that prices can be usefully forecast using this approach. To see why this occurs, (14) should be viewed in terms of forecasting models and information sets. In essence, this formula attempts to forecast P_{n+1} from the information set $I_n: E_{n-j}, D_{n-j}, j \geq 0$, but there is no sensible reason why the past of the price series should be ignored. If the expanded information set $I'_n : E_{n-j}$, $D_{n-j}, P_{n-j}, j \geq 0$, using past earnings, dividends, *and* prices is employed one might, for example, consider a model of the form

$$P_t = k + rE_{t-1} + sD_{t-1} + \omega P_{t-1} + e_t. \tag{15}$$

If this model is fitted to data, however, it is almost inevitably found that r and s are insignificantly different from zero, ω is near unity, k is small, and the errors are white noise so that (15) effectively reduces to

$$P_t = P_{t-1} + \varepsilon_t, \tag{16}$$

where ε_t is white noise, at least to a good degree of approximation. This is the well-known random walk hypothesis for stock market prices and essentially says that stock price changes are white noise and so cannot be forecast from their own past. As it is price changes that one needs to forecast in order to make money on the stock market, the model is not helpful in the search for ways of making a fortune. This is exactly what one should expect, as if a simple method of predicting stock prices existed it would not be published widely, for otherwise its value would soon be removed by overuse.

This discussion of dividends, earnings, and stock prices is a very brief summary of a few of the main empirical relationships that have been observed in this field. Further details and some references can be found in the book by Granger and Morgenstern (1970). The results have been presented in some detail as they do provide good examples of a number of important points concerning simple forecasting methods based on regression models. These points are reexamined in the following section.

5.3   CAUSAL MODELS: THE GENERAL CASE

It is very frequently the case that the value taken by a variable is at least partially determined by the values taken by other variables, either at the same time or in previous time periods. The quantity of some good sold in a day will probably depend on the price at which it is offered, for example, or the amount of electricity used by a household may depend both on the price of electricity and the income of the household. Models based on such ideas are often called causal models, although they are usually just observed, empirical relationships. The idea of causality is a difficult and subtle one, a proper discussion of which is beyond the scope of this text.

An explanatory model is then one that presents an equation explaining the value of the variable of interest in terms of present values of one or more other variables, and possibly also the past values of these variables.

Equations (3) and (13) provide examples. By inserting plausible values of the explanatory variables, conditional forecasts are obtained directly. To achieve unconditional forecasts, further equations are required for each of the explanatory variables to provide forecasts for these variables. These forecast values for the explanatory or causal variables are then used to form a forecast for the variable of interest. Equations (7) and (9) provide examples. If x_t is the series one wishes to forecast and y_t and z_t are possible explanatory series, then a further example of an explanatory model is

$$x_t = a + by_t + cz_{t-1} + dy_{t-1} + e_t. \tag{17}$$

To forecast one step ahead, write this as

$$x_{n+1} = a + by_{n+1} + cz_n + dy_n + e_{n+1}. \tag{18}$$

Another model is therefore required to provide a forecast for y_{n+1} so that a forecast for x_{n+1} can be constructed. To forecast two or more steps ahead, a further equation is required to provide forecasts for $z_{n+j}, j \geq 1$. Once the necessary models are obtained, it is obviously quite easy to construct forecasts; the main problem is to achieve the correct explanatory or forecasting model in the first place. The discussion of the dividends, earnings, and stock price example suggests the following two rules:

(i)   Do not rely too heavily on a theory that merely appears to be sensible and is not founded on a sound base or on comprehensive empirical testing; and
(ii) there is little or no point in attempting to explain a variable just in terms of past values of *other* variables. It is almost always worth also including the past of the series being explained in the information set used to form a forecast. Equations (11) and (15) provide examples.

There are some circumstances where rule (ii) may seem not to apply, such as when the series being explained, x_t, is known to be made up of past and present values of the explanatory series y_t. For example, the number of people leaving a hospital in a week can only comprise patients who entered previously; the number of automobiles leaving the Lincoln Tunnel in a five-minute interval must be made up on automobiles that entered the tunnel in previous periods; after removing the effects of borrowing, the amount spent by a household in a period consists of money earned in earlier periods, and so forth. This last example is also true for corporations, but not for central governments, or at least they behave as though it is not true. These examples appear to lead to models of the form

$$x_t = ay_t + by_{t-1} + cy_{t-2} + \cdots + e_t \tag{19}$$

and are called distributed lag models by economists. Although they may appear to be sensible, such models do not have a great deal to recommend them, and the output series x_t may contain features that are not related to the input series y_t. For example, the income series y_t for a family may be free of seasonal effects, but the spending series x_t may have a strong seasonal component. Equally, there may be some congestion in the Lincoln Tunnel which will have a large effect on the output series but not affect the input series for a considerable period. In both cases, if a distributed lag model such as (19) is fitted to data, the error series will not be white noise. This has two effects. First, for technical reasons the estimates of the coefficients of the model obtained by a standard regression procedure may not be satisfactory, and second, the forecasts for x_{n+1} have to be altered. For example, if the model fitted is

$$x_t = by_{t-1} + cy_{t-2} + e_t, \tag{20}$$

then the forecast for x_{n+1} made at time n is

$$f_{n,1}^x = by_n + cy_{n-1} + \text{forecast of } e_{n+1}, \tag{21}$$

where the forecast of e_{n+1} is obtained by building a single-series model on past errors. It is possible that the need to forecast the error series exists in all of the models so discussed in this and the previous section wherever the time series properties of the error series were left indeterminate. If the coefficients of the model are known, or well estimated, then the sequence of past errors e_t can be extracted and a single-series model found to fit this series, using the methods outlined in Chapter 3. Suppose, for example, that an AR(1) model seems appropriate, so that

$$e_t = \alpha e_{t-1} + \varepsilon_t, \tag{22}$$

where ε_t is white noise. The appropriate forecast of e_{n+1} to insert into (21) is then αe_n, which from (20) gives

$$\text{forecast of } e_{n+1} = \alpha[x_n - by_{n-1} + cy_{n-2}].$$

Substituting this into (21) shows that the best forecast of x_{n+1} should involve x_n as well as further lagged y's. This then suggests that the original model would have been improved if it had used $x_{n-k}, k \geq 0$, in its information set. It is generally true to say that, if a model uses sufficient lagged values of the variable being explained as well as lagged explanatory variables, the resulting error series should be white noise.

The usual stages in forming a causal or regression model are as follows:

(i)   For the variable to be forecast, list likely explanatory or causal variables. The list should be based on some specific theory, if possible, but introspection is an acceptable source.

(ii) Gather relevant data to be used to estimate and evaluate the model. Time series will be required for all of the variables involved, and the series should be as long as possible in time span, although very ancient data may not be relevant. Exactly what data to use has to be a judgment call, both for the time span and the time interval between observations, if data are available daily, weekly, monthly, etc. In practice, there may be little choice, as only a few years of monthly data, say, will be available.

(iii) Propose a model of the following form (assuming x_t is to be forecast and two explanatory variables y_t and z_t are being used):

$$x_t = \alpha_0 + \alpha_1 x_{t-1} + \alpha_2 x_{t-2} + \cdots + \alpha_k x_{t-k}$$
$$+ \beta_0 y_t + \beta_1 y_{t-1} + \cdots + \beta_p y_{t-p}$$
$$+ \gamma_0 z_t + \gamma_1 z_{t-1} + \cdots + \gamma_q z_{t-q} + e_t$$

and estimate it from the data, using ordinary least squares. If more than two explanatory variables are being used, then they should be added to the equation, both lagged and unlagged. The question of how many lags to use is a very difficult one, and it is doubtful if a satisfactory but simple method exists capable of answering it. If sufficient data are available, at least one lag for each variable may be recommended, but if the data contain a seasonal component, a value of x_{t-12} should also be included. In practice, various alternative lagged models should be fitted to the data and the most satisfactory chosen, that is, the model which leads to the smallest sum of squared errors. There are some very sophisticated techniques available, generalizations of the single-series method or the Box–Jenkins procedures outlined in Chapter 3, but these methods lie outside the scope of this text.[1] One very important aspect of the model eventually chosen is that its error or residual series should be white noise. This can be checked by looking at the correlogram of the residuals of the model. The reasons for requiring the errors to be white noise is that if this is not so the estimation procedure can lead to unsatisfactory estimates, as will be further explained below, and also because the full forecasting possibilities are not being realized if the errors are themselves somewhat forecastable.

A frequently used technique to correct for serial correlation in the residuals, proposed by Cochrane and Orcutt, is to transform every variable in the equation, such as x_t, into

$$x_t^* = x_t - \rho x_{t-1}$$

---

[1] Very much more sophisticated methods of modeling relationships between variables are discussed by Granger and Newbold (1986).

where ρ is a coefficient to be determined so that the equation involving the new variables fits as well as possible, in terms of minimizing the sum of squared residuals. Thus, for example, a model

$$x_t = a + by_t + \text{residual}$$

becomes

$$x_t^* = a^* + b_t^* + \text{residual}^*$$

where $a^* = a(1 - p)$, b and ρ are chosen to minimize the variance of residual*. The resulting equation can be rewritten in terms of x_t, x_{t-1}, y_t, and y_{t-1}. The method effectively models the original residuals as AR(1).

An alternative procedure is to add a lagged dependent variable to the equation so that

$$x_t = a + by_t + \text{residual}$$

becomes

$$x_t = c + by_t + cx_{t-1} + \text{residual}.$$

Neither method is consistently better than the other, and since both are quite simple to use if the relevant computer program is available, it may be better to use both and compare the results.

The extent to which economic theory should be used in the specification of a model is still rather controversial. Some modellers will believe in a theory so strongly that they will insist on constraining parameters to agree with this theory. Others have so little confidence in theories that they are totally ignored and their specification comes just from analysis of the data. A correct theory can be very helpful in pointing towards a satisfactory model specification, limiting the class of models that need to be considered, or at the very least suggesting which explanatory variables should be included. Very rarely will a theory completely specify the model, including exactly what lags to use.

Some of the most venerable economic theories take the form of equilibrium relationships, which say for example that a pair of economic variables x and y will obey an equation of the form $ax + by = 0$ in equilibrium. In practice, equilibrium rarely occurs, and the quantity

$$z = ax + by$$

may be called the equilibrium error. The z_t variable measures the extent to which the economy is out of equilibrium. For example, it may be suggested that the "natural rate" of unemployment is five percent, giving the equilibrium relationship

$$\text{unemployed} = 0.05 \text{ (total workforce)}.$$

A specification that takes such a theory into account takes the form

$$Dx_t = \alpha + \beta z_{t-1} + \text{lagged changes in } x_t, y_t + \text{residuals}$$

where $Dx_t \equiv x_t - x_{t-1}$. There will be a similar equation for Dy_t. The idea behind this type of model is that if the economy is out of equilibrium so that

$$z_t = ax_t + by_t$$

is not zero, then the variables Dx_t, Dy_t will take this into account in their generation process. Such models are known as "error-correcting" and allow a possible theory to enter into the model, through z_{t-1}, but the model is not constrained to have this theory true, as β can be zero. An application of this idea is shown in Section 5.5.

5.4 SOME PRACTICAL PROBLEMS

Once a regression equation has been obtained, it is not difficult to form forecasts from it, but unfortunately there are often several possible alternative formulations of the equation, and they do not necessarily produce similar forecasts. There are various diagnostic checks that can be applied to the model, and methods of comparing alternative models are available to help make a choice. This section considers such questions. It is necessarily rather technical and is not required reading for users of regression models, although it is important for those involved with constructing such models.

A convenient starting point is consideration of the statistics provided by most computer regression packages to help evaluate the quality of the model. Three types of statistics are usually given:

(i) Attached to every estimated parameter in the model is a "t value," though occasionally a "standard error" is provided instead. The usual rather inexact convention is to say that the parameter is significantly different from zero if the t value is at least 2 in magnitude or if the estimated parameter is at least twice the standard error in magnitude. These interpretations are appropriate and correspond to using an approximate 95% confidence region, provided certain assumptions about the form of the model are correct. Unfortunately, as will be seen, these assumptions are often not correct, which makes interpretation of t values very difficult.

(ii) A value of R^2 or of R_c^2, which is R^2 corrected for degrees of freedom so that the number of explanatory variables used is accounted for, is almost always provided. These are interpreted as measures of the goodness of fit of the model and are defined by

$$R^2 = 1 - \frac{(\text{variance of error terms in model})}{(\text{variance of variable explained by model})}$$

and

$$R_c^2 = 1 - \frac{n}{n-k}(1 - R^2).$$

where n is the sample size and k the number of explanatory variables used. The general interpretation given to these quantities is that a model with a larger value is preferred to one with a smaller value.

(iii) The Durbin–Watson d statistic. To a close approximation

$$d = 2(1 - r_1),$$

where r_1 is the estimated first-order autocorrelation for the residuals or errors in the model. Thus, if the errors are white noise, d will approximately equal 2, but if the errors have a positive first autocorrelation, so that an above average error is inclined to be followed by another above average error, d will be less than 2. If d is far from the value 2, this indicates that the errors of the model have a strong time series structure, and are thus capable of being forecast from past errors using the methods discussed in Chapter 3.

Probably the most important of these three statistics is the last, the d statistic. Many unsophisticated users of regression techniques are content to get a high R^2 value and ignore an unsatisfactory value for d, but this can lead to very poor models. It can be shown that if least-squares estimates of a regression model are formed when the errors are not white noise, then the t values are overestimated in magnitude, so that parameters that are actually insignificant from zero may appear to be significant. In the extreme case, when r_1 for the error series is near 1, so that d is very small, both theory and statistical experimentation have shown that spurious results not only can, but are very likely to occur. This is particularly likely if the levels of economic variables are used in the model. As was discussed in Chapter 3 such variables often need to be differenced to achieve stationarity. Using them in an indifferenced form can easily lead to spurious regressions, which can be distinguished by very low d values even though the R^2 values may seem to be satisfactory or even rather high. If differenced data are used, the problem of non-white-noise errors will not totally disappear, but the effect is likely to be very much less important. For forecasting purposes, there is no preference for a model on levels rather than on changes, as forecasts are easily produced from either model, but there should be a strong preference for a model in whose structure and estimated parameters one can have some confidence.

The R^2 or R_c^2 values cannot be usefully interpreted in absolute terms. It is not correct, for instance, to say that a model with R^2 greater than 0.8 is satisfactory but that one with R^2 less than 0.3 is unsatisfactory. The value achieved for R^2 depends solely on how explainable one variable is in terms of another. R^2 can only be used to *rank* alternative models that are trying to explain the *same* dependent variable. For forecasting purposes the criterion one is most interested in when comparing different models is the variance of the error term, as this will be a guide to the variance of the forecast errors when the model is used to form forecasts. For example, if one has the pair of models

$$X_t = 18 + 0.64Y_{t-1} + e_{1t}, \qquad R_c^2 = 0.86,$$

and

$$\Delta X_t = 0.23 \, \Delta Y_{t-1} + 0.13 \, \Delta Z_{t-1} + e_{2t}, \qquad R_c^2 = 0.22,$$

with $\mathrm{var}(e_{1t}) = 3.6$ and $\mathrm{var}(e_{2t}) = 1.3$, then the second model is more useful for forecasting, as its variance of error is smaller. The R^2 values are of no importance as the form of the dependent variable is not the same for the two models. In any case, the d values for both models should also be considered, as one at least may indicate serial correlation in the errors. If such serial correlation is observed, improved methods of estimation for the parameters need to be employed. Descriptions of these more sophisticated estimation procedures can be found in the better econometrics texts.

One further problem that often occurs when economic data over a span of several years are used in forming a model is called heteroscedasticity. It is often noted that as the level of some economic variable, such as price or consumption, increases so does the variance of the errors of any model using this variable, even if the differenced form is used. Heteroscedasticity is a particularly strange word meaning unequal variance, and if a model is estimated for a situation in which the errors have this property, again somewhat unsatisfactory estimates of the parameters and, particularly, of the associated t statistics, will usually occur. A frequently used strategy for at least reducing this problem is to build models on the logarithms of the data rather than on the raw data. This is a perfectly reasonable strategy, but it does have the unfortunate consequence that one ends up with a model that is capable of producing forecasts of the logarithm of a variable rather than of the variable itself, as is usually required. For example, denote the original variable to be forecast by X_t and its logarithm by $x_t = \log X_t$. For simplicity, suppose that Y_t is the only explanatory variable to be used and that $y_t = \log Y_t$. Further suppose that a model is selected and estimated of the form

$$x_t = 0.2x_{t-1} + 0.4y_{t-1} + \varepsilon_t,$$

where ε_t passes the usual tests for white noise and has variance σ^2. A one-step forecast of x_{n+1} is then given by

$$f_{n,1}^x = 0.2x_n + 0.4y_n,$$

but what is really required is a forecast of $X_{n+1}, f_{n,1}^x$. It is easily shown that a forecast of the form

$$f_{n,1}^X = \exp f_{n,1}^x$$

is biased and that a better forecast is given by

$$f_{n,1}^X = \exp(f_{n,1}^x + \tfrac{1}{2}\sigma^2).$$

The main point is that if transformations of the data are used in modeling, then great care has to be taken in unraveling this transformation when using the model to forecast.

It is hoped that this section will at least give an indication of the very real and important practical problems that arise when using regression models. These problems are often ignored by unsophisticated users of such models and often result in unsatisfactory or suboptimal forecasts. A complete description of all aspects of these problems and the strategies to overcome them is well beyond the scope of this text. Descriptions can be found in the more advanced texts in econometrics and forecasting, but completely satisfactory solutions to all of the problems have not yet been discovered and advances are to be found in recent research literature.

5.5   REGRESSION MODELLING — TWO EMPIRICAL EXAMPLES

The two examples shown here are designed to illustrate the approach and problems discussed in the previous two sections. Not all possible specifications are considered, and so the final model achieved is not necessarily the best possible. The models are chosen to be useful for forecasting.

5.5.1   Dividends and Earnings

The objective is to forecast an aggregate, economy-wide measure of dividend yield, that is the dividend divided by share price. An obvious explanatory variable is aggregate earnings (profits) divided by share prices. The data used are

D_t— Dividend yield, aggregate dividend/price ratio
E_t— Aggregate company earnings/price ratio

The series are observed quarterly, starting in 1947. The sample size is $n = 137$, and the source is Standard and Poors.

One method of modelling would relate D_t to past D_t. For example,

$$D_t = 0.19 + 0.957\, D_{t-1} \qquad \begin{array}{cc} \text{D/W} & \text{SSR} \\ 1.81 & 16.13 \end{array} \qquad (23)$$
$$(37.9)$$

D/W is the Durbin–Watson statistic, SSR is the sum of squared residuals, and the figure in brackets is the ordinary least squares estimate of the t-statistic. In all equations the error term is not shown.

An alternative model might try to explain D_t by lagged E_t.

$$D_t = 1.29 + 0.35\, E_{t-1} \qquad \begin{array}{cc} \text{D/W} & \text{SSR} \\ 0.70 & 30.97 \end{array} \qquad (24)$$
$$(26)$$

However, the very low Durbin–Watson statistic suggests that the equation is badly misspecified. The Cochrane/Orcutt method of correction forms the new variables

$$D_t^* = D_t - \rho D_{t-1}$$
$$E_t^* = E_t - \rho E_{t-1}$$

and estimates ρ to get the best fit for

$$D_t^* = \text{constant} + b E_{t-1}^*.$$

The result was

$$D_t^* = 3.23 + 0.12\, E_{t-1}^* \qquad \rho = 0.92 \quad \text{SSR} = 14.91 \qquad (25)$$
$$(3.44)$$

An alternative way to allow for the autocorrelation in the residuals in (24) is to add a lagged dependent variable. This is equivalent to starting with (23) and adding E_{t-1} as a possible explanatory variable, giving

$$D_t = 0.34 + 0.753\, D_{t-1} + 0.084\, E_{t-1} \qquad \text{D/W} = 1.83$$
$$(12.2) \qquad\quad (3.6) \qquad\qquad \text{SSR} = 14.72 \qquad (26)$$

This model appears to be basically satisfactory. The residuals have little or no serial correlation (of lag 1), both lagged D_t and E_t are significant, having large t-values, and the SSR is the lowest of all of the models, although it is almost identical to that with (25). Note that the SSR for (25) is very much lower than for (24), showing the advantage of not ignoring serial correlations in residuals. The SSR for (26) is about 9% lower than for (23), indicating that using lagged earnings helps forecast dividends.

Equations (24) and (25) can be compared to two nonforecasting models

$$D_t = 1.29 + 0.35 \, E_t, \quad \text{D/W} = 0.22 \quad \text{SSR} = 28.5 \qquad (27)$$

which has a low D/W value, indicating a high serial correlation in the residual. Correcting this gives

$$D_t^* = 1.41 + 0.33 \, E_t^* \qquad \rho = 0.883 \quad \text{SSR} = 5.96 \qquad (28)$$
$$(16)$$

As D_t is being explained by current E_t, this equation cannot directly be used to forecast, and the SSR is seen to be much smaller than for the forecasting models. This type of model merely suggests that D_t and E_t are jointly influenced by current events. This example illustrates both the usefulness of forecasting a variable by both its own past and also the past of another variable and the advantage to be gained from correcting for serial correlation in residuals.

5.5.2   Prices and Money

The Federal Reserve Bank controls part of the money supply and attempts to use this variable to control prices and thus restrict the level of inflation. For this to be successful, a change in money supply should cause a subsequent change in price, and thus money should be useful to predict the level of prices. The objective of this exercise is to determine whether information about money supply does help forecast changes in prices.

P_t The GNP price deflator, 1972 basis.

M_t Money supply, being currency and demand deposits, seasonally adjusted (average of daily figures).

Y_t Gross national product, seasonally adjusted.

R_t Treasury bill interest rate (3 month) average of daily figures.

Data is quarterly, starting in 1959 and going through 1981. For a series x_t, Dx_t will denote the change series, i.e., $Dx_t - x_t - x_{t-1}$. With differenced data, the sample size is $n = 88$. The series to be explained by these forecasting models is DP_t. An obvious model is to use past price change, giving

$$DP_t = 0.12 + 0.93 \, DP_{t-1} \qquad \text{D/W} = 2.4$$
$$(22.6) \qquad\qquad\qquad \text{SSR} = 17.48 \qquad (29)$$

where D/W is the Durbin-Watson statistic and SSR is the sum of squared error. An alternative approach is to model price change in terms of just previous change in the money supply giving

$$DP_t = 1.22 + .07\ DM_{t-1} \qquad D/W = 0.17$$
$$SSR = 116 \qquad (30)$$

The very low Durbin-Watson statistic indicates strong serial correlation in the residuals. This can be corrected by forming new variables

$$DP_t^* = DP_t - \rho DP_{t-1}$$
$$DM_t^* = DM_t - \rho DM_{t-1}$$

and the new model becomes

$$DP_t^* = 2.01 + 0.023\ DM_{t-1}^* \qquad D/W = 2.6$$
$$(1.87) \qquad SSR = 16.7$$
$$\rho = 0.945 \qquad (31)$$

The t-statistic on DM_{t-1}^* is marginally significant. A rather different way to allow for the serial correlation in the residuals in (30) is to add DP_{t-1} to this equation which is the same as adding DM_{t-1} to (29), giving

$$DP_t = 0.26 + 0.92\ DP_{t-1} + 0.043\ DM_{t-1} \qquad D/W = 2.7$$
$$(23.6) \qquad SSR = 15.4 \quad (32)$$

This appears to be an improvement over both (29) and (31), with a lower SSR. The parameter on DM_{t-1} is now clearly significant, suggesting that money supply does influence next quarter's price change.

Other possible exploratory variables are GNP and interest rates. Adding changes in these variables to (2) gives

$$DP_t = 1.38 + 0.055\ DM_{t-1} - 1.42\ DY_{t-1} + 0.14\ DR_{t-1}$$
$$(1.49) \qquad (-1.22) \qquad (1.33)$$

$$D/W = 0.22$$
$$SSR = 113 \quad (33)$$

Correcting for the obvious serial correlation in the residuals gives

$$DP_t^* = 1.92 + 0.003\ DM_{t-1}^* - 0.03\ DY_{t-1}^* + .066\ DR_{t-1}^*$$
$$(0.2) \qquad (-.07) \qquad (2.2)$$

$$D/W = 2.5$$
$$SSR = 15.61$$
$$\rho = 0.94 \quad (34)$$

This is not an improvement over (32), and only DR_{t-1} appears to be significant. Using the alternative approach of including DP_{t-1} gives

$$DP_t = 0.93\ DP_{t-1} + 0.04\ DM_{t-1} - 0.07\ DY_{t-1} + 0.52\ DR_{t-1}$$
$$\quad\ (3.0)\qquad\qquad (3.16)\qquad\qquad (-0.2)\qquad\quad (1.4)$$

$$\text{D/W} = 2.75$$
$$\text{SSR} = 15.0 \qquad (35)$$

This is now virtually the same as (32), as the two new variables, DY_{t-1}, DR_{t-1} do not enter significantly and SSR is similar.

One further model uses the error-correction form as discussed in Section 5.3. The well known economic identity

$$\text{money} \times \text{velocity of circulation} = \text{price} \times \text{income}$$

with the unobserved velocity assumed to depend on interest rates suggests a possible linear equilibrium relationship between M, R, Y, and P with any temporary deviation being an equilibrium error. If price change is driven by this error, one gets the model

$$DP_{t-1} = -0.37 + (0.03\ M_{t-1} + 0.17\ R_{t-1} - 0.03\ P_{t-1} - 0.33\ Y_{t-1})$$
$$\qquad\qquad (4.5)\qquad\qquad (6.5)\qquad\qquad (-1.8)\qquad\quad (-3.13)$$

$$\text{D/W} = 1.55$$
$$\text{SSR} = 11.1 \qquad (36)$$

Note that the term in brackets may be thought of as the equilibrium error and involves levels, rather than changes, of the variables. This appears to be the best fitting model of those considered, with clearly the lowest SSR.

This example illustrates the potential gains in the goodness of fit of the model after considering various alternative specifications, including the error-correction form.

The models discussed in these examples have been evaluated in terms of their in-sample goodness of fit measured by SSR. It is not always the model that fits best in sample that forecasts the best, particularly if many different specifications have been considered, a process sometimes called "data mining." If a model with just a few parameters is being compared with a much more complicated one, the corrected R^2, as discussed in Section 5.4, should be used rather than SSR to make comparisons between models.

5.6   ECONOMETRIC MODELS

Any economics textbook or course in macroeconomics emphasizes the considerable extent to which economic variables are interrelated. Production will depend on consumption and consumption on employment and employment on production, for example. Such feedback relationships, or relationships holding simultaneously for groups of variables, not only introduce particular problems of modeling but also suggest the existence of true, important relationships that can be utilized to produce improved forecasts in economics.

An example of a simple, simultaneous national income model is as follows:

$$C_t = a_1 + b_1 Y_t \hspace{4cm} + e_{C_t}, \hspace{1cm} \text{(37i)}$$

$$I_t = a_2 \hspace{1cm} + c_2 P_{t-1} \hspace{2cm} + e_{I_t}, \hspace{1cm} \text{(37ii)}$$

$$T_t = \hspace{2cm} d_3 \text{GNP}_t \hspace{1cm} + e_{T_t}, \hspace{1cm} \text{(37iii)}$$

$$P_t = a_4 + b_4 Y_t \hspace{2cm} + f_4 I_{t-1} + e_{P_t}, \hspace{1cm} \text{(37iv)}$$

$$\text{GNP}_t = C_t + I_t + G_t, \hspace{3.5cm} \text{(37v)}$$

$$Y_t = \text{GNP}_t - T_t, \hspace{3.5cm} \text{(37vi)}$$

where C is consumption, I investment, Y disposable national income, GNP gross national product, G government expenditure on goods and services, T taxes, P profits, and e_{C_t}, e_{I_t}, e_{T_t}, and e_{P_t} are error terms.

The model consists of two different types of equations. The first four are called structural equations and involve parameters (a_1, b_1, etc.) that need to be determined. These equations arise from some economic theory and determine the four variables C, I, T, and P. Thus, for example, Eq. (37i) states that aggregate consumption is a linear function of national income and Eq. (37iii) has aggregate taxes as a fixed proportion of GNP, although both equations do not fit exactly and so contain error terms. The final two equations are identities and are simple definitions linking different variables. An identity is known to hold exactly and thus has neither error term nor parameters to be estimated. It would be possible to substitute for the variables defined by the identities in the structural equations and thus reduce the total number of variables involved in the system, but there may then be some loss of interpretability.

The variables can also be subdivided into important classes. Variables C_t, I_t, T_t, and P_t are called endogenous, which means that they are determined by structural equations in the system. Variables P_{t-1} and I_{t-1} are called predetermined because at time t there is little or no doubt about their values. G_t is an exogenous variable, meaning that its value at time t is determined outside the system, presumably as a result of various government decisions. The two remaining variables GNP_t and Y_t are determined by identities and so are completely determined from the other variables.

Because of the two identities, the set of endogenous variables can in fact be almost any four of the group C, I, T, P, GNP, and Y, provided the identities are obeyed.

The error terms will be taken to be white noises, for the moment. If one tries to use the structural equations to form forecasts, difficulties immediately arise because of the simultaneous nature of the system. For example, replacing t by $n + 1$ in (37i) gives

$$C_{n+1} = a_1 + b_1 Y_{n+1} + e_{c,n+1},$$

and so a "forecast" for C_{n+1} can be written

$$f_{n,1}^C = a_1 + b_1 f_{n,1}^Y,$$

but a forecast for Y_{n+1} is required for this equation to be usable. The simultaneous form of the model also makes estimation of the parameters of the system difficult. However, econometric texts invariably include extensive discussions of this estimation problem, and it would be quite inappropriate to try to summarize this area here. In what follows, it will be assumed that good estimates of the parameters have been obtained so that attention can be focused on the use of the model for forecasting purposes.

A different formulation of the model is particularly useful for forecasting, known as the reduced form. A reduced form expresses each endogenous variable just in terms of exogenous and predetermined variables, plus error. Suppose the above model is to be used to provide a forecast for GNP. Adding the first two equations and using the identities, one gets

$$\text{GNP}_t - G_t = (a_1 + a_2) + b_1(\text{GNP}_t - T_t) + c_2 P_{t-1} + (e_{C_t} + e_{I_t}).$$

Substituting for T_t from (37iii), rearranging, and dividing through by $H \equiv 1 - b_1 + b_1 d_3$ gives

$$\text{GNP}_t = A + \frac{G_t}{H} + \frac{c_2 P_{t-1}}{H} + e_{G_t}, \tag{37vii}$$

where $A \equiv (a_1 + a_2)/H$ and $e_{G_t} = (e_{C_t} + e_{I_t} - b_1 e_{T_t})/H$.

The other endogenous variables can be expressed in similar ways. Equation (37ii), for I_t, is already in a reduced form, as it only involves the predetermined variable P_{t-1} and substituting from (37vii) for GNP_t into equation (37iii) immediately gives the reduced form equation for T_t. Finally, writing (37iv) as

$$P_t = a_4 + b_4(\text{GNP}_t - T_t) + f_4 I_{t-1} + e_{P_t}$$

and then substituting for GNP_t from (37vii) and for T_t from (37iii) gives the reduced form equation for P_t, which can be written

$$P_t = h_1 + h_2 G_t + h_3 P_{t-1} + h_4 I_{t-1} + e'_{P_t}, \tag{37viii}$$

where the parameters h_1, h_2, h_3, h_4 are all functions of the parameters of the structural equations and the error e'_{P_t} is a linear function of the errors in the original set of equations.

From (37ii), which is a reduced form equation, a one-step forecast for I_{n+1} is easily formed:

$$I_{n+1} = a_2 + c_2 P_n + e_{I, n+1}$$

and so

$$f^I_{n,1} = a_2 + c_2 P_n$$

if e_{I_t} is white noise, as has been assumed. The rule, as in previous chapters, is to write down the equation that you believe will determine the future value of the variable of interest and then to replace all explanatory variables by either their known values or by their optimum forecasts. To use (37vii) to forecast GNP_{n+1}, one has

$$\text{GNP}_{n+1} = A + \frac{G_{n+1}}{H} + \frac{C_2 P_n}{H} + e_{a,n+1},$$

and so

$$f^{\text{GNP}}_{n,1} = A + \frac{G_{n+1}}{H} + \frac{c_2 P_n}{H} \qquad (37\text{ix})$$

The question immediately arises of how to forecast future government expenditure. If an economist is employed by a company and has no inside information about what are the government's intentions, he can take one of two alternative approaches. The first is to list a set of plausible values for G_{n+1} and, for each of these values, to then use equation (37ix) to give *conditional* forecasts of GNP, as was discussed in the second section of this chapter when relating dividends to earnings. The alternative technique is to try to determine a model relating past government expenditure figures to other economic variables, such as unemployment levels, national income, or price changes. This model essentially completes the system by treating G_t as though it were endogenous rather than exogenous. The resulting reduced form of this extended system will then have each exogenous variable in terms of just predetermined variables, so that forecasts are easily formed. This approach gives *unconditional* forecasts for the GNP. The only problem with this method is that it is difficult to take into account nonnumerical information, such as rumors one might have about government interactions. It is usual to use a model to forecast G_{n+1} and then to alter this forecast subjectively if relevant extra information is available to the forecaster. The success or lack thereof of such adjustments clearly depends on the quality of the information being utilized and the abilities of the forecaster who tries to use it.

An economist employed by the government may use Eq. (37ix) in a quite different fashion. If the viewpoint is taken that the government has some considerable flexibility in the value that G_{n+1} can take, since this value is determined by governmental decisions, Eq. (37ix) can be used as a control equation, with the value of G_{n+1} chosen so that $f_{n,1}^{\text{GNP}}$ is at or near some target value for the GNP in the next period, as determined by those in control. Discussion of control theory would take us too far from the central theme of this chapter, but the importance of correct forecasting models for control purposes should be clear.

Due to the simultaneous nature of an econometric model, the information set being used to form a forecast can become substantial. The form taken by any individual structural equation may be quite simple, but this is because many of the variables in the information set are excluded from the equation, due to the constraints on the model imposed by the economic theory that is being referred to when the model is being specified. The main advantage of basing an econometric model on a specific economic theory is the resulting simplification in the structural form and a consequent saving in the number of parameters that need to be estimated. The reduced form may well involve many predetermined and exogenous variables and so not be simple in form. The difficult estimation problem with a set of structural equations can be circumvented by applying ordinary least squares to each individual equation of the reduced form. For example, the h's in equation (37viii) could be estimated directly, rather than derived from the parameters of the structural equations, and the resulting equation used to form forecasts. However, if this is done for every reduced form equation, the total number of parameters to be estimated may become very large, and so suspect if the total amount of data available is not large. Further, any simplifications suggested by the economic theory will not have been utilized, and so the estimates may be less efficient than is achievable. If one has available a correct theory, or at least a good approximation to one, it is clearly better to base one's forecasts on this theory. The timing of high tides is an example of forecasts based on a sound theory.

On the other hand, a model based on an incorrect or incomplete theory will produce suboptimal forecasts. A problem with economic theories is that they are not obviously correct. There are often competing theories which econometricians have not been able to decide between, possibly because neither theory is correct and many theories are insufficiently precise for a full-scale econometric model to be based upon them. In particular, few theories specify the lag structure of the variables entering into the model with an acceptable degree of precision. These effects often result in models having non-white-noise errors, plus many of the other problems discussed in the previous section. Because of this, a certain amount of experimental modeling is conducted with econometric models, particularly with the error terms.

The correct size of the model, that is, the number of equations that it should contain, is also a source of controversy. The larger the model, the more likely it is to capture all the important feedback loops in the economy, but the likelihood of misspecification also increases and estimation of the parameters of the model necessarily becomes more difficult. Some econometricians prefer a "small" model of only 20 – 30 structural equations, but models of 1000 or more equations are considered to be necessary by other experts. A worldwide model, linking individual country models with trade flows, has also been constructed and consists of several thousand equations. As one bad egg can spoil an omelette, there must be a worry with such large models that one poorly specified sector of the model may have bad effects throughout, unless special care is taken.

In practice, most of the really influential macroeconomic forecasts of developed economies are based on econometric models. It is also true that the forecasts produced by the model are not necessarily the forecasts issued by the model's constructors. If a forecast for some segment seems strange or out of line with other forecasts or the econometrician's own judgment, then it will probably be altered to look more reasonable. This application of "tender loving care" has been shown to result in improved forecasts and, to some extent, overcomes the most important misspecifications that inevitably occur when constructing a large-scale model.

It could be claimed that the construction of a really well specified model for the economy should be the ultimate goal of all statisticians concerned with economic data, as such a model would both result in the very best possible forecasts and also allow governments to efficiently control the economy. It is also clear that econometricians are a very long way from achieving this objective.

The question of how forecasts from econometric models can be evaluated and how well they perform in practice compared to alternative methods will be discussed in Chapter 8.

One practical problem that has arisen in recent years is the use of nonlinear forms of the variables in the structural equations. For example, consumption may be explained by income and also the square root of income. Such transformations may well lead to improved structural equations, but the reduced form cannot always then be derived and so forecasting becomes more difficult. The usual practice is to "linearize" the model and then to find the corresponding reduced form, but this is probably a suboptimal solution to the problem.

5.7   AN ACTUAL ECONOMETRIC MODEL

To further emphasize some of the more important points made in the previous section and also to introduce a little more reality, use will be made of an actual econometric model published by Fair (1984). In his book he discusses a medium size model, called the "US model," involving 30 estimated structural equations, 98 definitions on identities, and a total of 233 variables. The model is based on economic theory and is estimated using various methods. To evaluate this model, a much simpler, linear twelve-equation model is also constructed (called LINUS) using some simple economic theory and many fewer variables. By comparing forecasts from the two models, one can get an idea of how much gain there is in going from a simple model to a more sophisticated one.

LINUS makes a good example of a simple econometric model. The first four equations concern expenditure of the household section.

(i)   Consumption of services (CS)

$$CS_t = -0.45 + 0.99\ CS_{t-1} + 0.009\ GNPR_t - 0.11 RS_t$$
$$\qquad\qquad (10.6)\qquad\quad (3.24)\qquad\quad (8.19)$$

$$R^2 = 0.99,\ DW = 2.13,\ \hat{\rho} = -.23$$

(ii)   Consumption of nondurables (CN)

$$CN_t = 2.7 + 0.80\ CN_{t-1} + 0.044\ GNPR_t - 0.07\ RS_{t-1}$$
$$\qquad\qquad (11.09)\qquad\quad (3.05)\qquad\quad (2.03)$$

$$R^2 = 0.99,\ DW = 1.94,\ \hat{\rho} = 0.21$$

(iii)   Consumption of durables (CD)

$$CD = -2.4 + 0.76\ CD_{t-1} + 0.037\ GNPR_t - 0.21\ RM_{t-1}$$
$$\qquad\qquad (13.34)\qquad\quad (4.83)\qquad\quad (4.29)$$

$$R^2 = 0.99,\ DW = 2.01,$$

(iv)   Housing investment (IH)

$$IH_t = 1.97 + 0.51\ IH_{t-1} + 0.026\ GNPR_t - 0.44\ RM_{t-1}$$
$$\qquad\qquad (4.17)\qquad\quad (4.37)\qquad\quad (4.75)$$

$$R^2 = 0.98,\ DW = 1.96,\ \hat{\rho} = 0.82$$

In these equations $GNPR_t$ is real GNP, RS_t is a short-term interest rate (bill rate), and RM_t is a long-term rate (mortgage rate). If the Cochrane-Orcutt procedure was used in the estimation, a value for $\hat{\rho}$ is shown. Figures in brackets below estimated parameters are t-statistics. Each expenditure item is a function of its lagged value, real GNP, and an interest rate. The similar equations in the full US model also include the price level, wage rate, and nonlabor income.

(v)   Production (Y)

$$Y_t = 9.93 + 0.18\ Y_{t-1} + 0.97\ X_t - 0.17\ V_{t-1}$$
$$(3.64) \qquad (17.20) \quad (4.32)$$

$$R^2 = .99,\ \text{DW} = 2.19,\ \hat{\rho} = 0.54$$

where X_t is total sales and V_t is total stock of inventories.

(vi)   Investment

$$\text{IK}_t = -1.21 + 0.82\ \text{IK}_{t-1} + 0.008\ \text{KK}_{t-1} + 0.06\ Y_t - 0.02Y_{t-1}$$
$$(17.1) \qquad\qquad (4.21) \qquad\qquad (2.88) \qquad (0.79)$$

$$R^2 = 0.99,\ \text{DW} = 1.90$$

where KK_t is the stock of capital.

(vii)   Mortgage rate (RM)

$$\text{RM}_t = 0.32 + 0.84\ \text{RM}_{t-1} + 0.28\ \text{RS}_t - 0.07\ S_{t-1} - 0.025\ \text{RS}_{t-2}$$
$$(28.6) \qquad\qquad (7.32) \qquad (1.31) \qquad (0.72)$$

$$R^2 = 0.99,\ \text{DW} = 2.11$$

which is the term structure equation relating long-term and short-term interest rates.

(viii)   Bill rate (RS)

$$\text{RS}_t = -0.3 + 0.85\ \text{RS}_{t-1} + 0.06\ \text{GNPR}_t - 0.05\ \text{GNPR}_{t-1} +$$
$$(14.2) \qquad\qquad (1.55) \qquad\qquad (1.41)$$

$$0.039\ \text{DM1}_t + 0.13\ \text{DUM793} \times \text{DM1}$$
$$(1.76) \qquad\qquad (3.92)$$

$$R^2 = 0.95,\ \text{DW} = 1.71$$

where DM1 is change in money supply (M1) and DUM793 takes the value 0 before the third quarter of 1979 and the value 1 afterwards, capturing a change in policy by the Federal Reserve Bank. This equation can be interpreted as an interest rate, government policy reaction function.

The final four equations are identities.

(ix) $$X_t = \text{CS}_t + \text{CN}_t + \text{CD}_t + \text{IH}_t + \text{IK}_t + Q_{1,t} \qquad \text{(total sales)}$$

(x) $$V_t = V_{t-1} + Y_t - X_t \qquad \text{(stock of inventories)}$$

(xi) $$\text{GNPR}_t = Y_t + Q_{2,t} \qquad \text{(real GNP)}$$

(xii) $$KK_t = (1 - \delta)KK_{t-1} + IK \qquad \text{(capital stock)}$$

where V_t is total inventories and δ is the rate of depreciation of the capital stock. Q_{1t}, Q_{2t} are simply exogenous variables defined to make the identities (ix) and (xi) be true. The equations were estimated by a technique known as two-stage least squares using quarterly data for the period 1954 to the third quarter of 1982.

This model contains twelve endogenous variables, although four can be easily removed by the identities, and the only true, directly observable exogenous variable is the change in M1 which enters nonlinearly in equation (viii). Four equations, (i), (ii), (iv), and (v), used the Cochrane-Orcutt procedure. The residuals of the equations contain little or no serial correlation, R^2 values are very large as the model generally deals with the levels of macroeconomic variables, lagged dependent variables are often included, and most of the parameters in the model have t-values that are greater than two in magnitude.

From its structure, it is rather difficult to obtain reduced form equations. To be used for forecasting, models would need to be derived for Q_1 and Q_2, possibly using simple time series techniques, and forecasts will also be required for M1. Because of the many contemporary terms in the model, and the consequent difficulty in finding the reduced form equations, forecasts have to be made by first assuming a value for key variables such as X or Y, deriving forecasts for other variables, then forecasting X or Y and repeating this process until convergence occurs.

In his book, Fair (1984) compares the forecasting ability of his full model and the much simpler LINUS model discussed above, for two variables, Real GNP (GNPR) and the bill rate (RS). The models were compared by the root mean squared (RMS) forecast errors for the period 1970 to 1982 using forecast horizons from one to eight quarters. The two models forecast the bill rate about equally, with the one-step RMS error being about half the eight-step RMS value. However, for real GNP, the full model forecast better than LINUS, about 10% better at the one-step horizon and up to 50% at the eight-quarter horizon. One substantial difference between the full and the simplified models is that the full model provides forecasts of many more variables than does the smaller model.

5.8   A NOTE ON THE CONCEPT OF CAUSALITY

Relationships have been called "causal" in this chapter, but it should be pointed out that there is some disagreement about the use of the word "causal." Most philosophers of science and research workers agree that a cause occurs before an effect and that the relationship between a caused variable and the variable that is being caused is a deep one, not easily disrupted by the inclusion of other variables in a regression, for example. It is also commonly believed that a cause does not inevitably lead to a specific effect, just that the probability of the effect occuring is changed by the appearance of the cause. The generally accepted causation of lung cancer from smoking is an example. One consequence of these ideas is that a causal variable should help forecast the variable being caused even after other information has been used in forming a forecast. This idea has resulted in a number of tests for causality between economic variables based on forecasting models. Further discussion can be found in Granger (1980).

5.9 FORECASTING AND CONTROL

One of the main objectives of governments, companies, universities, and other institutions is to control their environments. A government may decide to try to bring down unemployment or inflation, to reduce a balance of trade or budget deficit, or to improve investment. A company will try to increase sales and profits by controlling prices and advertising expenditures. Provided that the number of control variables, whose values can be strongly influenced by the institution, is equal to the number of variables to be controlled, then in theory control can be achieved. However, the relationships between variables have to be well understood and various forecasts have to be formed carefully.

Suppose, for example, that Y_t is the gross national product (GNP) of some economy, being a measure of the size of the total flow of the economy. It will be asssumed that Y_t is well modelled by an equation of the form

$$Y_t = a + bY_{t-1} + cG_t + dX_t + \varepsilon_t \qquad (38)$$

where G_t is government expenditure and X_t is GNP of an important neighboring country. For example, Y_t could be the GNP of Canada and X_t the GNP of the U.S.A. Suppose for the moment that the government can choose the future value of G_t so that it decides at time $t-1$ what value G_t will take. Suppose that we are now at time t and that the government has a target value Y_{t+1}^* that it would like Y_{t+1} to take. The problem that it faces is how to choose the control variable G_{t+1} so that Y_{t+1} is as near as possible to the target Y_{t+1}^*. It is necessary to have a measure of nearness corresponding to the cost function discussed in Chapter 1. As was true there, a convenient measure is the squared difference between the variable one is trying to control and its target, i.e.,

$$C = E_t(Y_{t+1} - Y_{t+1}^*)^2 \qquad (39)$$

where E_t is the expectation taken at time t so that everything that occurs at or before time t can be treated as a constant.

Replacing t by $t + 1$ in (38) and substituting into (39) gives

$$C = E_t(a + bY_t + cC_{t+1} + dX_{t+1} + \varepsilon_{t+1} - Y^*_{t+1})^2.$$

Both C_{t+1} and Y^*_{t+1} are selected by the government at time t in this assumed situation. Let $f^*_{t,1}$ be the optimum forecast of X_{t+1} made at time t, then expanding the squared expression and taking expectations gives

$$C = (a + bY_t + cC_{t+1} + df^*_{t,1} - Y^*_{t+1})^2 + \mathrm{var}(\varepsilon_{t+1} + e^*_{t,1}) \qquad (40)$$

where $e^*_{t,1} = X_{t+1} - f^*_{t,1}$ is the one-step forecast error for X and is assumed unforecastable at time t. The government needs to select G_{t+1} so that C is minimized, and this is easily seen to be achieved by making the first term in (40) zero, so that

$$G_{t+1} = -c^{-1}[a + bY_t + df^*_{t,1} - Y^*_{t+1}].$$

This analysis is an example of a more general theory that proves that proper forecasting of important variables in the area of consideration is necessary for successful control. If X_{t+1} is poorly forecast, the control value selected will be suboptimal and unfortunate surprises can occur. In practice, control by governments is less simple as they typically have great difficulty in achieving the required values for their control variables, such as government expenditure or money supply, because of political and institutional factors.

5.10   THE PROJECT

Models will now be considered which can be used to forecast the series of interest from other series. If x_t is the series to be forecast, at least one other series, say y_t, should also be collected to help in the forecasting exercise. The y_t series should be chosen from economic or managerial theory, or from common sense. For example, if one is forecasting an exchange rate, then an inflation measure in one of the countries may be appropriate. If the series being forecast is a U.S. macroeconomic variable, the weekly index of leading indicators published in Business Week could be useful.

Assuming that both x_t and y_t have any trends and seasonals removed, and using all of the available data at this time, a variety of models can be tried, with x_t the dependent variable and combinations of lagged x_t and lagged and contemporaneous y_t as explanatory models. For example, we might try

  (i) x_t explained by y_t;
 (ii) x_t explained by x_{t-1}, y_t;
(iii) x_t explained by x_{t-1}, y_{t-1} etc.

The quality of the models will be judged by the Durbin-Watson statistic (should be near 2), the relative sizes of the variances of the residuals or, better, the corrected R^2 values, and the significance of the coefficients as measured by the t-values (the magnitude of t should be about 2 or more), as explained in Section 5.4.

The exercise project uses the data given in Table 1.3 plus the following values which can be thought of as having become available since the start of the project:

$t =$	31	32	33	34
x_t	8	-6	-2	4
y_t	-0.8	0.1	0.5	-0.6

It has been decided to use lags up to two, so to make the evaluation statistics comparable, the values of x_t for $t = 3, 4, \ldots , 34$ are used, giving the sample size of 32 for all models, which are fitted by least-squares methods.

The first model fitted is

$$x_t = \text{const} + by_t + \text{residual}, \tag{41}$$

The estimates are

	estimate	t-value
const	2.46	0.65
b	6.17	2.50

$R^2 = 0.17$ \qquad $R_c^2 = 0.12$
s.d. = standard deviation of residual = 21.43
d = Durbin/Watson statistic = 1.77

The model looks hopeful, with an acceptable Durbin/Watson statistic, and the coefficient on y_t is apparently significantly different from zero. The fit is not very high, with a corrected R^2 of only 0.12.

The next model considered is

$$x_t = \text{const} + by_{t-1} + \text{residual} \tag{42}$$

which gave estimates

	est.	t-value
const	2.48	0.76
b	9.16	4.33

$R^2 = 0.38$, $R_c^2 = 0.34$
s.d. = 18.49, $d = 1.95$

This is a better model, as s.d. is smaller and (equivalently) R_c^2 is higher.
The next model is

$$x_t = \text{const} + ax_{t-1} + by_t + \text{residual} \tag{43}$$

which gave

	est.	t-value
const	1.92	0.51
a	0.22	1.31
b	5.51	2.22

$$R^2 = 0.39, R_c^2 = 0.32$$
$$\text{s.d.} = 18.78, d = 2.13$$

This model is seen to be somewhat inferior to (42).
The next model extends (42), taking the form

$$x_t = \text{const} + ax_{t-1} + by_{t-1} + \text{residual}, \tag{44}$$

and giving estimates

	est.	t-value
const	2.38	0.71
a	0.037	0.23
b	8.93	3.76

$$R^2 = 0.386, R_c^2 = 0.32$$
$$\text{s.d.} = 18.78, d = 2.10$$

which is also slightly inferior to (42), having a lower R_c^2 and a higher *s.d.*
The final model tries several explanatory variables:

$$x_t = \text{const} + a_1 x_{t-1} + a_2 x_{t-2} + b_1 y_{t-1} + b_2 y_{t-2} + \text{residuals}. \tag{45}$$

The estimated equation has

	est.	t-value
const	2.95	0.87
a_1	0.15	0.08
a_2	-0.21	-1.33
b_1	7.14	1.92
b_2	3.19	0.70

$$R^2 = 0.42, R_c^2 = 0.32$$
$$\text{s.d.} = 18.85, d = 2.05$$

Again, this model is inferior to (42), as the extra terms are not significant and R_c^2 is slightly lower, although R^2 is higher.

The best model is seen to be (42) and should be selected to provide forecasts. Even though the constant in this model is not significant it is suggested that it is retained when forming forecasts.

From the form of the model, it is seen that h-step forecasts of x made at time n are given by

$$f_{n,h}^x = 2.48 + 9.16\, f_{n,h-1}^y \qquad (46)$$

where $f_{n,h-1}^y$ is the $h-1$ step forecast of y_{n+h-1} made at time n. In particular the one-step forecast of x_{n+1} is

$$f_{n,1}^x = 2.48 + 9.16\, y_n$$

as y_n is known at time n. The forecast for y can be found from the univariate ARMA model found in Chapter 3. The model identified and estimated there for y_t was the AR(1)

$$y_t = 0.81\, y_{t-1} + \text{white noise,}$$

which gives forecasts

$$f_{n,h-1}^y = (0.81)^{h-1} y_n$$

using the formula provided in Section 3.3.

As the most recent piece of data is $t = 34$, with $y_{34} = -0.6$ and forecasts are being made to time $t = 39$, the horizon now is $h = 5$. The forecast of x_{39} is thus

$$f_{34.5}^* = 2.46 + 9.16(0.81)^4(-0.6)$$

$$= .09.$$

From (42) and (46), it is seen that

$$x_{n+h} - f_{n,h}^x = 9.16(y_{n+h-1} - f_{n,h-1}^y) + \varepsilon_{n+h}$$

so that the h-step forecast error of X is

$$e_{n,h}^* = 9.16\, e_{n,h-1}^y + \varepsilon_{n+h} \qquad (47)$$

where ε_t denotes the residual in (42). Throughout, it is assumed that this residual is white noise with zero mean. Squaring both sides of (47) and noting that ε_{n+h} and $e_{n,h}^y$ should be uncorrelated, it follows that

$$\operatorname{var}(e_{n,h}^x) = (9.16)^2 \operatorname{var}(e_{n,h-1}^y) + \operatorname{var}(\varepsilon_{n+h})$$

From model (42), $\text{var}(\varepsilon) = (\text{s.d.})^2 = (18.69)^2$ using the results at the end of Section 6.6,

$$\text{var}(e^y_{n,4}) = 0.72 \left[\frac{1 - \alpha^8}{1 - \alpha^2} \right]$$

where $\alpha = 0.81$, so that

$$\text{var}(e^y_{n,4}) = 1.71.$$

Hence

$$\text{var}(e^x_{n,4}) = 485.4$$

and

$$\text{standard dev}(e^x_{n,4}) = 22.03.$$

The approximate 95% conference intervals are thus:

$$f^x_{54,5} \pm 1.96 \times 22.03$$

i.e.

$$-43.09 \text{ to } 43.27.$$

QUESTIONS

1. Explain the main differences in approach between forecasts formed from econometric models and time series models. Outline any advantages or disadvantages the two methods possess.

2. An econometrician fits the following multiplier–accelerator model to some data:

$$I_t = \alpha + \beta C_t + \text{error},$$

$$C_t = \delta I_t + \gamma I_{t-1} + \lambda G_t + \text{error},$$

where I_t is investment in period t, C_t consumption in period t, and G_t government expenditure in period t.
The coefficients are estimated to be

$$\alpha = 0.03, \qquad \beta = 0.8, \qquad \delta = 0.5, \qquad \gamma = 0.2, \qquad \lambda = 0.5$$

and the errors can be taken to be white noise.
If $C_n = 1000$, $I_n = 500$, and $G_n = 300$, forecast C_{n+1} and I_{n+1}
   (a) using a conditional forecast, and
   (b) using a forecast for G_{n+1} of 350.

3. A report by a market researcher states, "I have found the following

relationship between total savings S_t and advertising by savings banks A_t,

$$S_t = 487 + 0.3A_t + 0.2A_{t-1} + \text{error},$$

and this will be useful in helping forecast future savings." Comment on how a forecast would be made and also on its likely quality.

4. A company econometrician builds the following model for his company relating sales S in a quarter, the wages W paid to salespersons in that quarter, and national income Y:

$$S = 0.2W + 0.5S_{-1} + 0.02Y + e_S, \qquad R^2 = 0.76, \, d = 1.9,$$
$$\quad (3.1) \quad\;\; (4.6) \qquad (2.2)$$

$$W = 82 + 0.3S + 0.01Y + e_W, \qquad R^2 = 0.82, \, d = 0.9.$$
$$\;\;(3.1) \;\; (4.0) \quad\;\; (1.1)$$

Critically discuss the quality of this second equation. Explain how you would use this model to forecast next quarter's sales.

5. A statistician wrote the following report: "My task was to forecast demand for new single family houses in Salt Lake City. I had available annual data for the period 1947–1976. As clearly this demand is largely due to population increases, I ran the following two regressions:

$$(\text{total houses in region})_t = a + b(\text{total population})_t + e_t$$

and

$$(\text{new houses built})_t = c + d(\text{change in population})_t + f_t.$$

The values for the coefficients were found to be

$$a = 10{,}526, \qquad b = 0.3, \qquad c = 122, \qquad d = 0.7.$$

The first equation had $R^2 = 0.62$ and e_t had variance 269, and the second equation had $R^2 = 0.24$ and f_t had variance 42. I then modeled the residual series and found that the following equations give good fits:

$$e_t = 0.9e_{t-1} + \varepsilon_t \quad\text{and}\quad f_t = 0.2f_{t-1} + \eta_t.$$

I noted that in the Salt Lake City region total population P_t appeared to have a linear trend of the form

$$P_t = 4629 + 2000t,$$

where $t = 0$ occurs in 1900. The two models give different forecasts and I could not decide which ones to use."

Comment on his report. Using whichever model you think is the better, forecast new house sales in Salt Lake City for 1977, 1978, and 1985. Discuss how you would try to obtain superior forecasts.

FURTHER READINGS

Fair, Ray C. (1984). *Specification, Estimation, and Analysis of Macroeconometric Models*, Harvard University Press.

Granger, C. W. J. (1980). Testing for causality: A Personal Viewpoint. *Journal of Economic Dynamics and Control.*

Granger, C. W. J., and Oskar Morgenstern (1970). *Predictability of Stock Market Prices*, Lexington, Massachusetts: Heath.

Discusses forecasting of stock prices, earnings and dividends and the random walk hypothesis.

Granger, C. W. J., and P. Newbold (1986). *Forecasting Economic Time Series.* Second Edition Chapter Six, New York: Academic Press.

A critical account of regression and econometric methods.

Klein, L. R. (1971). *An Essay on the Theory of Economic Prediction*, Chicago: Markham.

A very sound account of the use of econometric models for forecasting.

Maddala, G. S. (1977). *Econometrics*, New York: McGraw-Hill.

Up-to-date textbook on econometrics.

6

Survey Data:
Anticipations and Expectations

If you can look into the seeds of time, and say which grain will grow and which will not, speak then unto me.

Shakespeare

6.1 OVERVIEW OF THE USE OF SURVEY DATA

Much of the value to be taken in the future by some economic variable may already have been determined by plans or commitments by the individual decision-making units of the economy. Examples are the following:

(i) A household may have decided to buy a new automobile in three months time and is already adjusting its spending plans to allow for this anticipated purchase. By aggregating up these anticipations over all households, part of the automobile sales that will occur in three months time will have been determined.

(ii) A company is planning to extend its factory in twelve months time and is already organizing the details of the construction and is also considering how to raise the necessary capital. Many major investments by firms require planning and long-term commitments have to be made. By asking companies about these plans, data on future investment can sometimes be obtained.

(iii) A firm knows that a new major piece of machinery will be delivered in two months time and that its arrival will affect the company's manpower requirements. The firm therefore has an anticipated change in employment levels.

A sensible way of gathering data that may well have a useful forecasting potential is to conduct a survey of households or firms and simply ask about

153

their plans for future spending, manpower needs, or other resource requirements. Such surveys will provide what is called *anticipations data*.

This idea can be extended to asking opinions of individuals or firms about what they expect will happen either in the economy at large or in sectors that particularly affect them. It is possible, for instance, that consumers are particularly sensitive to clues that precede a substantial price change in an item they buy frequently. The consumers may therefore have an aggregate opinion about forthcoming price changes that is potentially useful. Surveys that ask opinions of essentially nonexpert forecasters provide what will be called *expectations data*. Even if the expectations of price changes are not very good forecasts of actual price changes, if consumers alter their expectations, they may consequently alter their consumption patterns. An expected large price increase may lead to panic buying of a commodity even though subsequent events show the expectation to be wrong. An indirect way of obtaining related data is to ask households or firms how contented they are with their present economic situation. It is possible that a happy group of consumers consistently behaves in a different fashion than an unhappy group. Data of this kind will be called *attitudinal*.

There is no reason why only forecasts by nonexperts should be considered when a large number of forecasts is being continually produced by professional forecasters in business, government, and universities. A survey of the opinions of these forecasters about the future value of some variable will give both a consensus opinion or expectation and also measures of the extent of disagreement to be found. For example, a panel of financial analysts, employed by large pension funds, banks and other financial institutions, could be asked each month for their opinions about future movements in the stock market. Presumably, the panel members will be able to apply more expertise and expend more time in weighing the various factors affecting the market than could the ordinary investor. They may also have access to relevant information not available to the general public, so that the combined opinion of this panel of experts could provide superior stock market forecasts. This type of data will be called *forecast survey data*.

A great deal of these types of survey data is collected, particularly anticipations and expectations data. But as collection costs are often high and the data is collected for commercial reasons, the results are sometimes not made public. A list issued in 1977, for example, mentions 88 different anticipations or expectations surveys in 33 countries. Of these surveys, 61 collected expectational data on business conditions, 41 were investment surveys, and 23 interviewed consumers on anticipations, expectations, or attitudes. Thirty of the surveys fell into more than one category. No attempt will be made in this book to survey the data that are available, as presumably any forecaster working in a particular industry, say, will be aware of survey data relevant to this field. However, a number of general points about how survey data can, or should, be utilized can be made and each of the main types are considered in the following sections. It is important to realize that survey data can either be used directly to form forecasts or it can be used simply to expand some information set. It is often in this second role that the main forecasting advantages of survey data can be realized.

6.2   ANTICIPATION DATA

Anticipations data consist of replies by a sample of companies, institutions, or individual households to questions put to them about their plans for some future period. For example, a sample of construction companies can be asked how many single-family housing units they plan to build in the next six months, or households can be asked how many new television sets they intend to buy in the next year. As will be seen, the usefulness of this data in improving forecasts is not always clear-cut. The least controversial and most obviously useful data relate to anticipations of investments by companies. Virtually all types of investment in plant and equipment take several months planning or prior commitment, and for a large investment such as a new factory or production line, plans need to be made several years ahead. The two major U.S. surveys of anticipated investments by companies have quite different horizons; that organized by the Department of Commerce produces anticipations up to four quarters ahead, whereas the survey conducted by McGraw-Hill lists investment anticipations for one, two, three, and four years ahead. The firms approached in these surveys do appear to take them seriously, and the survey forms are often signed by high-ranking officers of the company. The Department of Commerce's Bureau of Economic Analysis conducts a quarterly survey of plant and equipment expenditures (P. and E.) and plans for over twenty nonfarm business industries. Results are published in the press and in the *Survey of Current Business.* For example, the survey made in January and February 1984 gave a planned 1984 P. and E. expenditure 13.6 percent above the previous year for the total industries considered, ranging from an increase of 2.5% for the food and beverage industry to a 34 percent increase for the motor vehicle equipment industry. Forecasts were actually somewhat low as the eventual total P. and E. figure for 1984 was 15% above 1983, with the food industry increasing by 11% and motor vehicle equipment by 52%. The data produced by the survey can either be considered as providing direct forecasts of future investments or as useful additional information to be added to a regression model, for instance. The evidence of empirical studies suggests that changes in aggregate company investment can be better forecast from changes in anticipations than from either econometric models not using anticipations or by simple time series models relating investments just to previous investments. It is thus seen that, in this case, anticipations data does not have clear forecasting value.

The evidence is much less clear-cut for other anticipation survey data, for instance, those of housing starts or inventories. As these quantities involve more guesswork or forecasting and less prior commitment than investments, the poorer quality is perhaps to be expected. A more controversial type of data is the result of surveying households about their consumption plans. A great deal of this type of data is collected for commercial reasons and strong claims are made about its usefulness, although these claims are often based on regression studies using improper information sets. These studies usually concentrate on consumer durable goods, such as automobiles, refrigerators, freezers, and air conditioners, which often involve considerable expenditure and therefore possibly some planning. The earlier surveys simply asked one or more members of the household if they intended to buy a freezer, say, in the next six months or year; the only allowable answers were yes or no. Because there is obviously some uncertainty in the buying plans, more sophisticated answers are now possible, usually on a scale of 10 to 0, with 10 meaning practically certain, 6 interpreted as a probability of 0.6, or in words "good possibility," 3 as a probability of 0.3 or "some possibility," 1 as very slight possibility, and 0 as almost no chance, or a probability of 1 in 100, say. Follow-up surveys do indicate that the higher the score given by the household, the higher the chance of a purchase being made. For example, an English survey found the relationship shown in Table 6.1. However, the majority of households did not expect to make a purchase and so answered 0; in fact in this particular survey, nearly 92% of replies were zero. Of these households,

TABLE 6.1

Answer in first survey	Percentage of this group making a consumer durable purchase in following twelve months
1 or 2	24%
3 or 4	27%
5 or 6	39%
7 or 8	43%
9 or 10	46%

only 6% did in fact make a consumer durable purchase in the next twelve months. Although this is a small proportion, because this was such an important and large group, it was found that almost two-thirds of all purchases were made by those households who claimed they had no plans to make a purchase. The main reason given for this occurrence was that some appliance broke down unexpectedly and had to be replaced. This aspect of the data does make interpretation of consumer durable anticipation surveys difficult, particularly as replacement of a somewhat deficient automobile or appliance can be postponed in difficult economic times. In general, it does seem that these surveys do possibly have some value but should be interpreted and used carefully.

6.3   EXPECTATIONS AND ATTITUDES

In several countries, surveys of companies ask their expectations of new orders, employment, sales, and prices. In some cases, these seem to be little more than company forecasts of these quantities based on publicly available information rather than true expectations using useful insider information. Although this type of data may have some forecasting potential, expectations elicited from households about the national economy are much less obviously useful. For example, the Gallup Poll asked cross sections of over 1000 persons aged 18 and over, "Will economic conditions get better or worse during the next six months?" at different dates. The replies did vary considerably, with about 15% saying "better" and 70% "worse" during 1974 and about 50% "better" and 25% "worse" in early 1976. Whether such figures have any extra forecasting information over other publically available data is doubtful. It was fairly obvious during 1974 that the economy was on a decline because of the oil crisis, whereas all indications were much better in 1976. Although there are few convincing reasons for expecting the general public to be better at forecasting the economy, their attitudes as to how they see the future could affect their behavior, such as making decisions on how much to put aside as savings. The probable inability of the general public to produce useful forecasts is reflected in the known inability of housepersons to estimate inflation during the previous six or twelve months. The general estimate is often widely exaggerated, reflecting the movement of the most variably priced item rather than an index or average value.

A more careful attempt to measure household attitudes about what the future is likely to bring has been conducted by the Survey Research Center at the University of Michigan, which regularly produces an "index of consumer sentiment." The index is based on the answers to five questions, which in 1982 took the following form:

(i) "We are interested in how people are getting along financially these days. Would you say that you and your family are better off or worse off financially than you were a year ago? Why do you say so?"

(ii) "Now looking ahead, do you think that a year from now you people will be better off financially, or worse off, or just about the same as now?"

(iii) "Now turning to business conditions in the country as a whole, do you think that during the next twelve months we'll have good times financially, or bad times, or what?"

(iv) "Looking ahead, which would you say is more likely, that in the country as a whole we'll have continuous good times during the next five years or so, or that we will have periods of widespread unemployment or depression, or what?" and

(v) "About the big things people buy for their homes — such as furniture, refrigerator, stove, television, and things like that — generally speaking, do you think now is a good or bad time to buy major household items? Why do you say so?"

For each question the percentage of answers that are unfavorable is subtracted from the percentage giving favorable or optimistic answers. These relative scores are then added to the number 100. The index can swing quite dramatically, taking a value near 95 for 1959 – 1968, with a peak of over 100 in 1965, dropping to 75 in mid-1970, increasing back to 95 in mid-1972, and thereafter declining steadily to 58 in 1974, possibly due to Watergate and the unusual inflation in 1974. It rose to 84 in 1978, was down to 52 in May 1980, was down again to 62 in March 1982, but was up to 99.5 in the first quarter of 1984, one of the highest values ever observed, certainly since 1969. Towards the end of 1985 the figure had declined slightly to 93 and was 87 in December 1987. The index is widely quoted in the media, but its actual value is certainly controversial. The Michigan group views its index as having clear relevance to consumer spending, but the plot of this variable against the index does not suggest any simple relationship. The prediction of turning points in the economy is an important problem and is discussed in the next chapter. The data produced by the attitudinal surveys are not consistently found useful for making such predictions. However, there is some evidence that the Index of Consumer Sentiment is of some use as a turning point indicator, particularly for the answers to questions (ii) and (v). A good discussion is Curtin (1982).

Once more, the expectations and attitudinal data might be relevant for improving forecasts when added to some other information set but are less clearly useful if used by themselves.

6.4 SURVEY OF FORECASTERS

Rather than use forecasts made by the public, who are not experts in this field, would it not be better to survey those who do claim to be experts? Two prestigious institutions, the American Statistical Association and the National Bureau of Economic Research, do collaborate to produce such a quarterly survey in the United States. Similar surveys do exist in a few other countries, although they are not always conducted so regularly. A postal questionnaire is used, but the response rate is not particularly high, with often only about 50 people replying. Of these, about 40% come from manufacturing and banking or other financial institutions, with the other major groups coming from consulting or research companies and the academic world. Forecasts are requested for a number of important economic variables, including gross national product, inflation, industrial production, unemployment rate, corporate profits, and new housing starts for each of the next four or five quarters. The forecasts are made both in terms of actual values and also percentage changes. The survey not only provides interesting average forecasts, but, for a few variables, the extent of agreement or disagreement between forecasters is indicated. For example, in December 1973, the forecasters produced the distribution of forecasts shown in Table 6.2 for inflation rates during 1974. Thus, the median forecast was for between 6.0% and 6.9% inflation and 90% of the forecasters suggested a value between 4% and 9%, which is quite wide. The actual inflation rate was just over 9%. In 1974, 70% of the forecasters predicted an inflation of 8%–10% in 1975 and the actual inflation was

TABLE 6.2

Percent change	Distribution	Percent change	Distribution
9% or more	3.8	5.0–5.9	26.1
8.0–8.9	4.0	4.0–4.9	9.8
7.0–7.9	13.7	less than 4%	8.1
6.0–6.9	34.5		

9.4%. Further, 90% of the forecasters named a value from between 7% and 11%. It seems that there was more agreement in 1975 than in 1974, and the forecast was better in this second year. No sophisticated evaluation of the sequence of forecasts produced by the survey has been published, but some unpublished work suggests that the forecasts are better than those produced by a single-series model of the type discussed earlier in Chapter 3. The survey also produces information on the techniques that the forecasters are employing and also on the kind of broad assumptions they are using. During the period 1968–1973, 54% of the respondents named an informal GNP model as their most important technique and 22% named an econometric model, although this percentage was increasing through time. For their second most important method, 35% named leading indicators, which are discussed in Chapter 7, 23% named econometric models, 22% anticipation surveys, and 16% informal GNP models. For the third most important method, the majority named leading indicators and anticipation surveys.

These surveys do appear to produce useful forecasts even though the various forecasts are combined totally uncritically. It is interesting to contemplate if superior forecasts would be produced if greater weight were given to those forecasters who had performed particularly well in recent periods and the obvious turkeys were given little weight. The possible advantages of combining forecasts is discussed in Chapter 8.

6.5   THE PROJECT

The procedures discussed in this chapter will probably not be useful for the project. However, if several students are forecasting the same variable, a survey of forecasters can be undertaken and their forecasts merged to provide an alternative forecast to those obtained from the statistical procedures discussed in earlier chapters. Similarly if one is forecasting sales of a company, a survey of salesmen or junior executives will provide a forecast. If such an alternative forecast is obtained, how should it be utilized? It is a question of judgment, if the new forecast agrees with that obtained from the statistical procedure, there is no reason to change. However, if the two forecasts are significantly different, for example if the forecast from the survey lies outside the 95% confidence interval around the statistical forecast, then it is possible that some people know something about the forecasting situation that you do not. You should try to find out what and, possibly, form a weighted average of the two forecasts with weights that add to one and whose values are determined (guessed at) by yourself.

QUESTIONS

1. A survey of college football head coaches asked what record, in terms of number of wins and losses, they predicted for their teams in the coming season. Would you classify this as expectations or anticipations data? Would you expect the forecasts to be of good quality?

2. It is important, when selecting a career during college, to find a field that will both have ample openings when you graduate and also one that is not too popular with your fellow graduates. Discuss how you would survey potential employers or career counselors to get an impression of the demand side of the job market for different kinds of jobs and also how you would survey undergraduates to help forecast the supply side.

3. Give your own answers to the questions used by the University of Michigan Survey Research Center to construct its index of consumer sentiment. Discuss any problems you encounter in giving answers.

4. Suppost that you want to construct an *index of political sentiment* to be applied separately to politicians of each of the major parties to gauge their feelings about the upcoming elections. Suggest three questions that you would ask and outline how an index would be formed.

FURTHER READINGS

Cohen, Morris (1976). "Surveys and Forecasting," in *Methods and Techniques of Business Forecasting* (W. F. Butler, R. A. Kavesh, and R. B. Plats, eds.), Englewood Cliffs, New Jersey: Prentice-Hall.
A constructively critical discussion of various actual survey data sources.

Curtin, R. T. (1982), " Indicators of Consumer Behaviour: The University of Michigan Surveys of Consumers." *Public Opinion Quarterly* **46**, 340–352.

Rippe, R. D., and M. Wilkinson (1976). "Forecasting Accuracy of the McGraw-Hill Anticipatory Data," *Journal of the American Statistical Association* **69** (December), 849–858.
Presents results of an empirical investigation.

7

Leading Indicators

A good forecaster is not smarter than everyone else, he merely has his igno-rance better organized.

7.1 SWINGS IN THE ECONOMY

Even the most casual observer of the economy will be aware that progress is typically not along a smooth curve, but is rather the accumulations of periods of relative decline and advance. Since 1950 there has been a tendency for the wealth of the nation, as measured by gross national product (GNP), to increase, but the actual slope of the curve can vary from about 10% per year down to zero, and there have been some pairs of years for which wealth has actually gone down, during 1974 and 1975, for instance. Prior to 1940 the swings in the economy were much more severe. Some examples of swings are shown in Fig. 7.1, which uses GNP in real terms as a measure of the state of the economy.

It is vital for both government economists and businessmen to deter-mine and predict the turning points of these long-term swings in the economy. The government may want to use policies to reverse a trend, particularly a decline, and management, when making investment deci-sions, needs to know if the economy will be expanding or contracting over the next couple of years. There are a number of reasons why it is difficult to decide whether or not a turning point has occurred. The GNP series does not consist only of trend plus long swings, but also includes much shorter swings of lesser amplitude which obscure the picture. The data also contain measurement errors and inevitably appear some weeks, or even months, after the date that they apply to. It is not too difficult to decide on a sensible month when it can be said that a turning point occurred, given data both before *and* after this point, but it is extremely difficult to pick a turning point given data before it but none, or virtually none, after it. The

163

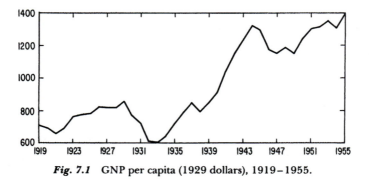

Fig. 7.1   GNP per capita (1929 dollars), 1919–1955.

reader should try covering the components of Fig. 7.2 immediately after
the indicated turning points and ask if the existence of the turning point is
then obvious with the data available.

Because so many decision makes view turning points as being of considerable importance, special attention has been given to producing forecasts
of when these turns will occur. One fairly obvious way to proceed is to try
to find sectors in the economy that lead the rest, so that an observed

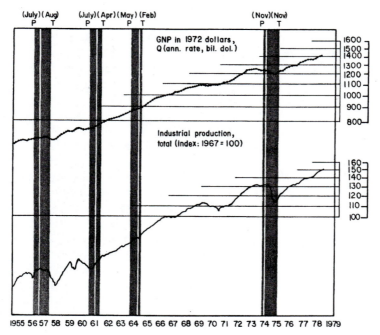

Fig. 7.2   GNP and industrial production, 1955–1979 (P, peak; T, trough).

turning point in these sectors suggests that the whole economy will soon turn. Individual economists are inclined to have their own favorite leading indicators. For example, some may want to look at the sales of the special paper used to make blueprints, as it is argued that firms have to order this paper in order to make plans for future investments, and so orders will increase when firms intend to invest. Other favorites are sales by large retail firms, such as Sears Roebuck in Chicago, or sales figures from the automobile industry. The main advantages of such series is their immediate availability and ease of interpretation. Monetary statistics are also much used, such as the inflow and outflow of New York mutual savings banks or the relationship between demand deposits and currency in circulation, all of which are published both quickly and frequently. Many company economists merely watch some of their own company's results, such as the percentage of cancellations relative to new orders, or they ask their own sales force for impressions about change in the marketplace. Some of the most used, and probably least useful, indicators are derived from the stock market. These favorite indicators may well produce useful forecasts on some occasions but are not necessarily reliable. As turning points may occur only every two or three years, on average, the casual observations of an individual economist may not allow sufficient evaluation in the typical length of a career for definite conclusions about their usefulness to be determined. What is needed is a more systematic approach, and this is discussed in the following section.

First, however, consideration has to be given to how the state of the economy should be measured and how turning points in historical data can be determined. There is clearly no ideal measure of the state of the economy, simply because all sectors are not affected in the same way. Near a turning point, for example, some sectors will be expanding whereas other parts will be in decline, which is the whole point of the leading indicator approach. The most obvious measure to use is the aggregate known as the gross national product, which is the total value of all goods and services produced in the economy over some period of time, and is, by definition, equal to gross national income. Although this is certainly the best understood measure of the state of the economy, it does have the disadvantage that it is complicated and costly to estimate, so that its value is only available on a quarterly time period for most advanced countries, such as the United States and Britain. Because a more frequently available measure is desirable, it has become more usual to use the index of industrial production, which is published monthly. Empirical studies suggest that this index and GNP do move very closely together, although the index of industrial production does ignore the important agricultural and service parts of the economy.

To decide on the location of a turning point in the economy in a historical series, a group of expert economists might be assembled and, from plots against time of GNP, the index of industrial production, and possibly a few other closely correlated, coincident aggregate series, a consensus opinion about the precise month in which the turn occurred might be reached after some discussion. In the United States, the National Bureau for Economic Research, which originated most of the work on leading indicators and is much concerned with business cycle research, has been responsible for dating the turning points, and these *reference dates* are needed for evaluation of indicators. The precise dating of a turn is sometimes difficult and the actual choice may seem arbitrary, especially after the initial estimates of the index of production have been updated. Figure 7.2 shows both GNP and the production index for the period 1955–1984 with the National Bureau's reference dates.

The figure also suggests that there has been a change in the character of business cycle swings since the 1940s. In the earlier period there were severe declines in aggregate personal income in some years, as the figures in Table 7.1 illustrate. Thus, GNP per capita in real terms was approximately the same in 1919, 1922, 1931, and 1935. During the 1950s and 1960s this measure of national income had less clear-cut swings, partly due to institutional changes designed to dampen the oscillations in the economy and partly due to better control techniques by the central government. However, since the mid 1970s there have been three substantial depressions, the worst being 1973–5 due to a combination of a sudden change in oil prices and poor crops. During three relatively stable growth periods, attention was being focused on an alternate measure, the difference between the actual and "potential" production. Thus, turning points were effectively sought in changes in the growth rate rather than in the

TABLE 7.1

GNP ($1929) Per Capita		GNP ($1929)Per Capita	
1919	$710	1930	$772
1920	688	1931	721
1921	660	1932	611
1922	689	1933	590
1923	766	1934	639
1924	775	1935	718
1925	781	1936	787
1926	821	1937	846
1927	817	1938	784
1928	817	1939	847
1929	857	1940	916

absolute level of national wealth. This new approach has not been emphasized in recent years, and although it has important practical implications, it is not crucial to the basic underlying ideas of the leading indicator forecasting procedures, which are described in the next section.

7.2 THE SEARCH FOR INDICATORS

One of the earliest attempts at using leading indicators was the system devised before World War I that became known as the Harvard ABC curves. The A curve consisted of a stock price index, representing speculation, the B curve used the dollar volume of checks drawn on bank deposits, representing business activity, and the C curve consisted of the rate of interest. Empirical studies had suggested that around turning points in the economy the three curves were inclined to move in sequence, with stock prices first, then bank debits, and finally interest rates. The economic theory underlying this selection of variables is that increasing interest rates lead to a decline in economic prospects and hence of stock prices, which causes a reduction in investment and so a recession in business. This recession leads to a reduction in interest rates which improves business prospects, thus raising stock prices and consequently generating an expansion of economic activity. This particular system came to grief in the tremendous depression of 1929, largely due to the fact that the stock market proved to be an unreliable leading indicator, but also because of poor interpretation by economists at that time.

Before the economy had fully recovered from the post-1929 Great Depression, a sharp recession occurred in 1937–1938, and this event caused Henry Morgenthau, Jr., the Secretary of the Treasury, in the fall of 1937 to approach the National Bureau of Economic Research and ask them to devise a system of indicators to help signal when the recession was nearing an end. Under the leadership of Wesley C. Mitchell and Arthur F. Burns, the National Bureau selected a number of series, using both observed empirical behavior and theories of the business cycle, that promised to be fairly reliable indicators of business activity. This list was presented to Morgenthau in late 1937 and published in 1938. Three classes of indicators were proposed — leading, coincident, and lagging — and this system of classification is still used by the National Bureau, although the economic variables used have changed in subsequent years.

The economic theory of the causes of business cycles that Mitchell and Burns proposed can be briefly summarized as follows:

(i) After a period of expansion, some parts of business begin to meet bottlenecks when trying to further expand production, such as shortages in raw materials, specialized labor, spare parts, or capital. When this occurs, businessmen become more cautious and reduce demand for capital goods, such as machinery and equipment. They may also reduce inventories, thus causing production slowdowns, and profits can become more uncertain. There could also be reductions in overtime and hours of work and the closing down of marginal activities at the same time.

(ii) Although some parts of the economy may be showing evidence of the end of the growth phase of the business cycle, other parts will still be carried along by the considerable momentum in the economy, so that current employment and production may continue to rise, perhaps to all time highs. However, eventually the decisions to reduce investment begin to affect production and employment and the downturn is experienced generally.

(iii) During the ensuing depression, production bottlenecks vanish, costs may decline and profit prospects improve, and the forces that lead to a new expansion gradually gain importance, sometimes helped by government policy decisions affecting government expenditure and interest rates. Thus, the economy begins an upturn and the cycle will eventually start to repeat itself once more.

It should be emphasized that this is a very simplified version of the Mitchell–Burns theory and that this is not the only theory available. Nevertheless, it does provide a framework to search for leading indicators, as well as coincident and lagging ones. Originally, series were simply stated to be leading, lagging, or roughly coincident. In 1966, 72 indicators had been selected by the National Bureau, of which 36 were leading indicators, 25 were classified as coincident, and 11 labeled as lagging. However, a revised list issued in 1977 considered the timing at peaks and troughs separately. Table 7.2 shows these various indicator series, now numbered 111, classified under different economic headings. It is seen that quite a few series are considered to be leading at peaks and lagging at troughs, particularly some of the employment and unemployment series, together with such diverse series as unfilled manufacturing orders in the durable goods industries, bank borrowing from the Federal Reserve, and materials and supplies, stocks in hand and on order.

The leading indicator series are those that might be expected to turn before the aggregate economy, so if some of these series are observed to make an apparent turn, this could suggest that a turning point for the whole economy is about to occur. The "roughly coincident" indicators turn at about the same time as the aggregate economy measures, but will sometimes be series whose figures are released quickly after the date to which they relate. Thus, if many of these coincident indicators appear to be changing in direction, this is taken to be evidence that a turn has already occurred in the economy. The lagging indicators are series that react slowly to changes of direction in the main part of the economy. Thus, if changes are observed in these lagging series, it becomes fairly certain that a turning point has occurred in the recent past. The lagging series are thus used mainly to confirm what the other indicators have been suggesting, if the system works properly.

The large number of indicators mentioned in Table 7.2 presents almost an excess of information when trying to predict a turning point, and so it is natural to try to distill out the most relevant information and form averages or indices, as are used in Figure 7.3 (see page 177). In fact, the indices used in that figure involved twelve leading indicators, four coincident ones, and six lagging indicators. The twelve series used to construct the index of leading indicators are average work week of production workers, lay-off rate, new orders of consumer goods and materials, net business formation, stock prices, contracts and orders for plant and equipment, building permits for private housing, vendor performance, change in inventories, percentage change in sensitive prices, percentage change in total liquid assets, and money supply (M1). The indices are not just simple averages, however, for various weights and adjustments are used, one hopes, to increase both the value and the interpretability of these composite indices. To decide which variables to use in an index, the National Bureau has assigned scores to every indicator within a range of $0-100$ under each of six headings in (i) economic significance, (ii) statistical adequacy, (iii) historical conformity to business cycles, (iv) cyclical timing record, (v) smoothness, and (vi) promptness of publication. Some examples of the scores assigned in 1967 are given in Table 7.3.

The scores are rather arbitrary and are based more on opinion than on any sophisticated empirical analysis. The average scores are used to weight the various indicators when forming an index, those with highest scores being given the highest weight. However, before this is done, two other adjustments are made. The first inverts any series that moves in an opposite direction to the major economic measures, an example of which is unemployment. The second adjustment divides each series by a measure of its average or usual amplitude or variability, so that the variability of all of these amplitude adjusted series is comparable. Finally, the leading group is also subject to a further adjustment, designed to make its long-run trend the same as that of the index of coincident series. This reverse trend adjustment is likely to make leads more uniform and is designed to improve the cyclical comparability among the leading, coincident, and lagging indices by removing most of the differences in long-run trend. How-

TABLE 7.2

Cross-Classification of Cyclical Indicators by Economic Process and Cyclical Timing

A. Timing at Business Cycle Peaks

Economic Process \ Cyclical Timing	I. EMPLOYMENT AND UNEMPLOYMENT (15 series)	II. PRODUCTION AND INCOME (10 series)	III. CONSUMPTION, TRADE, ORDERS, AND DELIVERIES (13 series)	IV. FIXED CAPITAL INVESTMENT (18 series)	V. INVENTORIES AND INVENTORY INVESTMENT (9 series)	VI. PRICES, COSTS, AND PROFITS (18 series)	VII. MONEY AND CREDIT (28 series)
LEADING (L) INDICATORS (61 series)	Marginal employment adjustments (3 series); Job vacancies (2 series); Comprehensive employment (1 series); Comprehensive unemployment (3 series)	Capacity utilization (2 series)	Orders and deliveries (6 series); Consumption and trade (2 series)	Formation of business enterprises (2 series); Business investment commitments (5 series); Residential construction (3 series)	Inventory investment (4 series); Inventories on hand and on order (1 series)	Stock prices (1 series); Sensitive commodity prices (2 series); Profits and profit margins (7 series); Cash flows (2 series)	Money (5 series); Credit flows (5 series); Credit difficulties (2 series); Bank reserves (2 series); Interest rates (1 series)
ROUGHLY COINCIDENT (C) INDICATORS (23 series)	Comprehensive employment (1 series)	Comprehensive output and income (4 series); Industrial production (4 series)	Consumption and trade (4 series)	Business investment commitments (1 series); Business investment expenditures (5 series)			Velocity of money (2 series); Interest rates (2 series)
LAGGING (Lg) INDICATORS (19 series)	Comprehensive unemployment (2 series)			Business investment expenditures (1 series)	Inventories on hand and on order (4 series)	Unit labor costs and labor share (4 series)	Interest rates (4 series); Outstanding debt (4 series)
TIMING UNCLASSIFIED (U) (8 series)	Comprehensive employment (3 series)		Consumption and trade (1 series)	Business investment commitments (1 series)		Sensitive commodity prices (1 series); Profits and profit margins (1 series)	Interest rates (1 series)

B. Timing at Business Cycle Troughs

Economic Process / Cyclical Timing	I. EMPLOYMENT AND UNEMPLOYMENT (15 series)	II. PRODUCTION AND INCOME (10 series)	III. CONSUMPTION, TRADE, ORDERS, AND DELIVERIES (13 series)	IV. FIXED CAPITAL INVESTMENT (18 series)	V. INVENTORIES AND INVENTORY INVESTMENT (9 series)	VI. PRICES, COSTS, AND PROFITS (18 series)	VII. MONEY AND CREDIT (28 series)
LEADING (L) INDICATORS (47 series)	Marginal employment adjustments (1 series)	Industrial production (1 series)	Orders and deliveries (5 series) Consumption and trade (4 series)	Formation of business enterprises (2 series) Business investment commitments (4 series) Residential construction (3 series)	Inventory investment (4 series)	Stock prices (1 series) Sensitive commodity prices (3 series) Profits and profit margins (6 series) Cash flows (2 series)	Money (4 series) Credit flows (5 series) Credit difficulties (2 series)
ROUGHLY COINCIDENT (C) INDICATORS (23 series)	Marginal employment adjustments (2 series) Comprehensive employment (4 series)	Comprehensive output and income (4 series) Industrial production (3 series) Capacity utilization (2 series)	Consumption and trade (3 series)	Business investment commitments (1 series)		Profits and profit margins (2 series)	Money (1 series) Velocity of money (1 series)
LAGGING (Lg) INDICATORS (40 series)	Job vacancies (2 series) Comprehensive employment (1 series) Comprehensive unemployment (5 series)		Orders and deliveries (1 series)	Business investment commitments (2 series) Business investment expenditures (6 series)	Inventories on hand and on order (5 series)	Unit labor costs and labor share (4 series)	Velocity of money (1 series) Bank reserves (1 series) Interest rates (8 series) Outstanding debt (4 series)
TIMING UNCLASSIFIED (U) (1 series)							Bank reserves (1 series)

From *Business Conditions Digest*, Washington, DC: U.S. Govt. Printing Office. Jan. 1986.

TABLE 7.3

	Criteria						
	(i)	(ii)	(iii)	(iv)	(v)	(vi)	Average
Leading indicators							
1. Average work week (production workers, manufacturing)	50	65	81	66	60	80	66
6. new orders (durable goods, industry)	75	72	88	84	60	80	78
19. stock prices, 500 stocks	75	74	77	87	80	100	81
Coincident indicators							
41. employment (not agricultural)	75	61	90	87	100	80	81
43. unemployment (inverted)	75	63	96	60	80	80	75
205. GNP, in constant dollars	75	75	91	58	80	50	73
52. personal income	75	73	81	43	100	80	74
Lagging indicators							
71. inventories	75	67	75	66	100	40	71
67. bank rate, short-term business loans	50	55	82	47	80	25	57

ever, the basic timing remains the same, with the leading index typically moving first, the coincident index next, and the lagging index last. In the more recent classification of indicators introduced in 1977, the components of the leading index are said to be leading at both peaks and troughs. Similarly, the series used in the coincident and lagging indices are consistently coincident and lagging, respectively.

One further group of indicators has been constructed to help understand current and prospective business conditions, the so-called *diffusion indices*. If some group of firms is considered, the diffusion index for employment shows the percentage of those firms that display an increase in employment in this month compared to the previous month. A diffusion index can be constructed showing the percentage of companies, industries, or geographic areas which are experiencing rises in some relevant variable over a month or a quarter. They can be used to indicate how widespread a recession or recovery is and whether it is continuing to spread. Diffusion indices that are considered to be leading indicators include average workweek, new orders, profits, and stock prices, whilst roughly coincident diffusion indices include employment, industrial production, wholesale prices, and sales of retail stores. In practice, these indices are extremely variable when monthly changes are considered and are still very variable and difficult to interpret if six- or nine-month changes are considered. Their use is only recommended for those experienced in all other aspects of indicators and their interpretation.

All of the main U.S. indicators and the various indices are presented, both in numerical and in an extremely convenient diagrammatic form, in the publication *Business Conditions Digest,* which is produced monthly by the U.S. Department of Commerce. They are also available for some other countries, such as Britain, Canada, and Japan, and are likely to become available in other countries in the near future. There is clearly a lot of interest in leading indicators and a great deal of money and effort is expended on their collection, construction, and publication. What now has to be asked is whether all this effort is worthwhile and if indicators are a useful forecasting tool.

7.3 EVALUATION OF INDICATORS

To a statistician, the problem of evaluating the effectiveness of leading indicators and measuring the extent of any lead is at first sight a straightforward one. If the index of industrial production is used as the ideal coincident indicator, there are a variety of statistical techniques of varying sophistication which can be used to test if some other time series on the average leads industrial production. These techniques include a number of versions of regression analysis and the use of cross correlations and spectral methods. When these methods have been applied, statisticians have often discovered that the National Bureau's leading indicators do lead, but often by a lesser extent than suggested by the National Bureau analysis and not in a consistent fashion. Thus, for example, a stock market index might be observed to lead the aggregate economy by a couple of months on average, but in practice it leads about 60% of the time and lags during the remaining 40%, say. This kind of behavior makes interpretation of indicators extremely difficult. However, it can be argued that these kinds of statistical analysis are virtually irrelevant to evaluate the National Bureau's approach. This is because these statistical methods investigate the average lead over *all* points in time, whereas the National Bureau is only concerned about leads just prior to a turning point in the economy and does not concern itself with the interim periods. Thus it might be argued that proper methods of evaluation should concentrate just on turning points in the indicator series. To do this, however, one immediately runs into the problem of how to identify when the series displays such a point. To use an entirely subjective method could lead to biases in the analysis, but there is no entirely satisfactory objective or mechanical method. One method of proceeding, although not ideal, is to record an upturn if the predictor series has been above a previous low for a specified number of months. Similarly, a downturn is said to have occurred if the series has been below a previous high for a set number of months. Thus, with a "two months up or down" criterion, a series must be below (above) its previous peak (trough) for two months before a prediction of a turn is said to occur. Consider, for example, the following constructed series and its plot, where P indicates a peak, T a trough.

The local peak at $t = 2$ is designated to be a downturn under both the one- and two-month criteria, as the values of x_t at $t = 3$ and 4 are both lower than at $t = 2$, but it is not a peak under three- or four-month criteria as x_5 is larger than x_2. However, $t = 5$ is a peak under all four criteria and $t = 8$ is a trough under one-, two- and three-month criteria, since the next three x values are all larger than x_8.

t	1	2	3	4	5	6	7	8	9	10	11	12
x_t	5	6	5	5	7	5	4	3	4	5	4	3
					x							
		x										
x_t	x		x	x		x				x		
							x		x		x	
								x				x

Criterion

Criterion												
1 month		P			P			T		P		
2 month		P			P			T		P		
3 month		—			P			T		—		
4 month		—			P			—		—		

Stekler and Schepsman (1973) used these criteria to choose turning points in the index of leading indicators (ILI) to see how well it predicts turning points in the index of industrial production (IIP), which is used as the economy-wide measure or main coincident indicator.

Using a four-month up-or-down criterion, the turning point in the ILI can be compared to the reference dates prepared by the National Bureau, which may be considered as the "official" dates for the turning points of the economy. This comparison is shown in Table 7.4.

Although the table appears to indicate that the ILI is a useful predictive devise, there remains the basic problem of "false signals," where a turn in

TABLE 7.4

NBER Designated

Date of turn in ILI		Turning point		Lead (months)
	Peaks			
July 1948		Nov 1948		4
March 1953		July 1953		4
Sept 1955		Aug 1957		23
May 1959		April 1960		11
April 1960		Dec 1969		8
March 1969		Nov 1973		8
March 1979		Jan 1980		10
April 1981		July 1981		3
			Average	8.9
	Troughs			
June 1949		Oct 1949		4
Nov 1953		May 1954		6
Feb 1958		April 1958		2
Dec 1960		Feb 1961		2
Oct 1970		Nov 1970		1
Feb 1975		March 1975		1
May 1980		July 1980		2
March 1982		Nov 1982		8
			Average	3.3

the ILI does not correspond to an actual turn in the economy. Table 7.5 shows the number of "true" and false turns in the period 1948–70 using different criteria. It is seen that using a less stringent criterion, such as two-up moves, gives many more false peaks than if a more stringent criterion is used such as five-up. It is seen that as a more stringent criterion is applied to identify a turn fewer false turns appear, but as one has to wait longer until the criterion can be applied, any lead will have been lost, on average. The existence of false signals is not a property only of the criterion used here, but will probably occur with any other method of choosing turning points amongst recent time periods. One further problem of practical significance is that the index of leading indicators is usually published at least a month after the index of industrial production, both relating to the same data, so any lead advantage is further reduced.

Other studies have also found similar problems with leading indicators in practice. Hymans (1973), for example, not only observed the false turns with the NBER index of leading indicators but also suggested that many of

TABLE 7.5

True and False Turns, Period 1948–1970

Criterion No. of months up or down	Peak		Trough	
	No. of true turns	No. of false turns	No. of true turns	No. of false turns
1	5	24	5	9
2	5	15	5	3
3	5	9	5	2
4	5	5	5	1
5	5	3	5	0

the twelve components of this index did not help its performance and that the weights used by the National Bureau were far from optimal. He went on to suggest a possibly superior index.

On the more positive side, Auerbach (1982) formed an autoregressive model for the changes of an index of production. He then regressed these changes on lags of the production index and also of the index of leading indicators. The second model had a 17% lower sum of squared residuals, suggesting that the ILI does not forecast production. A similar result was found when the series being forecast was a measure of unemployment.

The leading indicator methodology as presently developed is not without its problems. This is unfortunate, as it is basically an obviously good idea and a great deal of effort has gone into producing the indicators. It can be argued that the evaluation and selection methods used by the National Bureau have not been sufficiently sophisticated and that superior indices and other ways of distilling the relevant information undoubtedly contained in the indicators could be devised. Until this is done, the present methods will continue to have a real place in forecasting a very important aspect of the economy. As the following examples show, they are not without value.

7.4   THE 1974–1975 DEPRESSION

The worldwide depression during 1974 and 1975 was one of the most severe since World War II. Figure 7.3 and Table 7.6 show a selection of six U.S. indicators:

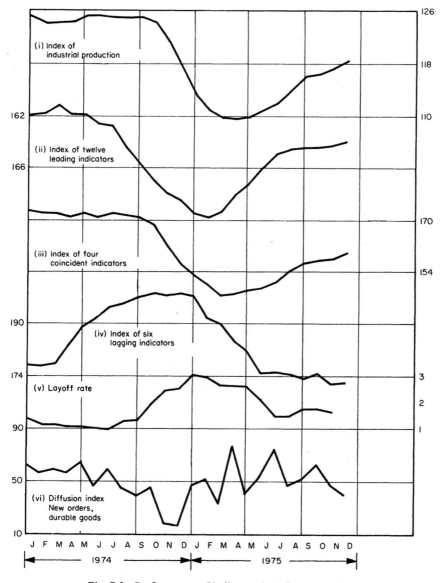

Fig. 7.3   Performance of indicators in 1974 and 1975.

TABLE 7.6

Selection of Indicators for 1974 and 1975[a]

		(i) Index of industrial production	(ii) Index of 12 leading indicators (reverse trend adjusted)	(iii) Index of 4 coincident indicators	(iv) Index of 6 lagging indicators	(v) Layoff rate in manufacturing per 100	(vii) Diffusion index, new durable orders
1974	Jan.	125.4	162.5	173.7	177.7	1.4	65.7
	Feb.	124.6	163.2	172.6	177.6	1.2	57.1
	Mar.	124.7	166.0	172.2	178.7	1.2	60.0
	April	124.9	163.4	171.8	184.0	1.1	57.1
	May	125.7	163.0	172.5	189.4	1.1	65.7
	June	125.8	160.0	171.6	192.3	1.1	47.1
	July	125.5	159.1	172.4	195.5	1.0	60.0
	Aug.	125.2	153.1	171.9	196.7	1.3	45.7
	Sept.	125.6	147.7	171.0	198.3	1.4	40.0
	Oct.	124.8	142.5	169.0	199.5	2.0	45.7
	Nov.	121.7	138.7	162.8	198.9	2.5	18.6
	Dec.	117.4	136.3	156.4	199.5	2.6	17.1
1975	Jan.	113.7	132.2	152.7	198.5	3.1	48.6
	Feb.	111.2	131.7	149.8	192.0	3.0	51.4
	Mar.	110.0	133.3	147.2	189.9	2.7	34.3
	April	109.9	138.0	147.5	185.5	2.6	77.1
	May	110.1	141.5	148.4	182.0	2.6	42.9
	June	111.1	146.4	148.9	175.3	2.1	54.3
	July	112.2	150.5	151.1	175.7	1.5	74.3
	Aug.	114.2	152.1	154.3	174.8	1.5	47.1
	Sept.	116.2	152.5	156.7	173.6	1.7	51.4
	Oct.	116.7	152.5	157.8	174.7	1.7	62.9
	Nov.	117.3	153.2	158.1	171.8	1.6	47.1
	Dec.	118.5	154.4	159.7	172.0	1.3	40.0

[a] Taken from the January 1976, issue of *Business Conditions Digest*, Washington, D.C.: U.S. Govt. Printing Office. Some of the figures are provisional.

(i)   The index of industrial production, which will be used in this illustration as the reference series, measuring the level of the aggregate economy. The series was remarkably level throughout virtually all of 1974, and it was not clear until early 1975 that a downturn had occurred by late 1974. The behavior of this series in 1974 shows how difficult it is to pinpoint the precise point at which a downturn occurred. By fall 1975, it was clear that an upturn had occurred in about April 1975.

(ii)   The composite index of twelve leading indicators, reverse trend adjusted (i.e., adjusted so that the trend in this series is similar to that of the index of coincident indicators). The series is seen to be trending down from March 1974, and so by mid-1974 evidence was accumulating that a downward turning point for the total economy was likely to occur. By the end of 1974, this evidence was overwhelming, so the leading indicator composite index did provide a correct forecast of a downturn before it became clear from the index of industrial production. From a low point in February 1975, the composite index consistently trends upward, suggesting that the upturn was about to occur in the economy, so that a correct prediction again was made.

(iii)   The composite index of four coincident indicators. The behavior of this series is very similar to the index of industrial production, as one would expect.

(iv)   The composite index of six lagging indicators. The lagging property of this index is clearly seen as there is no evidence of a downturn until February 1975 (which is almost when the upturn occurs in the rest of the economy), and there is no clear indication of an upturn up to the end of 1975. The extent of the lag in this composite index is so large that its usefulness is doubtful.

(v)   The fifth series is a particular, individual leading indicator, layoff rate in manufacturing industries, per 100 employees. This variable records just the percentage of employees that are removed from employment, ignoring the number of workers that may gain jobs in the same period. Some studies have found this indicator to be a consistent, long-lead one. It obviously has to be inverted to be used as an indicator of the main economy. By October or November 1974, a clear upturn had occurred in layoff rate, not only from the trend but also from the sizes of the numbers involved, indicating that a downturn will be occurring. Thus, a useful prediction was made. By July 1975, a clear downturn is observed to have occurred in layoff rate, providing a somewhat earlier indication of an upturn in the economy than found in the index of industrial production. However, this individual indicator provides less successful predictions than does the composite index of leading indicators over the example time period.

(vi)   The final series illustrated is a leading indicator diffusion series, based on the value of manufacturer's new orders for the durable goods industries. The diffusion index represents the proportion of cases that new orders increase over a one-month span for a sample of 35 durable goods industries. The figures in 1974 show how unstable a one-month diffusion index can be, but the values strongly indicate a downturn in November and December 1974, and also an upturn in April 1975. Thus, this diffusion index does appear to contain some useful predictive information about the timing of economy-wide turning points, but interpretation is made difficult by what seems to be the inherent variability of diffusion indices.

In general, it is seen that in January 1976 the leading indicators do seem to have been useful in predicting turning points during the previous two years, although the extent of the leads is not impressive. In interpreting these results it should be noted that by the time sufficient GNP data had become available it was clear that in 1976 the index of industrial production had turned down about three months later than did GNP.

7.5 THE DEPRESSIONS OF 1979–80 AND 1981–82

The following two depressions were rather less severe than that of 1974–5 and so constitute a more difficult test for the index of leading indicators. Figure 7.4 shows the plots for this index together with that of the index of industrial production (IIP). The ILI is seen to lead the downturn of IIP by about twelve months in 1978/9 and to lead the subsequent upturn by a couple of months. The lead at the downturn of 1981 is less clear, but the

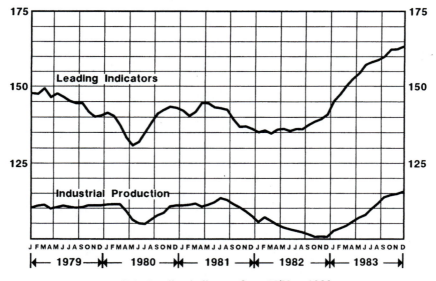

Fig. 7.4   Leading indicators from 1979 to 1983.

ILI does show a fairly clear upturn in 1982, several months before that of the production index. Thus, the index of leading indicators has proved to be a useful forecasting device over these two periods.

The success of the leading indicator index at turning points, for which it was devised, does not necessarily mean that it is helpful in forecasting the economy at all other times. However, reports on the ILI in the media often try to misinterpret its abilities and imply that it is a useful forecast indicator at all phases of the business cycle.

7.6 THE PROJECT

Leading indicators are used for medium- or long-run forecasting situations and so are unlikely to be relevant for the project. In the United States, the weekly magazine, *Business Week*, does publish a weekly index of leading indicators, which can be used in a causal model or combined judgmentally with your statistical forecast. Weekly indices are not available in other countries, to my knowledge.

QUESTIONS

1. The board of directors of a company manufacturing consumer non-durable goods receives a forecast that the economy will very soon experience a downturn. Discuss how this could affect decisions made by the board. How different would your answer have been if the forecast had been of an upturn? Would your answers have been different if the company manufactured an investment good such as heavy machinery? If not, why not?

2. List the properties that a good leading indicator should possess. Do you think that any of the following series would be good indicators of anything?
   (a) the number of requests per week for Sears catalogs,
   (b) the number of speeding tickets issued per week in Dallas, or
   (c) the number of firms going bankrupt in a month in California.

3. The small Caribbean island of Tabasco has two sources of income, tourists from the United States and sales of capsicum berries. The berries are all exported to Mexico, where they are made into a some-what edible concoction, half of which is exported to the United States and the rest used in Mexico. Suggest three leading indicators, a coincident indicator, and a lagging indicator for the Tabasco economy.

4. An enthusiastic investor states that he has observed that the number of children born to local stockbrokers in a month is a good leading indi-

cator of the Dow Jones stock market price index. Briefly describe how you would try to evaluate the truth of this claim and also the quality of this potential leading indicator.

5. Discuss how you would investigate the usefulness of the U.S. leading indicators for forecasting turning points in the Mexican and Canadian economies.

6. The dictator of a Caribbean island wants you to predict the effect on inflation in this country of the introduction of controls on money supply. Unfortunately, he has read an elementary forecasting book and suggests that you use either the method of leading indicators or Box–Jenkins ARIMA modeling. How would you try to persuade him that these techniques are inappropriate but that a small econometric model would probably do a better job. Discuss how this econometric model would actually be used to suggest an appropriate control policy for money.

FURTHER READINGS

Auerbach, Alan J. (1982). "The Index of Leading Indicators, 'Measurement Without Theory' Thirty-five Years Later," *Review of Economics and Statistics*, **64**, 589–595.

Hymans, Saul H. (1973). "On the Use of Leading Indicators to Predict Cyclical Turning Points," Brookings Papers on Econometric Activity, No. 2, pp. 339–384.

Moore, G. H. (1975). "The Analysis of Economic Indicators," *Scientific American* **232** (January), 17–23.
Excellent, but uncritical, general account.

Shiskin, J., and L. H. Lampart (1976). "Indicator Forecasting," in *Methods and Techniques of Business Forecasting* (W. F. Butler, R. A. Kavesh, and R. B. Platt, ed.), Englewood Cliffs, New Jersey: Prentice Hall.
Much more detailed account.

Stekler, O., and M. Schepsman (1973). "Forecasting with an Index of Leading Series," *Journal of the American Statistical Association* **68**, 291–295.

CHAPTER

8

Evaluation and Combination
of Forecasts

A. Did you know that some people can foretell the future?
B. I knew you were going to say that.

8.1 EVALUATING AN INDIVIDUAL
FORECASTING METHOD

At first sight the problem of how to evaluate the quality of a set of forecasts might seem to be a simple, straightforward one. Suppose that a sequence of one-step forecasts $f_{n,1}$ of the series values x_{n+1} is available over some period, giving the set of data $f_{n,1}, x_{n+1}, n = 1, 2, \ldots, N$, say. As $f_{n,1}$ is, in a sense, an *estimate* of x_{n+1}, an apparently sensible method of establishing how good an estimate is to plot both $f_{n,1}$ and x_{n+1} against n. It might be thought that if the $f_{n,1}$ are good forecasts, then the two plots should look similar. This plot is much used in books and articles involving forecasting, but in fact it is by no means as easy to interpret as the literature implies. There is no convincing reason why the two plots should be similar, as the shapes depend on the forecastability of the series x_t. As an extreme example, suppose that x_t is a white noise series, with zero mean; then x_{n+1} will be this white noise and so will have a very irregular plot, whereas $f_{n,1} = 0$ for all n and so will look completely different. Generally, the time series properties of $f_{n,1}$ will not be the same as those of x_{n+1}, the series being forecast, as can be seen both by the white noise example or by considering the case where x_t is generated by an MA(1) model, so that

$$x_{n+1} = \varepsilon_{n+1} + b\varepsilon_n.$$

The optimum forecast in this case was shown in Chapter 3 to be

$$f_{n,1} = b\varepsilon_n,$$

so that a plot of $f_{n,1}$ against n will be that of white noise. Thus, again, the plots of the forecasts and the series to be forecast will look quite different.

A further reason why the two plots look different is seen by considering the variances of the two series. Writing

$$x_{n+1} = f_{n,1} + e_{n,1}, \tag{1}$$

where $e_{n,1}$ is the one-step forecast error; it was shown in Chapter 4 that if $f_{n,1}$ was an optimal forecast, according to some proper information set, then $e_{n,1}$ will be a zero-mean white noise series that is uncorrelated with $f_{n,1}$. If the errors $e_{n,1}$ were not white noise, they could be partly forecast from their own past, which is itself a function of past and present x's and f's and thus of the information set used to form the forecasts, which is contradictory. The zero correlation between the forecasts and errors may be thought to be sensible as the forecasts are based on the information set I_n, whereas the errors consist of events that cannot be forecast from I_n (at least in a linear fashion). It follows that

$$\text{var}(x_{n+1}) = \text{var}(f_{n,1}) + \text{var}(e_{n,1}).$$

Since virtually all series met in economics and business are such that they can never be consistently forecast without error, it follows that

$$\text{var}(e_{n,1}) > 0,$$

so

$$\text{var}(x_{n+1}) > \text{var}(f_{n,1}).$$

Thus, the two series will have different variances and the plots against time will not be similar. If x_t is a stationary series, that is, if it is trend free or has been sufficiently differenced according to the rules given in Chapter 3, then a reasonable measure of its forecastability relative to an information set I_n is given by

$$R^2 = \frac{\text{var}(f_{n,1})}{\text{var}(x_{n+1})} \equiv 1 - \frac{\text{var}(e_{n,1})}{\text{var}(x_{n+1})},$$

where $f_{n,1}$ is the optimal forecast derived from f_n. For series that cannot be forecast, such as white noise, R^2 will be zero, but for all other series R^2 will lie between zero and unity. Only if a series can be forecast without error will $R^2 = 1$, and this is very unlikely to be true for any economic series. If a series is not stationary, such as a random walk, then a value of R^2 very near 1 can be obtained, but this situation was specifically excluded from the above definition. The reason for the exclusion is that the theoretical variance for such series is infinite, so that if the second of the two equivalent definitions of R^2 given above is used and the variance of the errors is finite, a value $R^2 = 1$ results, even though x_t cannot be perfectly forecast. It should be clear that if the forecasts $f_{n,1}$ are given by some technique, and the components of the ratio

$$\frac{\text{var}(f_{n,1})}{\text{var}(x_{n+1})}$$

are estimated from the available data, then one cannot look at the resulting value and state that the forecasts are "good" or not, as there is no satisfactory or unsatisfactory level of the ratio. The possible value of the ratio depends on the degree of forecastability of the series. Some series are high forecastable, whereas others cannot be forecast at all.

From (1), and the properties of $f_{n,1}$ and $e_{n,1}$, it follows that, if from an observed set of forecasts and of the series being forecast a regression of the form

$$x_{n+1} = \alpha + \beta f_{n,1} + \text{residual}$$

is calculated, then an optimal forecast will give $\alpha = 0$, $\beta = 1$ and the residuals will be white noise. If a regression obtained from an actual set of forecasts does not display these properties, then it follows that the forecasts can easily be improved. For example, if α is not zero, it can mean that the forecasts are consistently biased, in which case the addition of an appropriate constant to each forecast will remove this problem. Unfortunately, the regression results are of limited use as, with a wide enough information set being available, various alternative techniques can produce the correct values of α and β and also a white noise residual. The correct way to choose the best amongst alternatives is discussed in the next section.

There is no really useful procedure for evaluating an individual forecasting technique, as any evaluation cannot be separated from the degree of forecastability of the series being predicted. As the *I Ching* says, "The best of hunters finds no game in an empty field." However, if the one-step forecast errors $e_{n,1}$ are *not* white noise, then the forecast is clearly suboptimal and can be improved simply by remodelling these errors.

It should be emphasized that to evaluate an individual forecaster or a technique a whole sequence of forecasters is required. It is virtually impossible to evaluate the quality of a single forecast about some unique event. Even when evaluating a sequence of forecasts it is important to insure that they are collected in controlled circumstances. As an example of the difficulty of evaluation in a noncontrolled situation, suppose a confidence trickster gets the names of 1000 individuals who all subscribe to an investment journal. To 500 he writes a letter recommending that they buy a particular stock as he forecasts that it will rise in price over the next month. To the other 500 he recommends they sell short this same stock because he expects the price to fall. If actually the price does fall, he writes letters only to this last 500, half of the new letters recommending that they buy some stock and the other half that they sell short. Again, 250 people will have received a "correct forecast." After other further rounds there will exist about 30 people who have received five correct predictions in a row and they may well be prepared to pay substantially to receive further "forecasts." Their evaluation problem is a difficult one and perhaps heavy weight should be given to one's prior beliefs about the probability of being given such consistently good advice about the stock market and why anyone with such apparent abilities should be willing to sell the forecasts rather than utilizing them directly.

8.2   EVALUATING A GROUP OF FORECASTING METHODS

It should be clear from the preceding chapter that there is usually not just a single forecasting method available for consideration but rather a variety of alternative methods. These methods may have different cost characteristics and depend on different information sets or on alternative philosophies about how to proceed. Suppose for the moment that just two forecasting methods are being considered, giving one-step forecasts $f_{n,1}^{(1)}$ and $f_{n,1}^{(2)}$ with corresponding one-step forecast errors

$$e_{n,1}^{(1)} = x_{n+1} - f_{n,1}^{(1)}$$

and

$$e_{n,2}^{(2)} = x_{n+1} - f_{n,1}^{(2)}$$

An obvious question to ask is which method is superior? This question was already answered in Chapter 1 when discussing cost functions. If the cost of making an error of size e is $C(e)$, then the preferable method is that which minimizes the average cost. Thus, if the cost is proportional to e^2, then the appropriate procedure is to form the sum of squared errors

$$\text{SSE} = \sum_{t=1}^{n} (e_{t,1})^2$$

or, equivalently, the mean square error

$$\text{MSE} = \frac{1}{n}\text{SSE}$$

and then to choose the method that produces the smaller value for these quantities over the data period being used for evaluation. It is strongly advised that this evaluation period be different from that used to form any model from which forecasts are produced. If several forecasts are available, the value of SSE should be found from the forecast errors of each method, and the best individual method is then that which produces the smallest sum of errors. It is thus possible to *rank* alternatively forecasting methods, although one is not able to say if the best of these available methods is the best of all possible methods, unless the SSE for the evaluation period happens to be zero, which is extremely unlikely.

The more statistically sophisticated forecasters will not want to just order a pair of methods but would also like to test if one method is significantly superior to the other. Suppose that the forecasts produce unbiased errors, so that the means of $e_{n,1}^{(1)}$ and $e_{n,1}^{(2)}$ are both not significantly different from zero. It is not correct to use the usual F test to see if the SSE's are significantly different, as generally one would expect the two sets of errors to be correlated. A way around this problem is to form the two series

$$P_n = e_{n,1}^{(1)} + e_{n,1}^{(2)}$$

and

$$Q_n = e_{n,1}^{(1)} - e_{n,1}^{(2)}$$

and then to test for any correlation between P_n and Q_n, using any standard test for zero correlation, such as the t test, Fisher's z test, or even a rank correlation test. It can be shown that if any significant correlation is found, then this implies a significant difference in SSE values.

SSE values can be used to rank a group of alternative forecasts of the same variable. Any other statistic makes no sense if the models have been estimated using a least-squares criterion. However, the ranking does not have very much operational significance. In particular, it does not imply that only the top method should henceforth be used and all the other methods ignored. As will be shown in the next two sections, the lower-ranked methods may contain important information that can be utilized to improve the "best" method.

8.3   THE COMBINATION OF FORECASTS

Table 8.1 shows one-step forecast errors of the total airline passenger miles, measured monthly, for the months of 1953 by two alternative forecasting methods; the first a Box-Jenkins model as discussed in Chapter 3 and the other an adaptive model similar to those discussed in Chapter 4. The original aim of the table was to illustrate the superiority of the Box-Jenkins approach.

TABLE 8.1

Forecast Errors of Passenger Miles Flown, 1953

Month	Box-Jenkins	Adaptive	Combined forecast	Month	Box-Jenkins	Adaptive	Combined forecast
Jan.	−3	1	−1	Aug.	2	−16	−7
Feb.	−10	18	−2	Sept.	−11	−12	−11.5
March	24	18	21	Oct.	−10	−9	−9.5
April	22	18	20	Nov.	−12	−12	−12
May	−9	3	−3	Dec.	−7	−13	−10
June	−22	−17	−19.5	MSE	188	196	150
July	10	−24	−7				

The scale involved in the table or the details of the forecasting methods are of no relevance in this example. The values of the mean square error (MSE) do suggest that the Box-Jenkins forecasts are better, on the average, than the forecasts from the model. This is equally true if data for the whole period 1951–1960 are used, with MSE values of 177.7 for the adaptive and 148.6 for the Box-Jenkins method. The final column in the table shows the errors from a simple combined forecast, where

$$\text{(combined forecast)} = \tfrac{1}{2}(\text{Box-Jenkins} + \text{adaptive forecasts}).$$

The errors from this combined forecast are simply the average of the errors from the two constituents. For 1953, the MSE for the combined is seen to be less than for the two original forecasts, and this holds true for the whole period 1951–1960, when the combined had MSE 130.2. Thus, a very simple method of combining has provided a set of forecasts that on average is superior to both constituent forecasts.

The approach can obviously be generalized, and hopefully improved, by considering more flexible weighting schemes. Suppose that f_n and g_n are both one-step forecasts of x_{n+1}, using different approaches, with resulting errors ef_n, eg_n. Further suppose that the forecasts have no consistent biases, so that the error series have zero means. A combined forecast given by

$$C_n = kf_n + (1 - k)g_n \tag{2}$$

will necessarily be unbiased, and the resulting forecast error will be

$$ec_n = x_{n+1} - C_n = kef_n + (1 - k)eg_n. \tag{3}$$

The value of k is of our choice and it may be possible to choose so that the variance of the combined forecast's error ec_n is smaller than either of the variances of the other two error series. Note that as means are assumed to be zero, variances and mean squared errors will be identical. The variance of ec_n is given by

$$\text{var}(ec) = k^2\text{var}(ef) + (1 - k)^2\text{var}(eg) + 2k(1 - k)\text{cov}(ef, eg), \qquad (4)$$

where $\text{cov}(ef, eg)$ is the covariance between the error series ef_n and eg_n. A little calculus will show that $\text{var}(ec)$ is minimized by taking

$$k = \frac{\text{var}(eg) - \text{cov}(ef, eg)}{\text{var}(eg) + \text{var}(ef) - 2\text{cov}(ef, eg)}. \qquad (5)$$

In the case when ef_n and eg_n are uncorrelated, this formula reduces to

$$k = \frac{\text{var}(eg)}{\text{var}(eg) + \text{var}(ef)}. \qquad (6)$$

If the first of these formulas for k, (5) is inserted into the formula for $\text{var}(ec)$, (4), then the resulting variance for the combined forecast error will generally be smaller than both of the variances of ef_n and eg_n and is never more than the smaller of these two variances. Thus, in theory, a combined forecast will usually be superior to either constituents. This means that one should never lose by combining and will usually gain. Unfortunately, a formula such as (5) cannot be used to find the combining weight k, for the variances and covariances required are never known. They can, of course, be estimated from past forecast errors if these are available. However, it is not clear how many past errors should be used, as the forecasters who are producing the forecasts being combined may be changing in ability, at least relatively. For instance, f_n may come from a simple regression model which is applied automatically, whereas the forecasts g_n could come from an econometrician who is continually updating and improving his model as well as applying subjective corrections and learning from past mistakes. It would be reasonable to expect that the econometrician's forecasts should be given increasing weights through time as his forecasting ability improves relative to f_n. Another problem with applying (5) directly is that often only a few previous forecast errors are available, and so it is very difficult to get a satisfactory estimate for the covariance term. To circumvent these problems, a time-varying weight k_n can be used, given by

$$k_{n+1} = \frac{\sum_{t=n-m}^{n} (eg_t)^2}{\sum_{t=n-m}^{n} [(eg_t)^2 + (efx)^2]}. \qquad (7)$$

Thus, formula (6) is used and the variances are estimated over just the last m error terms. An appropriate value for m would be 12, although this is a rather arbitrary choice, and if less than twelve previous errors are available, the sums are just over those errors that are known. An appropriate starting up value for k_n where no previous forecasts have been made is obviously $k_1 = \frac{1}{2}$.

For example, using the data in the above table, with $m = 12$, the two forecasts for January 1954 would use weight

$$k_{13} = \frac{196}{188 + 196} = 0.51$$

and so

$$C_{13} = 0.51(\text{Box-Jenkins}) + 0.49(\text{Adaptive}).$$

The weight k_{14} for February 1954 would be calculated by dropping the errors for January 1953 and adding those for January 1954 into the formula (7). The weights k_n are seen to be proper weights in that they only depend on information available at the time the combined forecast is made. They are also seen to be necessarily positive, which is not necessarily a good thing, although it does imply the belief that both forecasts have something positive to contribute to the combination. There do exist alternative methods of forming the weights which do allow these weights to go outside the range (0, 1). Occasionally giving one of the forecasts a negative weight does appear to produce a superior combination, but if the constituent forecasts have been prepared at all carefully and are based on some relevant data, only nonnegative weights should be appropriate.

To gain an improved forecast by using this combination technique is usually worth considering as it is easy to do, is often successful, and at the very least removes the necessity of deciding which of a pair of forecasts is preferred. These are very pragmatic reasons, but if the combination is successful, there are some further implications. The reason a combined forecast may be preferable is that neither constituent forecast is using all of the data in the available information set in an optimum fashion. Thus, success of combination suggests that a more general model should be attempted, including the better features of the models underlying the constituent forecasts. This also suggests that combining forecasts will be particularly successful when using constituents based on quite different philosophies, such as those using a time series Box-Jenkins model and a regression model. It is also possible to insert nonnumerical information into one's forecasts by using such a combination. If an economist produces a sequence of forecasts based on whatever information he decides to use, including rumors or gut feelings about the situation, these can be combined with forecasts based on a standard data analysis. If the nonnumerical data have any consistent predictive value, the economist's forecasts should obtain a positive weight.

A final use of combining forecasts is to help evaluate forecasts based on a wide information set, such as those derived from an econometric model. The wide-based forecasts should be better than those using a subset of the information set. For example, a forecast based on a regression model using the past and present of series including that being forecast should be better than a single-series forecast, such as one from a Box-Jenkins model. As one information is a subset of the other, the wider-based forecast should not merely have a lower mean squared error, but, if combined with the other forecast, should have a weight very near 1, provided a long enough series of errors is available and weights based on (5) are used. This is a very strong condition to be used when evaluating forecasts from an econometric model.

The combining technique can be generalized to the combination of more than two forecasts, of the form

$$C_n = k_{1,n} f_{1,n} + k_{2,n} f_{2,n} + \cdots + k_{p,n} f_{p,n}.$$

If $e_{j,n}$ are the errors from the jth forecast $f_{j,n}$, with the notation

$$A_{j,n} = \left[\sum_{t=n-m}^{n} (e_{j,t})^2 \right]^{-1},$$

$$B_n = A_{1,n} + A_{2,n} + \cdots + A_{p,n},$$

then a simple method of estimating the jth weight is to use

$$k_{j,n} = \frac{A_{j,n}}{B_n}.$$

However, it is better to discard any really bad forecasts, that is, those with particularly small A values, as quickly as possible and then to apply the above procedure to combine the remainder.

A rather easier way of combining that has been shown to be superior is just to regress the actual value on its various forecasts and a constant without constraining the combination weights to add to one. (See Granger and Ramanathan (1984).

The potential benefits to be gained from combining forecasts will be discussed in the following section.

8.4 HOW WELL DO THE METHODS WORK?

As has been seen in this and the previous chapter, there is a variety of methods for producing point forecasts. In fact, there are also many others that have not been discussed, although a few more are mentioned in

Chapter 12. There naturally have been many studies that have tried to evaluate the relative success of the competing methods. It is not easy to summarize the results of these studies, as different sets of data have been used with differing groups of forecasting methods and no clear-cut consensus of conclusions has been achieved. Some of the studies have difficulties with their interpretation because improper procedures have been used, such as using information, like the future values of some series, that a real forecaster could not possibly have available. Some studies have used models estimated by a least-squares criterion and then have tried to evaluate forecasts from these models using a different criterion, which is obviously a dubious procedure.

There is a number of general rules that the theory presented in earlier chapters suggests are at least plausible:

(i)   The further ahead you forecast, the less well you do;
(ii) the bigger the information set, the better the forecast, provided that the extra information is relevant;
(iii) the more data analysis conducted, the better the forecast; and
(iv) if two forecasts based on quite different approaches are combined, the result will often be better than the constituents.

On occasion these rules clash. For example, if one has the choice of forecasts from 1000- or a 50-equation econometric model, the larger model will be based on a larger information set but the smaller model will generally have been more carefully constructed, analyzed, and evaluated. It is often found that for key economic variables the smaller model produces superior forecasts but, of course, if one wants a forecast of a variable that is not in the smaller model, it is necessary to turn to the bigger model.

At this time there has been no comprehensive study comparing forecasts from a variety of different methods on may economic series. Only small group comparisons exist between several econometric models and AR(4) models, or between a single econometric model and ARIMA forecasts, or between regression equations using anticipations data and an econometric model not using these data, or between three different time series methodologies, for example. In attempting to summarize the results from these studies, which are not always in agreement, or even consistent, it is difficult to remain totally objective and not to reflect one's own preferences. However, it can be said that the results do generally support each of the above rules, at least to some extent. It is usually difficult to forecast further ahead, sophisticated data analysis does often produce somewhat superior forecasts, and combining often improves matters. On the other hand, it is frequently difficult to improve forecasts significantly based on a proper, but small information set by adding further information. To illustrate some of these conclusions, the results obtained by Granger and Newbold

TABLE 8.2

h	1	2	4	6	8
B-J versus Adapt.	73	64	58	57	58
B-J versus S-A	68	70	62	61	63
Adapt.versus S-A	48	50	57	56	59

(1976) when applying three time series methods to 106 economic series can be quoted. The three methods were the Box-Jenkins ARIMA models discussed in Chapter 3 and the stepwise autoregressive and adaptive or exponentially weighted moving average methods described in Chapter 4. These methods are denoted B-J, S-A, and Adapt., respectively. All use the same information set, just the past and present of the series being forecast, and the second two are purely automatic, with any analysis being conducted by a computer, whereas the first requires the decision making abilities of a trained statistician. Some of the results obtained from making just pairwise comparisons are shown in Table 8.2, which gives the percentage of occasions that the first-named method outperforms the second for various forecast horizons h.

It is seen that the method involving the most analysis, B-J, outperforms the two automatic techniques for one-step forecasts and generally has a mean squared error about 15%–20% smaller, but that the advantage dissipates somewhat as longer horizons are considered. There is little to choose between the other two techniques for small h values but the adaptive method does rather better for higher h values. Using the notation $C(A, B)$ for the combination of methods A and B, Table 8.3 shows how well the various combinations performed in pairwise comparisons for one-step forecasts, the number being the percentage the first named method outperforms the second. The combinations shown in this table used m = 12.

In an earlier study, Cooper (1972) compared the forecasts for 33 economic variables from seven of the most prestigious econometric models

TABLE 8.3

	Percentage first method wins
C(B-J, Adapt.) versus B-J	56
C(B-J, S-A) versus B-J	55
C(Adapt., S-A) versus Adapt.	69
C(Adapt., S-A) versus S-A	76
C(Adapt., S-A) versus B-J	46
C(Adapt., S-A, B-J) versus B-J	63

with those from fitted AR(4) models. The series were recorded quarterly. Comparing mean squared one-step forecast errors, the autoregressive models beat all of the econometric models for over half the series. The best individual econometric model beat all the other forecasts on seven occasions. Although these results show something of the power of single-series methods of forecasting, they do have to be interpreted with some caution. First, the results given were for one-step ahead forecasts, but when looking further ahead the econometric models perform much better. Secondly, Cooper did use the forecasts just as produced by the models and without the subjective corrections usually made by econometricians and which generally improve matters. Finally, it can be said that econometric models have certainly improved since the Cooper study, partly because of the appearance of such results, by better model specifications. Nevertheless, forecast-produced ARIMA models are not at all easy to beat for most economic variables.

There is not a great deal of experience with the combination of time series and econometric forecast in the published literature, but what is available does suggest that combining often produces a forecast superior to both components.

It is not possible to give a definite answer to a question such as, "What is the best forecasting method?" In any particular forecasting situation, some methods may be excluded either because of insufficient data or because the cost is too high. If there are no such limitations, it is still not possible to give a simple answer. All methods are based on simplifying assumptions about the true world, and one method will produce a good approximation to the truth on some occasions, a different method in other occasions. For macro-economic variables, it should be expected that the Box-Jenkins ARIMA models and econometric models should be superior to most simple alternatives. For microeconomic variables, ARIMA and carefully constructed causal regression models should generally be the best. However, one of the advantages of combining techniques is that it is not necessary to make a definite choice between alternative methods, as both can be retained and given a weight determined by recent performance.

The question of which methods to use is considered further in Chapter 12.

8.5   EVALUATING THE PROJECT

The project has been a very simplified version of a real forecasting exercise and so a complete evaluation process will not be possible. The project should have produced at least two forecasts of the variable of interest for the designated horizon, such as the 9 weeks suggested in Chapter 1. The basic evaluation will consist in comparing these point forecasts, possibly together with their confidence intervals, with the actual value taken by the variable at the designated time, which has to be available for evaluation. If your forecasts are perfectly correct, so that there is little or no forecast error, you can consider yourself either very good or extremely lucky, probably the latter. If there is a substantial difference between your forecast and the actual value, it is worth searching for a reason. The difference may be rationalized by the occurrence of some important, unforecastable event, such as a strike, a stock market crash, a heavy storm, the introduction of a new product by a competing company, or a change in some law. Of course, you just could have been unlucky, or the statistical model chosen may have been a poor one. It is worth plotting the actual data for the whole in-sample and post-sample periods and throughout the post-sample compare the forecasts made by your model.

In a complete forecasting exercise a sequence of h-step forecasts would have been made, each compared with the actual value, and the sums of squared forecast errors calculated and compared for different forecasting models. With the forecasting project this evaluation method is not possible.

QUESTIONS

1. A retired engineer has been attempting to forecast the local index of production for the past five years. He is under the impression that he is doing better than a forecast produced by the local newspaper but is unsure how to evaluate his forecasts. What advice would you give him?

2. To try to evaluate the quality of his forecasting technique, a statistician suggests using the correlation between the forecasts $f_{n,1}$ and the quantity being forecast x_{n+1}. Explain why this is not likely to be a useful method of evaluation.

3. A large company that manufactures frozen peas as well as many other products makes two sets of forecasts of the price of fresh peas, one set by statisticians in the Head Office and the other by market researchers in a subsidiary company's offices. There is need for a company forecast, so each quarter the two groups of forecasters meet, discuss their differences, and try to reach a compromise figure. These discussions are often acrimonious. Discuss how you might try to sell the idea of producing combinations of forecasts to the head statistician of the company.

4. A group of large oil firms provide anticipations of oil price changes over the following six months. A regression study finds

$$\text{(actual change)} = 5.0 + 1.0(\text{anticipated change}) + (\text{residual}),$$

where the residual series appears to be white noise. Over the last five periods the forecast errors [(error) = (actual change) − (forecast change)] from the anticipation data and an autoregressive model were those given by the following tabulation:

Errors	Period				
	1	2	3	4	5
Anticipation	8	−1	9	1	2
Autoregressive	−1	3	1	−2	2

Suggest an appropriate method of combining the two forecasts made for the next period.

5. If X_t is a trend-free series with no seasonal component, $f_{n,h}$ and $g_{n,h}$ are two forecasts made at time n of X_{n+h}, and

$$C_{n,h} = k_{n,h} f_{n,h} + (1 - k_{n,h}) g_{n,h}$$

is a combined forecast, where the k's are chosen from past h-step errors, then if both $f_{n,h}$ and $g_{n,h}$ have the same mean (average) value as X_{n+h}, show why you would expect $k_{n,h}$ to tend to the value $\frac{1}{2}$ as h becomes large.

FURTHER READINGS

Armstrong, J. Scott (1978). *Long-Range Forecasting, from Crystal Ball to Computer*, New York: Wiley.

Cooper, R. L. (1972). In *Econometric Models of Cyclical Behavior* (B. Hickman, ed.), New York: Columbia Univ. Press.

Granger, C. W. J., and P. Newbold (1986). *Forecasting Economic Time Series*, Second edition, Chapter 8, New York: Academic Press.

Granger, C. W. J., and R. Ramanathan (1984). "Improved methods of combining forecasts" *Journal of Forecasting* **3**, 197–204.

CHAPTER

9

Population Forecasting

My interest is in the future because I am going to spend the rest of my life there.
C. F. Kettering

9.1 STATING THE PROBLEM

Virtually everyone is aware of the dramatic increases in world population that have occurred in the past 100 years or so. World population has increased from well under half a billion (i.e., 500 million) to around four billion in less than 1000 years, with the most spectacular increases happening since 1800. The figure is confidently expected to reach over six billion by the year 2000, a year which is always accorded special attention for purely numerological reasons. In this chapter we shall be solely concerned with the problem of how such forecast population figures are produced. No attention will be paid, in any direct fashion, to the question of how population might be controlled, although this is obviously a question of overwhelming and immediate importance. Virtually no one opposes the view that there now exist sufficient human beings for any conceivable purpose, although some nationalist politicians apparently feel that the mix could be improved. Many dramatic statistics can be quoted in an attempt to bring home the extent of the population problem. For example,

(i)   the population of the world at the time of the birth of Christ was probably less than the present population of the United States and Mexico;

(ii) there are more scientists alive at this moment than the total of all who have died in the past; or

(iii) it is expected that world population will have grown from two billion in 1930 to over six billion by 2000.

Such figures should make it clear why it is important and necessary to

197

produce reliable forecasts not only of the population of the world or of separate geographic regions but also of how the population will be divided between different age groups. For governments, such forecasts are required in order to plan food and energy requirements and to organize long-run services, such as the size of universities and schools and even road construction. For firms, the forecasts are relevant to long-term investments in power stations or steel plants, to research into alternative raw materials and products, and possibly to decisions on whether or not to introduce brands aimed at specific age groups. The forecasts are essentially long run, over a decade or more, because significant changes generally do not occur over shorter intervals.

Population figures are often somewhat more easily interpreted and assimilated by considering changes or growth rates. At the start of the 1980s, the world population was growing at a rate of about 76 million people a year, which is almost 209,000 per day. Thus, in 4 days the world adds as many people as now live in San Diego, in 71 days as many as live in Australia, in 70 days the whole New York metropolitan area, all of France in 259 days, and all of Africa in just over 6 years.

A population is said to have a growth rate of 5% if for every 100 people alive at the start of the year there are 105 alive at the end. It can be shown that if a population has a growth rate of $g\%$ and this continues every year, then the population will double in $69/g$ years. Some figures for 1970 and 1986 on growth rates are given in Table 9.1. If the 1986 figures hold up, then from 1970 to 2000 the population of India will increase from 555

TABLE 9.1

	Population (millions)		Growth rate		No. of years to double	
	1970	1986	1970	1986	1970	1986
World	3632	4942	2.0	1.7	35	41
Africa	344	583	2.6	2.8	27	24
Asia	2056	2876	2.3	1.8	31	39
Kuwait	0.7	1.8	8.3	3.2	9	22
Japan	103.5	121	1.1	0.7	63	107
India	555	785	2.6	2.3	27	31
North America (U.S.)	205	267	1.0	0.7	70	87
Mid-America (including Mexico)	67	108	3.4	2.3	21	30
Europe	462	493	0.8	0.3	88	248
Britain	—	57	—	0.2	—	462

million to 1017 million, that of Kuwait from 0.7 million to 2.7 million, and that of Europe from 462 million to 508 million. Of course, it can be argued that these growth rates will not continue, that death rates will not continue to fall in Europe, that people will be rational and induce lower birth rates, that Malthusian effects will limit population in India due to shortages of food and space, and that the boom in the Kuwait population is due to a high rate of immigration caused by oil wealth and will not be allowed to continue. Such speculations certainly suggest factors that will affect population sizes and need to be carefully considered when forecasting. It is nevertheless true that rather good forecasts have been achieved in recent decades in most countries by simply fitting an exponential curve to past figures and then using this curve to extrapolate into the future. One would certainly expect more sophisticated, causal models to provide better forecasts, and these are considered in the next section.

The most remarkable change has been for China who has reduced its population growth ratio to 1.0% due to the implementation of very strong policies to limit fertility rates. Despite this change, China's population is still expected to reach 1190 million by the year 2000, an increase of 140 million over 1986.

As the population of the United States will be used as an example in later sections, it is perhaps worthwhile at this point to give some actual figures based on U.S. census figures (Table 9.2).

The United States' population is currently increasing at over 2 million people a year, made up of about $3\frac{1}{2}$ million births, 2 million deaths, and $\frac{1}{2}$

TABLE 9.2

Year	U.S. population (millions)	Year	U.S. population (millions)
1790	4	1890	63
1800	5	1900	76
1810	7	1910	92
1820	10	1920	106
1830	13	1930	123
1840	17	1940	132
1850	23	1950	151
1860	31	1960	179
1870	38	1970	203
1880	50	1980	226.5
		1986	241.0
		2000 (projected)	268

million net immigration. Thus, the United States is adding the populations of Detroit and Dallas each year. California is the state with the largest population with above 24 million inhabitants and is growing at almost half a million people a year, half of these coming from net immigration.

9.2 POPULATION EXTRAPOLATION

The problems considered in this section are of the form: how many twelve-year-old children will be requiring education in 10 years time? Clearly, answers to such questions are of vital importance to school directors or supervisors. A problem of this form will be called one of extrapolation, rather than forecasting, because all the children involved are already alive, so that future births need not be considered. This makes the problem much easier, for the required extrapolation is

Number of children = (Number of 2-year-old children now alive)
×(survival rate over next 10 years)
+(net immigration).

Suppose, for the moment, that the last term is small and can be ignored and let N_2 denote the number of 2-year-olds now alive and P_x the probability of a person aged x living to age $x + 1$. The answer to the above problem can then be stated as

$$Number = N_2 P_2 P_3 P_4 P_5 P_6 P_7 P_8 P_9 P_{10} P_{11}.$$

N_2 can certainly be taken as known, from birth registration figures, and death rates for children in their first 2 years. Values for P_2, P_3 etc. can be estimated from the experience of the previous *cohorts* of children. For example, P_2 is estimated by looking at the children who were aged 2 *last* year and asking how many survived the year and so are now aged 3. Similarly, P_3 is estimated by looking at the cohort of children who were aged 3 last year and observing how many survived to become aged 4 now, and so forth. Merely by looking at available data, all of the constituents of the extrapolation formula can be estimated and so a forecast obtained. There would be equally little problem in providing forecasts of segments of the population, such as boys or girls, for different races or regions, provided that suitable data have been collected in recent years. However, in some cases, some care may have to be taken with the net immigration component.

Denoting by N the total number alive and by N_x the number of people alive aged x, so that

$$N = \sum_x N_x,$$

then the number expected to be alive next year is

$$\sum_x N_x P_x$$

and the number expected to die is

$$N - \sum_x N_x P_x = \sum_x N_x(1 - P_x).$$

P_x is estimated by

$$\frac{N_{x+1} \text{ this year}}{N_x \text{ last year}}$$

The *crude death rate* is then defined as this quality divided by N, i.e.,

$$\text{Crude death rate} = \sum N_x(1 - P_x)/N.$$

The *crude birth rate*, which is discussed in the next section, is defined by

$$\text{Crude birth rate} = \frac{\text{Number born this year}}{N}$$

The estimates of the P_x can also be used to estimate the mean or expected length of life of a baby just born. To see how some of these figures have varied in the United States this century, we show some values in Table 9.3. The effects of improvements in health science, sanitation, and hygiene are clearly seen, as would be the small likelihood of the average man enjoying a long retirement if the retirement age had stayed at 65. For comparison, in 1986 the life expectancy at birth in Africa was 50 years.

TABLE 9.3

Year	Crude death rate per 1000 population	Expectation of life length at birth	
		male	female
1900	17.2	46.3	48.3
1910	14.7	48.4	51.3
1920	13.0	53.6	54.6
1930	11.3	58.1	61.6
1940	10.8	60.8	65.2
1950	9.6	65.6	71.1
1960	9.5	66.6	73.1
1970	9.5	67.1	74.8
1980	8.7	70	77.5
1986	8.6	71	78.5

9.3   BIRTH-RATE FORECASTING

Now consider the question, how many 6-year-old children will be entering school in 10 years' time? To make a forecast, a formula that can be used is

Number of children = (Number born in 4 years' time)
$\qquad$ ×(survival rate over first 6 years)
$\qquad$ +(net immigration).

This is clearly a more difficult problem than that discussed in the previous section, as it deals with children yet to be born. To predict the number of children to be born in 4 years' time, a sensible method would be to estimate the number of women aged 15–44 that will be alive then and to multiply by a forecasted *fertility rate.*

There are two methods of defining a fertility rate, and they have different uses. The *general fertility rate* is defined as

General fertility rate
$\quad$ =(Number of births in a year per 1000 women aged 15–44).

In 1983, this rate had the value 65.8 in the United States. The *total fertility rate* is an estimate of the number of children that a representative sample of 1000 women would bear in their lifetime. This estimate is based on present, age-specific birth rates, as follows.

Let r_x equal the birth rate per woman aged x at the start of the year (r_x is said to be an age-specific fertility rate). Then a woman aged Y would be expected to bear

$$r_Y + r_{Y+1} + \cdots + r_{44}$$

more children in the rest of her life. The total fertility rate is then defined as the sum of the r_x for all x values between 15 and 44 (or possibly 49). The total fertility rate assumes that the present age-specific fertility rates will continue unchanged in the future and ignores the possibility of a woman not surviving throughout the potential childbearing years. This total fertility rate is considered easier to interpret than some of the alternative measures. In colonial times, the average American woman bore about eight children, but infant mortality rates were also extremely high then. In the early 1970s, the rate fell to 2.1 and below in the United States. This is a particularly significant figure because, at this rate, enough girls are born to replace the generation of mothers that bore them. In other words, 1000 females must bear 2098 children so that there will be 1000 females for the next generation, as more males are born than females, at a ratio of about 51 to 49, and some females do not live to childbearing age. The total fertility rate in 1985 was 1.8. Although the total fertility rate is now below

2.1, it does not mean that the number of babies born will necessarily decline, as the children of the postwar baby boom are now reaching ages that traditionally have the highest age-specific fertility rates.

For most countries, fertility rates have been falling, and virtually all developed countries have rates under 2.1. However, in 1986 the world fertility rate was 3.7 and Africa had a value of 6.3.

Suppose that the age-specific fertility rates r_x have been estimated for the last twelve months and let F_x be the number of females aged x presently in the population. Then, by assuming that the r_x values will continue into the future without altering, the expected number of children to be born next year is given by

$$\sum_x F_x r_x,$$

where the sum is over x values from 15 to 44, say.

Similarly, the expected number of children to be born the following year is

$$\sum_x F_{x-1} P_{x-1} r_x,$$

where again x goes from 15 to 44. The number of births expected the subsequent year is

$$\sum_x F_{x-2} P_{x-2} P_{x-1} r_x,$$

as $F_{x-} P_{x-2} P_{x-1}$ is the estimate of the number of females that will be aged x at the start of that year, and so forth.

It is reasonable to expect that these forecasts will be fairly accurate when forecasting just a few years ahead, but when considering, say, 25 years hence, very little confidence could be displayed. Not only are fertility rates very likely to have changed, but the estimate includes children by mothers that have yet to be born themselves, so the possibility of errors cumulating obviously increases.

It should now be clear how the population for some country in a future year is estimated: The likely number of those alive who survive until the year is calculated, and the predicted number of children born is then added for each year to make up the total. When forecasting from, say, 1980 to 2000, the children to be born are not only a major part of the projected population, but are also the most difficult part to estimate. In practice, death rates and immigration figures are fairly stable for at least the advanced countries, but the fertility or birth rates are changing quite quickly. To provide a sound long-range population forecast, it is necessary to forecast future fertility rates. To show how important fertility rates are, consider the following four projections:

(i)   Series 1 assumes a slight decline in life expectancy, a historically low total fertility rate of 1.6 births per woman and a 250,000 annual net immigration. This may be taken to be a low growth series.

(ii) Series 2 is a middle growth series with no change in life expectancy, 1.9 births per woman and 450,000 net immigration.

(iii) Series 3 is a high growth series, with an increase in life expectancy of 83.3 years for women, 2.3 births per woman, and 750,000 net immigration.

(iv) Series 4 is a nonimmigration series and uses 1.9 births per year and a life expectancy of 79.6 years.

The U.S. census bureau continually makes projections of future population under a variety of assumptions about the movements in fertility rates. It must be emphasized that they are projections, being essentially conditional forecasts. To make true forecasts of population, a particular scenario has to be selected as being the most likely. The projected populations for the United States are (approximately, in millions) given in Table 9.4. Fairly small changes in family size are seen to make a tremendous difference in eventual projected population size. The actual census bureau projections are based on a more sophisticated model than that mentioned above, although the essence is the same. It is fairly clear that different subsections of the populations can be considered separately, based on race and geographical location, and married women can be considered separately from unmarried ones when using fertility rates. Precisely how useful this decomposition is in producing superior projections is not clear, as while a better model is certainly produced the estimates of essential values such as the age-specific fertility or survival rates may be less reliable.

TABLE 9.4[a]

Series	1990	2000	2025
I	246	256	260
II	250	268	301
III	255	282	357
IV	245	258	274

[a] Figures taken from the *Statistical Abstract of the United States, 1984*, Washington, D.C.: U.S. Dept. of Commerce, U.S. Govt. Printing Office.

It should be clear that to produce good population forecasts, future fertility rates need to be forecast. Once these are available, the projection procedure is fairly straightforward. The methods of forecasting fertility rates are similar to those discussed in earlier chapters when considering economic variables. The main methods seem to be the following:

(i)   Trend fitting and time series modeling, producing forecasts based just on previous rates.

(ii) Anticipations data. In 1960, a survey of married women aged 18–24 showed that they expected to have an average of 3.1 children. It seems likely that this age group will actually end up with a fertility rate of 2.9. In 1967, a similar survey of women aged 18–24 showed that they planned to have 2.9 children on average. By 1972, however, the anticipated average by women then aged 18–24 was down sharply to 2.3. By the early 1980's the figure fell to about 2.0 but later increased slightly.

(iii) Causal models. By far the most satisfactory way to proceed is to find out why people's anticipations and behavior change, if possible to find the main causes of these changes, and to build a suitable model. Unfortunately, this appears to be a difficult and complicated task and one that is very far from being satisfactorily answered. Change in the age that women get married is obviously a factor, but is it a cause or merely an effect of more fundamental causes? Changes in job opportunities for women, the tendency for more women to want to work, improvements in birth-control techniques, and changes in moral attitudes are also doubtlessly important, but the full impact of these changes has yet to be appreciated. Economic reasons may also be relevant and the more general awareness of the population problem, with its consequent overcrowding may also have an impact. Doubtless there is no single main cause, but many causes are working simultaneously and almost certainly not in a linear or simple additive fashion.

Until satisfactory answers are found to the question of what makes fertility rates change, high quality long-range population forecasts will not be possible.

9.4 WHAT OF THE FUTURE?

Despite the obvious difficulties in making projections, various important international organizations such as the United Nations and the World

Bank do keep producing "most likely" forecasts for future population. A way to present the projections is to list the estimated timing of each billion of the world population:

	Time taken to reach	Year attained
First billion	2 to 5 million years	1800 A.D.
Second billion	130 years	1930
Third billion	30 years	1960
Fourth billion	15 years	1975
Fifth billion	12 years	1987
Projection		
Sixth billion	11 years	1998

To put these figures into perspective, in 1986 the population of the USA was just under a quarter of a billion, Europe (excluding USSR) was just under a half a billion, and the USSR was rather more than a quarter of a billion. Thus, the world will increase in population in the eleven years starting in 1987 an amount equal to the current size of the USA, the USSR, and all of Europe. If fertility rates were to continue at present levels, a world population of 18 billion would be expected by the end of the next century.

Fortunately, in most countries fertility rates are declining, but because of the preponderance of youth in populations, the total number of people in the world will continue to increase. For example, China is using considerable pressure to reduce its birth rate and trying to limit couples to no more than one child each, in most cases. Even with these policies, Chinese population is expected to increase from its present one billion to a steady level of about one and a half billion towards the end of the next century. By then the population of India will have increased from its present 785 million to a size greater than China's one and a half billion. Over the same period, the population of Nigeria will increase from the present 105 million to over 500 million to become the third most populous country. Many countries will continue to increase into the following century before reaching steady levels. The total world population projected for 2100 is just over 10 billion, with the major increases occurring in Africa, Asia, and Latin America. A forerunner of the stationary population is the point of time when a replacement level of fertility is reached of about 2.1 children per woman. China has recently reached this point. Delays in reaching this point can have enormous effects on the eventual population size, as the following estimated figures for India show:

Year replacement fertility reached	Year stable population reached	Level of Stable population (millions)
2000	2060	1,420
2020	2080	1,900
2040	2100	2,600

The population of India in 1980 was 690 million.

There are many detailed implications from these projections; age distributions will change, growth of standards of living will be affected, city sizes could grow to 30 million or more (compared to 10 million currently for New York City), and the numbers dying from starvation could also increase. Some of these problems will be discussed in Chapter 11.

QUESTIONS

1. Suppose that you are approached to forecast the population of a small country town and also of a popular ocean-side resort this year and also 25 years hence. Write an essay how you would approach this problem and the kind of data that you would require.

2. The diaper supplier wants to forecast how many babies will be born in each of the next four quarters in some region. Briefly outline how one might make forecasts based on each of the following approaches: trend line fitting, indicators, survey and anticipations data, and seasonal time series modeling.

3. Given the following population figures for a small town:

	Number in population (N_x)				Number in population (N_x)	
Age x	1985	1986	Age x	1985	1986
1	1026	1033	4	980	990
2	1010	1020	5	971	980
3	992	1000	6	960	970

Forecast the number of children aged 6 who will enter school in 1987. Also forecast the total number of children aged 2–6 in 1987, assuming in both instances that there is zero net immigration.
Find the crude death rate for 1986 of children aged 1–5.

4. Considering further the small town mentioned in the previous problem, the accompanying table shows the number of women aged 14 – 23 in the town in 1985 and 1986 and also the number of births to each age group in 1985. Forecast the number of children born to women aged 16 – 23 in 1987 and the number born to women aged 22 in 1989.

Age	No. of women (1985)	No. of births (1985)	No. of women (1986)
14	6132	0	6120
15	6242	0	6100
16	6140	0	6201
17	6100	130	6020
18	6090	292	6030
19	6090	343	6003
20	6073	488	6005
21	6082	561	6000
22	6070	502	6010
23	6060	492	6010

FURTHER READINGS

Pressar, R. (1972). *Demographic Analysis,* Chicago: Aldine-Atherton.
  Contains extensive discussion of population projection.
Various issues of *Population Bulletin,* published by the Population Reference Bureau, Inc., Washington, D.C.

CHAPTER

10

Technological Forecasting

A religious sect is predicting that the world will end at 10 P.M. tonight. For more details, watch the news at eleven.

T.V. news flash

To expect the unexpected shows a thoroughly modern intellect.

Oscar Wilde

10.1 INTRODUCTION

The majority of the forecasting methods considered in previous chapters have been concerned with short- and medium-term forecasts, the only exception being the trend-curve fitting procedures. Over periods of less than five years, it is reasonable to make forecasts against a background of no technical change, so that the objects on sale will not change dramatically and neither will productivity. Of course prices can change as well as the values of other important economic variables, but the forecasts will largely be concerned with reactions of economic variables to behavioral, policy, or exogenous variable changes. However, when considering longer-run forecasts, an assumption of no technological change becomes quite unreasonable. One may expect that over periods of twenty years or more ahead the major changes in the economy and society will be due to changes in technology or in largely exogenous variables such as population size, distribution, or climate. Population forecasting was discussed in the previous chapter, and current evidence suggests that there is no clearcut trend in climate, although there may be long swings which have important effects.

Technological forecasting is generally concerned with the fairly long term and asks what technology will be likely to be available in particular years in the future and what the impacts of important technological developments and innovations will be. It is clearly related to problems of long-term planning so that companies can try to identify new markets and the decline of present markets and governments can foresee future bottle-necks in the growth or development of society in some proposed direction. Like any new and potentially exciting field, it has attracted both some extremely good researchers and some who certainly do not deserve such an accolade. The obvious major problem with the field is that it is inher-ently very difficult to evaluate the work of any individual or the usefulness of any technique. This difficulty of evaluation occurs whenever long-term forecasting is attempted, as it takes so long to decide if a forecast was adequate or not, and this means that it takes a great deal of time to generate sufficient evidence for the quality of one method to be seen to be better than another. It must be said that most of the techniques available for technological forecasting are neither very sophisticated nor highly developed. This is partly due to the evaluation problem just mentioned, but mostly to this kind of forecasting's being inherently difficult, as might be imagined. However, if it can be done well, the potential rewards are immense. As an illustration of both of these points, it is reported that in the very early days of electronic computers a European electrical company asked for a forecast of the potential sales of these new machines. The forecast made was that there would never be more than twenty computers sold, and so the company decided not to enter the field. Later events suggest that the forecast was incorrect in that IBM did quite well by selling thousands of computers. Of course, the company's decision may well have been the correct one, as many manufacturers did start to make computers in the beginning and nearly all lost a great deal of money.

Technological forecasting may be defined as "a prediction of the future characteristics or applications of useful machines, techniques or proce-dures." The forecasts are generally concerned with the characteristics of a technology rather than how these are achieved. For example, one might try to forecast the speed of computing or the efficiency of a gasoline engine, carefully defining these concepts, rather than forecasting how such speed or efficiency can be achieved. It is these characteristics which have impact on other fields of development.

To illustrate the basic features of technological forecasting, suppose one is in the year 1950 and is asked "Will there be commercially available color T.V. available in the future?" At that time most people would have ex-pected such a development would occur at some time. The problem rather becomes "When will this occur?" If the question about color T.V. had been asked to a group of scientists in 1910, say, it would have been possible to ask the question in some form, but the technical possibility would have been difficult to envisage or forecast. In the year 1800, before electricity was even available, it would have been very difficult even to have asked the question. In the future, a comparable question might be "Will there be commercially available three-dimensional color T.V.?'' Most people would say yes, so the question again becomes one of timing. However, what is the equivalent question for a 100 years ahead? For much of technological forecasting, in the very long run, knowing what question to ask is a large part of the problem.

There are basically two approaches to technological forecasting, which may be called exploratory and normative. Exploratory techniques provide specific forecasts of what will happen, such as when a particular medical breakthrough is thought most likely to occur. These forecasts can be in terms of probability statements, such as "with probability 0.75 by the year 1993 automobile engines will be twice as efficient as now." One difficulty with such forecasts is that they implicitly include a forecast of how much money is going to be invested in trying to reach some goal. It seems possible that rockets would have been less developed in 1970 if the United States had not decided to put a man on the moon. Normative forecasts start with an objective for some future period and then by working back to present time and state of the art determine what areas or technological parameters need improvement and by how much, by what means the required improvements will be attained, and what the costs, consequences, and major potential bottlenecks will be attaining the goal. Regulations about future automobile emissions fall into this category. The most successful example was the effort by NASA to put a man on the moon by a specific date and at a specific cost, both of which, it has been stated, were attained. It was known that certain developments in electronic miniaturization, rocket design, and new materials would be required, and by assigning good enough scientists and sufficient investment the intermediate goals were all attained in time for the final objective to be achieved. It was a truly remarkable piece of long-range planning coupled with excellent management and scientific research. In general, it is clear that normative and exploratory forecasts have to be linked, for it is pointless setting impossible objectives—such as having a colony on the sun by the year 2000, or eradicating all poverty, disease, and starvation on the earth by 1994. Some inventions and developments can simply be required and usually achieved by sufficient allocation of researchers, whereas others clearly cannot. However, there is a large penumbra of uncertainty consisting of developments that are neither clearly attainable or clearly unattainable, and penetration of this region is obviously of central importance in providing good technological forecasts.

Before discussing techniques for producing forecasts, it is worth asking the question whether there is any hope of predicting an invention or technological development. As might be expected, a wide range of views exists on this question. At one extreme, it is argued that invention is by its very nature unforecastable, being achieved by a flash of inspiration by some genius. At the other extreme, it is claimed that most inventions occur when in some sense "the time is right," as illustrated by several workers making the same invention or breakthrough at the same time, and that someone with sufficient knowledge could have observed precursors and thus forecast the invention. The truth is usually somewhere in between. It is certainly true that many inventions and breakthroughs do occur almost simultaneously. It is said that the telegraph, the reaper, the motion picture, the filament electric lamp, the sewing machine, and the elevator are all examples of inventions that occurred more than once, and many other examples exist. At least two instances come from the field of forecasting itself. Both Kolmogoroff, in Russia, and Norbert Wiener, in the United States, in the early 1940s developed the theory of optimum forecasts which was briefly mentioned in Chapter 4. At a less sophisticated level, the idea of combining forecasts, as discussed in Chapter 8 was suggested by Bates and Granger in 1969 and very soon after, and quite independently, by C. Nelson, using a different approach. Every research worker can supply similar examples. However, the fact that examples of simultaneous invention can be found does not necessarily mean that the inventions could have been predicted. There are many examples of what might be called the Pearl Harbor syndrome; situations in which it was later shown that information existed such that they could in theory have been predicted, yet in fact were not. Even after an invention has been made, it is not clear that it will be a success. In the early days of the automobile, most engineers were uncertain whether the electric car, the steamer, or the gasoline car would turn out to be the most successful.

The question of how well breakthroughs can be forecast, if at all, has still to be answered, and work is being conducted on the types of precursors that were available before the first release of nuclear power or the invention of the jet engine, for example. Once sufficient experience from the past has been gained, it may well be possible to monitor the research literature and the requests for patents so that improved forecasts are achieved.

Although breakthroughs in science and in other fields are naturally very important in the long run, they are perhaps less important when forecasting in the middle run, say from seven to twelve years ahead. Most of the changes in technology that will occur in the middle run will consist of developments of the present technology and of inventions that have already occurred and are being currently discussed in the research literature. There are eight basic stages in the development of a technological innovation:

Stage 1 the original scientific suggestion or discovery or the recognition of an achievable need or opportunity,

Stage 2 crystallization of a theory or design concept,

Stage 3 laboratory verification of the correctness of the theory behind the innovation,

Stage 4 laboratory demonstration of the successful application of the theory,

Stage 5 full scale or field trial,

Stage 6 commercial introduction or first operational use,

Stage 7 widespread adoption, and

Stage 8 proliferation, including adoption in areas other than that for which it was intended, plus impact on other products or parts of science.

By recognizing in which state a particular innovation now resides and by using case studies of the development of previous comparable inventions it may be possible to forecast when it will reach later stages. The full process, through all stages, will usually take at least 10 years, with 20 – 25 years being more likely. It has been suggested that the speed of an innovation going from stage 1 to stage 6 has been increasing, but it is not clear that this is true for the more complicated modern inventions, such as fission and fusion nuclear power, for example.

To give more structure to the procedures whereby forecasts are made about technological breakthroughs or developments, a variety of techniques has been suggested. The most important two, trend-curve fitting and Delphi, are described in the following two sections, and some of the other methods are summarized in the final section of this chapter.

10.2 GROWTH CURVES

For many purposes it is sufficient to forecast what the state of some technology will be in a specific year rather than how that state will be achieved. For example, a forecast that computing costs will be reduced will have many important implications for the ever increasing use of computers both in industry and in homes. It would not matter how this cost reduction is achieved provided that it does occur. Such a forecast could be based on observations of how costs have declined in the past. It could be noted that while in 1952 it cost \$1.20 to do 100,000 multiplications on an IBM computer, six years later the cost had dropped to 26¢. By 1964 the same calculations could be executed for 12¢, by 1970 for 5¢, and in 1975 for just 1 ¢. By fitting a trend curve, such as one of those discussed in Chapter 2, to these figures, it would be easy to produce a forecast of future costs.

The question, as always, is which curve to fit. The most popular, by far, is the exponential curve, in which the logarithms of the values being fitted are explained by a linear time trend. Other popular curves are the linear, the logistic (also called Pearl), and the Gompertz curves. It will be recalled from the discussion in Chapter 2 that these last two curves tend to an asymptote or upper limit. This upper limit may be estimated or it can just be selected from other considerations. For instance, if a curve is being fitted to the number of telephones per 1000 members of the population, then an upper limit of 800 might be selected and this will fix one of the parameters of the model. The obvious problem with this approach is that very poor forecasts result if this upper limit is badly selected.

Examples of exponential growth curves given by Martino (1972) include

(i)   the efficiency of light sources, in terms of lumens per watt, going from the paraffin candle in 1850, through the tungsten filament lamp in 1908 and the mercury lamp in 1936, to the gallium arsenide diode in 1960;

(ii) the gross take-off weight of U.S. single-place fighter aircraft;

(iii) the top speed of U.S. combat aircraft;

(iv) the maximum thrust from U.S.-built liquid and solid propellant rocket engine;

(v)   electric power production in the United States;

(vi) the installed technological horsepower per capita in the United States;

(vii) the ratio of the size of random access memories, in bits, to access time in microseconds, for digital computers; and

(viii) the time required for inversion of a 40×40 matrix by a digital computer.

With the exception of the last of these examples, the fitted exponential trends are upward. To illustrate the kind of result achieved, the logarithm of the ratio in (vii), denoted by Y_t, when regressed on time, gives

$$Y_t = -1080.82 + 0.5513t,$$

where $t = 0$ corresponds to 1945 and data up to about 1967 are used in the estimation. One way to interpret any such exponential growth curve is to use what is known as "the rule of 70." Suppose that the curve

$$Y_t = Ae^{bt}$$

is fitted to some data. On taking logarithms, the equation becomes

$$Y_t = a + bt,$$

where $y_t = \log Y_t$, $a = \log A$, and one asks how long it takes for Y_t to double in size. Some easy algebra gives the result that this doubling time is given by $0.6931/b$, which is often approximated by $0.70/b$. Thus, for the computer memory ratio, the doubling time is $0.70/0.55 = 1.23$ years. Thus, the ratio will expand eightfold in $3 \times 1.23 = 3.7$ years. This is a tremendous rate of growth, but not at all uncommon in technology.

Not all of these exponential curves forecast very well from their time of estimation, particularly those for electric power production (v). Because of increased prices for electricity following the 1976 oil crisis and consequential changes in behaviour and improvement of appliance efficiency and house insulation, demand for electricity increased much slower than forecast by the exponential curve.

It has been found that trend-curve fitting can provide useful forecasts, at least for the middle run. However, these forecasts are of technological parameters rather than of actual technology. No attempt is made to forecast how technological changes will be achieved. The curve fitting approach is also basically unsatisfactory in another way in that it is essentially based on an assumption that things will keep on going in the same way that they have in the past. Although this could often be the case, there may be information available suggesting that such an assumption is incorrect. Policy changes concerning environmental effects could limit growth in certain directions and the policy of reduced support to the U.S. space program may well be expected to reduce the growth in rocket maximum thrust, for example. Simply examining past data can miss such potential change in growth. A method of expanding the information set to include such possible policy changes is discussed in the next section.

As an example of the dangers of uncritical use of growth curves, a speaker at an international conference on the quality of life stated, "Computerized estimates of the world's end need not be accurate. Had there been a computer in 1872 it would have predicted that by 1972 there would be so many horsedrawn vehicles that the surface of the globe would be covered with six feet of manure."

10.3   THE DELPHI METHOD

When trying to make a technological timing forecast, such as when some breakthrough will occur, it is clearly of little value to ask the opinion of anyone who is not an expert in the technological field concerned. Most people, including scientists in other fields, would not have sufficient technical competence or knowledge about current research or problems needing to be overcome to give a relevant forecast. If, however, it is possible to identify a group of experts, there still remains the problem of how best to extract a useful forecast from them.

One obvious procedure is to select the best expert — a genius — and ask that person for a forecast. Although this is basically a sound idea, it is difficult to achieve in practice. It is not easy to select the genius and different selections may not give similar forecasts. It is not sufficient to pick the best-known person in a field as this position may have been achieved through a sound marketing effort rather than real eminence or because of an important discovery ten years earlier, which does not necessarily mean that the person is still in the forefront of research or ideas. The most relevant single individual to make a forecast might well be some fairly young, unknown scientist who is about to make a real breakthrough, but it is usually virtually impossible to identify such a person. More established research workers are likely to be most concerned with developing earlier ideas rather than discovering new techniques.

If the single-genius method is risky, would a meeting of minds in a committee or seminar format be any more successful? Personal observation by the author suggests that most minds become moribund when on a committee for reasons that presumably only psychologists can explain. Many scientists are not used to defending their views verbally and so a small committee is likely to be dominated by a few superegoists who do not necessarily have superior forecasting abilities. Similarly, a large seminar involving, say, 100 participants may not be able to hear the views of more than a few. The other extreme from face-to-face meetings is to conduct a postal poll or survey. The problem here is that although all opinions now have equal weight, there is no opportunity for those with particularly convincing arguments to present them, so that the likelihood of a consensus opinion's being obtained is low.

A suggested procedure to circumvent most of these problems and to squeeze out reasonable forecasts from a group of experts was developed at the RAND Corporation in 1963. The necessary ingredients are a carefully selected group of experts and an organizer. At the first stage, a set of properly worded questions are given to each expert, such as the following:

Q.1.   When will a reliable automated language translator be available?
Q.2.   When will it be economically feasible to commercially produce synthetic protein for food?
Q.3.   When will it be possible to breed intelligent animals, such as apes, for low grade labor?

Q.4.   When will there be two-way communication with extraterrestrials?
Q.5.   In what year will the percentage of electric cars amongst all cars reach 50%?

To each such question the expert is supposed to give a specific date, usually in the form of a year, which he or she thinks is the most likely to be correct. An answer of "never" is also allowed. A somewhat different form of question that might be used is

Q.6.   What is the probability of a world war occurring in the next twenty years?

The answer may be any number between 0 and 1 inclusive.

Once the answers have been returned to the organizer, the next task is to summarize them, to obtain both an average forecast date and a measure of how much the experts disagree. A sensible way of doing this is to find the median year and the two quartiles of the distribution of forecasts. This is done as follows. Suppose that all of the years named are placed in order from the nearest to the furthest. If a year is named several times, then it appears that number of times in the list. The median year is such that half of the list lies on each side of it. The first quartile has a quarter of the list before it and three quarters after. The last quartile has three quarters before it and a quarter after. Thus, for example, assume twelve experts gave the following dates in order:

1979, 1980, 1983, 1985, 1986, 1987, 1989,
            ↑   ↑
     first quartile   median
1990, 1990, 1990, 2010, never.
            ↑
     last quartile

Then the median lies between 1987 and 1989 (and so is recorded as the average of these two years, i.e., 1988), the first quartile lies between 1983 and 1985 (and so is 1984), and the last quartile is between 1990 and 1990 (i.e., 1990). The median guess, or forecast, is thus 1988 and represents an average value, and the interquartile range (IQR) is 1984–1990 and is a measure of the extent of agreement or disagreement of the experts. The use of these measures is recommended because of their ease of calculation and interpretation and because the reply "never" creates no problems with the analysis.

As an example, a sample of people attending a forecasting conference in 1967 replied to question Q.5, generating a median of 1990 and an IQR of 1985–2012. Such replies are frequently represented diagrammatically as shown in Fig. 10.1.

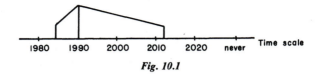

Fig. 10.1

The forecasts produced at this stage represent simply the result of a survey of possible experts and, although possibly useful, allow no form of debate. Rather more sophistication occurs at the second stage, where the experts are sent the results of the initial survey and asked if, given this extra information, they wish to alter their views. An expert who finds his view to be quite different from that of everyone else might decide that his views cannot be supported and so change his forecast toward the median. There is, however, no pressure for him to so change his viewpoint. He may well think that everyone else is out of step. Any expert who wishes to maintain a viewpoint or forecast outside of the interquartile range is invited to state briefly the main reasons for holding such a viewpoint.

Returning to the question of when electric automobiles would make up 50% of all automobiles, in the second round the experts changed their opinions somewhat, giving a median now of 1995 and an IQR of 1985–2020. The organizer of the experiment summarized the arguments in favor of an earlier date. "The first use will be for local travel, which will rapidly exceed 50%, in view of urban development. Developments in nuclear power cost-effectiveness and energy storage point to an earlier date." The arguments in favor of a later date ran. "Pollution will force improvements in the combustion engine. Batteries don't provide enough power or range. Battery recharging is too inconvenient. The oil industry will adjust this."

Once more, the participants are sent a summary of the second stage, their revised aggregated forecasts, plus the summaries of arguments for holding extreme views, and again they are asked to provide revised forecasts. They can also provide further arguments for holding a particular viewpoint and try to combat the arguments for the opposite viewpoint. For the electric car question, the third round produced little change, with a median of 1995 and an IQR of 1985–2011. The counterarguments in defense of an earlier date included, "The later-date arguments overlook the political pressure. Battery and fuel cell improvements will, in the 1970s, provide sufficient power and range. Inconvenience will be minimized because recharging can be automatic upon garaging." Those in defense of a later date included, "If it were not for pollution, this would occur even later than 2000. Energy storage would have to improve by 10 orders of magnitude. Consumers buy cars for long-distance, high-speed driving."

The sequence of questioning could continue almost indefinitely, with developing arguments, provided the participants' patience remained, but cost constraints usually stop the sequence after three or four rounds. For the forecasting conference views on electric cars, a fourth and final question produced a median of 1995 with an interquartile range of 1985–2000. A review of these results and arguments twenty years later shows a great deal of sense to have been generated. The lack of development of a greatly improved battery still prevents electric cars' becoming popular, and a median of 1995 now appears unreasonable, despite considerable changes in attitude towards electric cars due to concern about dependence upon foreign oil.

The original large-scale Delphi experiment was conducted by Gordon and Helmer at the RAND Corporation around 1965 and the technique was immediately widely accepted as being both sensible and potentially useful. The panel used in this first study consisted mainly of highly intelligent, well-respected scientists, social scientists, and intellectuals, who were asked to provide forecasts on a very wide range of topics, most of which were outside the field of expertise of the majority of the panelists. Some of the forecasts made in 1965 concerning scientific breakthroughs are given in Table 10.1.

Some of these forecasts now seem optimistic and others still reasonable. These figures illustrate a problem common to all long-term forecasting techniques: How can they be evaluated? It can take many years until one knows whether or not the forecast proves to be accurate. Although this problem is insurmountable, it is possible to conduct experiments that

TABLE 10.1

	Question	Median	Interquartile range
1.	Economically useful desalination of seawater	1970	1970–1983
2.	Automated language translators	1972	1968–1976
3.	New organs through transplanting or prosthesis	1972	1968–1982
4.	Reliable weather forecasts	1975	1972–1988
5.	Controlled thermonuclear power	1985	1980–2000
6.	Feasibility of limited weather control	1990	1987–2000
7.	Economically useful farming of ocean to produce at least 20% of world's food	2000	2000–2017
8.	Use of drugs to raise level of intelligence	2012	1984–2023

throw some light on the value of the Delphi technique. One such experiment goes through the full set of stages but using questions of fact rather than forecasts. The questions are selected so that the experimenter can know the true answer but the panelists will merely have an opinion and are very unlikely to know the truth. The kinds of questions used are illustrated by the following:

(a) How many divorces, in thousands, were there in the United States in 1960?
(b) How many prime numbers are there between 1000 and 2000?
(c) What was the year of birth of the inventor of FM radio?
(d) What is the area of Los Angeles county, in square miles?
(e) How many telephones were there in Africa in 1965?
(f) How many women Marines were there at the end of World War II?

Table 10.2 gives an example of the results obtained.

Although the experiments are hardly ideal, and the participants are rarely "experts," they do provide some interesting results, which may be summarized as follows:

(a) There was a tendency to converge, although the movement occurs less in the median than in reduction in the interquartile range.
(b) Panelists holding views outside the interquartile range were very much more likely to alter their views, toward the median, than other panelists. Thus, if the true answer fell inside the original IQR, there would appear to be a tendency for the panel to reach a consensus somewhere near the truth. However, if the truth lies outside the original IQR, it is unlikely that it will be approached in later rounds.

TABLE 10.2

	Median and IQR				
Question	Round 1	Round 2	Round 3	Round 4	True answer
(a)	500	500	500	400	393
	100–1000	250–750	350–750	400–500	
(b)	130	150	150	150	135
	50–200	100–200	118–200	120–200	
(c)	1893	1890	1890	1890	1890
	1884–1900	1885–1898	1885–1898	1885–1895	
(d)	1600	1800	2000	2000	4060
	500–4000	1200–4000	1500–3000	1500–2500	

(c) There is a tendency for participants to change their views toward the median opinion rather than toward the true value.

(d) If participants are allowed to rank themselves as "experts" or not on a particular question, the expert panel does no better than the full panel.

(e) If two panels are used, the one receiving feedback, i.e., information about the results of previous rounds, forecasts better than that not getting this information.

(f) A Delphi panel is much more likely to converge towards the truth than a panel involved in face-to-face discussion.

Although the results of such experiments do confirm that Delphi is a sensible procedure, the actual value of the technique still needs evaluating by observing the eventual accuracy of the forecasts made. The success or lack thereof of a particular Delphi forecasting survey naturally depends on the care with which the panel is selected, the questions formulated, and the arguments summarized. It is important for inexperienced survey directors to undertake a small pilot study before the full-scale survey is conducted, so that ambiguously worded questions are avoided for example. One obvious problem that has to be avoided are questions that are ambiguous or sufficiently imprecise that their resulting forecasts cannot be properly evaluated. Some of the questions in Table 10.1 are not easy to evaluate as phrased. For example, what does "economically useful" mean in the first question?

There are many possible criticisms of the Delphi approach, and doubtless ways of improving it can be found. One criticism is that most of the participants appear to be playing a game rather than thinking deeply about their position, trying to defend their views, or attacking the views of others. A method of generating more active participation might involve using groups of experts already committed to a position. For example, suppose a technological forecast is required about the relative importance of future energy sources. Groups active in conducting research into nuclear energy, solar energy, tidal sources, and oil shale usage could each be asked to state their reasons for being optimistic about their own specialization and the relative disadvantages of the alternative sources. These arguments could then be circulated to the other groups, who would try to defend their own positions and undermine those of the competing groups. This procedure, which might be called Competitive Delphi, could produce acrimonious arguments but also deeper expert thinking about the various problems to be solved. Whether or not it would eventually produce a forecast about the portfolio of energy sources that the nation would be using in the future is less certain.

10.4   OTHER TECHNIQUES

Just a few of the many other available techniques will be reviewed in this section. Most of them are even less scientific than those already described in this chapter. They are inclined to involve considerable subjective judgment and may not provide very reliable forecasts if used individually. However, they will sometimes release a research worker's thought patterns from the inhibitions that are often present and thereby enable him or her to produce more realistic long-range forecasts.

10.4.1   Forecasting by Analogy

When considering a particular forecasting problem it is occasionally possible to find a situation in an earlier time and perhaps in a different location, society, or technology that has many similar features to the situation being investigated. By studying the analogous situations, the timetable or sequence of events that occurred in the earlier case may be helpful in the later case. For example, if a community is planning to build from scratch a good quality university to teach 6000 students, it may well be worthwhile looking at the experiences of those building a similar university in some other state. The times required to recruit suitable faculty; to plan, design, and build the teaching facilities; to order, have delivered, and debug a computer system; and to collect together an adequate library need to be known before the university can fully open its doors. The observed times taken by other new universities would clearly provide valuable information when making forecasts. It is unlikely that the forecasts will be exact because the analogy will not be complete. For example, that other universities have been set up may make the buying of a workable computer system easier but the finding of available back issues of academic journals for the library more difficult. The decision whether a proposed analogy is apt or not has to be subjective. Presumably the lessons learnt in building a new university in an adjacent state will be more appropriate than experiences with building a new hospital locally, for example.

Examples of the use of analogies can be found in the fields of weather and stock market forecasting. In the 1960s, one method used to forecast British weather a month ahead was to compare the current weather map with all previous maps for similar parts of the year, using a computer. If, for example, the map for March 23, 1962, was found to be most similar in appearance to that of April 2, 1953, then the forecast for the month starting March 24, 1962, would be the same as what actually occurred in the month starting April 3, 1953. Experience with this procedure indicated that it is slightly better than choosing at random, which, given the well-known complexity of Britain's weather, is not totally unimpressive. For the stock market, a group of analysts known as chartists plot a stock price index or the price of a particular company's share against time and look for certain patterns. These patterns or shapes are given names such as "head and shoulders," and it is claimed that when such a shape occurs the market index or the price of the share is inclined to go in a specific direction afterwards. The value of this method of forecasting stock market prices is still controversial; there is little evidence that chartists all retire rich, although they may retire somewhat richer than the average speculator.

These are examples of unambitious analogies; the following example is more controversial. Fifteen or so years ago the problem of how to dispose of the incredible amounts of garbage generated by a large city was an important and worrisome one. Advances in technology have now made garbage a desirable product, to produce energy, animal feed, and raw materials. Some cities, in a sense, cannot get enough. Can the same sequence occur with radioactive waste, the disposal of which is causing so much heartache to some governmental agencies now? It might be suggested, from the analogy, that a technology will soon arise which will convert this waste into useful, and safe, materials so that the demand will be for more of it rather than less.

The difficulty in finding reliable analogies is an obvious problem, but in some circumstances use of analogies may enhance the available information set upon which a forecast is made in a useful way. Certainly historians would like this to be generally agreed upon, as it increases the importance and acceptance of their discipline.

10.4.2   Precursor Events

The identification of precursor events in a technology and their use for forecasting is similar to the use of leading indicators in time series forecasting, as discussed in Chapter 7. If the introduction of an innovation in one technology or society is frequently signaled by a similar innovation in another technology or society, this observation clearly has forecasting value. Examples would be developments in commercial aircraft design first appearing in military aircraft, developments in transmission, engine, or brake design in family cars first being seen in racing cars, or innovations in marketing usually first appearing in the United States and later occurring in Europe and Australia. Managers and research workers in some areas will usually be aware of such precursor events, but a search for others may sometimes prove worthwhile. One more, the identification of what events are relevant and how the information should be incorporated is generally necessarily very subjective.

10.4.3   Scenarios

Starting with some specific situation, such as the observed present, a scenario attempts to set up a logical sequence of events to indicate how some future state or situation can evolve step by step. As alternative developments occur, such as a breakthrough happening early or late, a set of alternative scenarios will usually arise. Thus, in considering future electricity production procedures, a "most probable" scenario might involve phasing out oil, phasing in more coal-burning plants in the short term, building more fission nuclear plants in the middle run, and relying on solar, geothermal, and fusion plants in the longer run. However, alternative and quite different scenarios would result if some states, or the federal government, restricted the building of nuclear plants, if more stringent air-pollution policies limited the use of coal or oil, if Australia decided never to export its large store of uranium, or if a breakthrough occurred in fusion technology and allowed commercial use of this technology in ten year's time. The use of the most probable scenario, or "surprise-free" viewpoint provides a basis against which to compare other alternative scenarios. The primary purpose of these scenarios is not strictly to predict the future but rather to facilitate a systematic exploration of branches or networks of critical events within some explicit time frame. By considering alternative scenarios, governments, states, or companies can devise contingency plans to meet these possible situations. Clearly, more attention will be given to the more probable scenarios, although lower probability but high impact situations should not be ignored in long-range planning.

Scenarios can be prepared either just for specific technologies, such as electricity production, water supply and quality, or military arms development, or for whole societies, such as the Saudi Arabian economy or the whole world. When this is attempted, it is not sufficient simply to run through sequences of possible events for each main part of the society or for each main technology as the interrelation, or cross impacts, of these events also need to be considered. Developments in one field may greatly affect developments in another. For example, it may be thought that the general acceptance of electric automobiles is dependent on the invention of a superior method of storing electricity than is provided by either conventional batteries or their foreseen developments in the shortrun. Thus electricity storage technology affects automobile technology. Similarly, a breakthrough in one field may increase the probabilities of innovative events in other fields. A formal way of proceeding is to attempt to estimate these cross-impact probabilities, using a Delphi procedure perhaps, and then to build scenarios taking these probabilities into account. Use of these ideas, either formally or not, should both increase the plausibility and self-consistency of the resulting scenario and also encourage the inclusion of all the critical and most relevant factors.

Scenarios are sometimes written by individuals, but more recently they have often become team efforts, bringing together opinions of experts in a variety of fields. This is particularly relevant when considering a bundle of alternative scenarios.

10.5 EXAMPLES OF SCENARIOS

As an example of scenario construction, consider the following evolution of the labor market in a developed economy. It may be expected that in the next decade there will be increased women's participation in the work force, in that there will be a substantial growth in the proportion of women in the age group 20 – 60 who earn wages for 20 or more hours per week. The similar proportion for men will decline slightly, but overall the total work force will increase. Relaxation of retirement rules will allow some people to extend their working life by five or so extra years, but many others will decide to retire early, although some of these will eventually attempt second careers. The declining birth rate will lead to a decrease in the number of school leavers entering the work force each year, and this will lead to a lessened seasonal component in the unemployed figures. Overall, there will be an increased demand for jobs. Automation will remove some jobs from the market, but other developments, particularly in the service industries, will create jobs. However, to meet the extra demand for jobs there will be a reduction in the average work week. Employers will find that they are employing more workers but for fewer hours each. Overtime will decline dramatically, and the pattern of hours worked during the day will become more varied.

During the following decade these tendencies will continue, but later retirement will become more common due to decreasing social security retirement benefits and improvements in health of the older sections of the work force. The money available for social security has been a continuing problem because of the general aging of the population, although it will be considerably alleviated by the increasing women's participation rate. Married couples both of whom are eligible for retirement benefits will observe that their combined benefits are less than that of two single persons, as the government relies on the "two can live as cheaply as one" adage. Consequently, the number of divorces involving couples in the 50 – 70 age group will increase considerably. Very much more attention will be paid to the legal problems of "common-law marriages," and, due to continuing changes both in the law and in attitudes, marriage rates will decline for all age groups. Partly as a consequence of this development, birth rates will decline further and many teachers will be required to retire early.

This is not intended to be a forecast of what will occur. It does emphasize some of the factors that will be important, such as women's participation rates, retirement, automation, birth rates, length of work week, and so forth. By making different assumptions about these factors, different scenarios result. If one is an administrator concerned with social security, for instance, the implications of these various scenarios should be of the greatest importance. The administrator would also require that the probability of its actually occurring be attached to each alternative scenario. This could either be his own subjective probability or could be obtained by using a Delphi-type panel.

A second and more carefully constructed example of a set of scenarios is that discussed by Herman Kahn (1976). Over period as long as 200 years, the important issues include population growth, the availability of scarce resources, economic growth, and the effects of technological innovations. Two extreme viewpoints are called the *neo-Malthusian* and the *technology-and-growth* positions. The first is a modern version of Malthus' argument that population will eventually grow faster than food supply, with consequent starvation for the poor. The opposite view is that technological developments will meet all needs, population will be controlled, the more advanced nations will develop superindustrial and then postindustrial economies, and the rest of the world will not be far behind. Two alternative versions of each of these viewpoints may be taken, the position of

A the strong neo-Malthusian,
B the moderate neo-Malthusian or guarded pessimist,
C the guarded optimist, or
D the technology and growth enthusiast.

These viewpoints provide the following alternative bases around which scenarios could be constructed.

10.5.1 The Strong Neo-Malthusian

(i) There is a finite pie of nonrenewable resources to be divided up. These resources will reach critical levels within 50 years. Any economic growth that makes the rich richer can only make the poor poorer.

(ii) The effect of technology and capital is largely illusory and counterproductive. Proposed technological solutions to problems of pollution or scarce resources are shortsighted illusions that only compound the difficulties. Any future economic development should be restricted to the Third World.

(iii) In management and decision making, failure is almost certain. The complexities, rigidities, and ideological differences among nations and their institutions make it inconceivable that present human organizations, even with computer assistance, could sufficiently comprehend and effectively act to solve our most important problems. More emphasis is needed on the community and regional level, much less on big business, big government, and big organizations generally.

(iv) There is a steady depletion of resources, including foods, fuels, and minerals. All signs point to catastrophe for the medium- and long-term future.

(v) Current growth is carcinogenic. Current population and economic production are akin to a spreading cancer. They are already more than the earth can sustain in a steady state. Future economic or population growth will hasten and increase the magnitude of the future tragedy.

(vi) New discoveries of resources, new technologies, and new projects may postpone the immediate need for drastic actions but not for long. The postponement could make the eventual collapse more severe.

(vii) Income gaps and poverty will grow worse.

(viii) Industrialization of the Third World would be a disaster and further growth of the developed world even worse.

(ix) The quality of life has already been ruined, particularly in the developed nations.

(x) The long-range outlook is bleak and desperate. Grave and even draconian measures are justified now to alleviate the extent and intensity of the future collapse.

10.5.2 The Guarded Pessimist

(i) The future supply and value of both old and new materials are necessarily uncertain. Prudence requires immediate conservation of remaining resources.

(ii) Despite some exceptions, the future will generally bring diminishing marginal returns from new investments, and the effort required for economic gains will increase dramatically. Until practical solutions to the problems of pollutions and shortages appear, we must turn away from technology and investment.

(iii) There will be a likely failure in attempts to manage resources, control pollution, and resolve social conflicts due to the increasing complexity of these problems.

(iv) The basic problem of limited resources may be insoluble, and so a more cautious approach to growth seems clearly desirable.

(v) There is a large potential for disaster in growth. Because of rapidly increasing population, even current levels of production must lead to exhausted resources and hazardous pollution. Few positive human values would be served by continued mindless growth.

(vi) Innovation and discovery will become increasingly ineffective. The basic solution is to limit demand rather than encourage a desperate search for new inventions, which could make basic problem even worse in long-run.

(vii) Income gaps and poverty are increasing and could become threatening. A more equitable income distribution has become an urgent matter.

(viii) Undeveloped nations would be better off preserving their cultural, environmental, and ecological values rather than entering headlong into industrial development.

(ix) The quality of life is in conflict with much growth.

(x) The long-run outlook is of contingent disaster. Although it is not possible to predict which disaster is most imminent, many possibilities exist even if we are careful and prudent today. Drastic actions should be taken soon to manage our resources and population more prudently.

10.5.3 The Guarded Optimist

(i) There is a growing pie to be shared out due to increased productivity. Progress in one region encourages similar developments elsewhere; thus as the rich get richer the poor also benefit. Some caution with regard to growth is necessary in selected areas.

(ii) Despite some dangers, only new technology and capital investment can increase production, protect and improve the environment, hold down the cost of energy, minerals, and food, and provide economic surpluses with which to improve living standards in the less developed countries. We must be alert for problems resulting from inadequately understood innovations, inappropriate growth, and natural causes.

(iii) Decision making should be fairly successful. Normal economic mechanisms can make most private organizations adequately responsive to most problems.

(iv) Resources should generally be sufficient. Given slow but steady technological and economic progress and an ultimate world population below 30 billion, it should be feasible to attain economic living standards markedly better than current ones.

(v) Concerning growth, we are on a probable transition to stability. There will be enough energy, resources, and space for a stable population to occur at a better standard of living provided that a relatively small number of people put forth the necessary efforts and others do not interfere.

(vi) Innovation and discovery are usually effective, do help solve current problems, although sometimes creating new ones, and provide some insurance against bad luck or incompetency.

(vii) The threat of worldwide absolute poverty and starvation is likely soon to be forever abolished. Some income gaps will increase and others decrease, but both rich and poor will have increased real income.

(viii) Industrialization of the less developed countries should and will continue, technical assistance being provided by the rich nations.

(ix) There will be more gains than losses in the quality of life, particularly in terms of the environment, health, and safety.

(x) The long-range outlook is a contingent success, the ultimate prospect being far superior to a world of poverty and scarcity.

10.5.4 The Technology and Growth Enthusiast

(i) The important resources are capital, technology, and educated people and there are no meaningful limits to growth in sight. The perennial doomsayers have always been scandalously wrong.

(ii) Technology and capital can solve almost all problems. Some current problems have resulted from careless application of technology, but none are without remedy. It is not paradoxical that the technology which has caused some problems can also solve them; it just requires mankind's attention and desire. The eventual colonization of the solar system will provide virtually unlimited living space.

(iii) Decision making is not a serious problem. We flatter ourselves that current issues are more important and difficult than ever: Actually there is nothing very special happening.

(iv) The earth is essentially bountiful in all of the important resources. Trust in the economics of the market system and have confidence in emerging technological solutions.

(v) Growth is desirable and healthy and no obvious limits are apparent. Even with current technological potential, growth (except perhaps in a few of the poorest nations) is and will be purely a matter of human choice, not of natural limitations. Problems always exist but solutions always emerge, often as a result of the dynamism of growth.

(vi)   Innovation and discovery are mankind's greatest hope and man is now entering the most creative and expansive period of his history.

(vii) Income gaps and poverty are a misformulated problem. All countries can expect to become wealthy in the next 200 years and income gap is a false issue, some inequalities being inevitable in a dynamic society.

(viii) Industrial development is necessary for wealth and progress.

(ix)   The quality of life is a meaningless phrase and issue.

(x)   The long-range outlook is one of high optimism and confidence. Mankind's ultimate goals cannot be known, but they include a solar civilization and a utopian notion of the quality of life on earth.

None of these viewpoints is strictly a scenario as it stands, as they need fleshing out with specific sequences of events. For example, the following scenario presented by Kahn corresponds approximately to the Guarded Optimist viewpoint. In this scenario a superindustrial economy is one whose enterprises are extraordinarily large, encompassing, and pervasive forces in both the physical and societal environments; a postindustrial economy is one in which the task of producing the necessities of life has become trivially easy because of technological advancement and economic development.

1956–1995. Four decades of worldwide and rapid economic and population growth; the initial emergence of a superindustrial economy, technological crises, and many other transitions, e.g., inflection points in world population and possibly also gross product curves — a decline in the rate of growth. In 1996 there are 4.1 billion people, and the Gross World Product (GWP) is $5.5 trillion, corresponding to an annual income of $1300 per capita. The first steps into space.

1996–2025. Another three decades for the initial emergence of postindustrial economies in European and non-Communist Sinic cultures, perhaps also in the Soviet Union. The full development of superindustrial societies and cultures in advanced countries. The first serious move to colonize space. A Gross World Product per capita of $2500.

2026–2175. 150 years for the emergence of postindustrial economies almost everywhere on earth. Possibly the establishment of an independent dynamic solar system society. By 2175 world population at 15 billion people (with a likely range of 7.5–30 billion), a per capita Gross World Product of $20,000 (range $7000–$60,000), and GWP at $300 trillion, give or take a factor of 5.

If this becomes true, prospects for mankind will be encouraging, to say the least. Again, it must be emphasized that this is a scenario and not a forecast, since it is designed to illustrate a possible future, to awaken minds to these possibilities, and to point out some bottlenecks that could occur in the future to delay mankind's objectives. Scenarios could be argued to be unscientific in that they are likely to deal in generalities without working out all the detailed implications. An approach that is in some sense more scientific is considered in the next chapter.

APPENDIX: SOME PROBABLE AND POSSIBLE SCIENTIFIC INNOVATIONS

The following are just a few of the expected or possible scientific and sociological changes that we can look for over the next 20–40 years:

1. Improved superperformance fabrics.
2. Major reduction in hereditary and congenital defects.
3. Effective appetite and weight control. Nonabsorbable sugar achieved by molecule alteration.
4. New and useful plant and animal species.
5. Nuclear reactors that cannot be used for the manufacture of atomic weapons.
6. Three-dimensional photography, movies, and television.
7. Electrical transmission of newspapers.
8. Substantial decrease in hours spent sleeping due to controlled relaxation.
9. Cheap and widely available major war weapons and systems.
10. Drugs to permanently raise the level of human and animal intelligence.
11. Ability to choose sex of unborn children.
12. Semiautomation of repairs.
13. Physically nonharmful methods of overindulging.
14. Chemical alteration of personality, applied to convicted criminals.
15. Extensive use of robots in the house.
16. Photon rockets.
17. Chemical methods for improving memory and learning.
18. International citizens.
19. New methods for rapid language teaching.
20. Home computers to run finances, to plan meals, and to communicate with the outside world, with an I.Q. of 50 or more.
21. Synthetic blood substitute.
22. Electrical control of pain, specific to location or as needed.

23.   Electronic sensors provide artificial "eyesight" for the blind.
24.   Artificial growth of new limbs and organs.
25.   Long-term suspended animation.
26.   Automated highways and location determination for automobiles.

A few very unlikely developments are

1.   Antigravity transportation systems.
2.   Compulsory genetic manipulation to improve the quality of the human race.
3.   Practical and routine use of extrasensory phenomena.
4.   Lifetime immunization against practically all diseases.
5.   Interstellar travel.

QUESTIONS

1.   A large soap manufacturer is worried by the rumor that a new type of shower is being investigated that uses low frequency vibrations. It is thought that the new technique could completely clean the occupant of the shower without the use of any soap or water. How would you try to investigate for the manufacturer the timing of the introduction and potential success of this invention?

2.   A manufacturer of an electric automobile, for purposes of future planning and design, would like an estimate of when a battery will be available with twice the present capacity, in terms of the amount of electricity stored, and at a quarter of the present size. Describe ways in which he can obtain such an estimate. Also discuss briefly the factors he should consider when trying to forecast sales for an automobile using such a battery.

3.   "The future of a society, an economy or a firm is too dependent on the decisions and desires of real individuals for a mechanical model based on mathematics, statistics, or computer simulation to be able to provide adequate forecasts. A clearly superior strategy is to base forecasts on mental modeling, analogies, opinions, expectations, anticipations, and rational thought." Comment.

4.   Because of the fast growth of knowledge in most academic subjects, a consultant's report suggests that all university degrees should lapse after ten years, to be renewed if a further six-month study at a university is undertaken. A university wants to study when such a scheme may be instituted and what the effect would be on its student numbers in future years. Discuss how you would provide forecasts for the university.

5. Write three alternative scenarios about how your local community might look in twenty years time, including a wild one of the "gold discovered in Central Park" variety.

6. Consider your favorite sport. Write a scenario about how it could change or develop over the next 30 years, considering the effects of new rules and new technological developments from the viewpoint of both the players and the spectators.

7. Write a criticism of the following scenario:

In the mid 1990s the government of both Britain and the United States, consisting largely of those who had been radicals in the 1970s, become particularly sympathetic to the masses of the world who are starving. Consequently, they decide to try to increase agricultural production in their countries. One aspect of this policy is a new law which prevents any land currently used for agriculture or forestry to be converted to any other use. There follows a decline in the construction of new houses and a sharp increase in housing prices. Old houses are pulled down in groups and replaced by high rise apartment buildings. The higher population concentration in cities leads to increases in pollution and crime. The new law also means that many speculator farmers who own land on the outskirts of cities are replaced by real, and more efficient, farmers. This leads to an increase in food production, which results in lower food prices. Americans begin to eat more and this leads to increases in deaths due to heart and blood circulation problems.

FURTHER READINGS

Gabor, D. (1963). *Inventing the Future,* London: Secker and Warburg.

Kahn, H. (1976). *The Next 200 Years: A Scenario for America and the World,* New York: Morrow.

Kahn, H., and A. J. Wiener (1967). *The Year 2000,* New York: MacMillan.

Martino, J. P. (1972). *Technological Forecasting for Decision Making,* (second edition, 1985) New York: Amer. Elsevier.

CHAPTER

11

World Models

This is the first age that's ever paid much attention to the future, which is a little ironic since we may not have one.

Arthur C. Clarke

The problem is not whether you can see the handwriting on the wall, but whether you can read it.

Evan Esar

11.1 INTRODUCING WORLD MODELS

For some years now there have existed models of the economy of a single nation, the econometric models discussed in chapter 5, and more recently these national models have been linked together to form an international model, called LINK. Although important difficulties have been encountered, both in model specification and in estimation, worthwhile progress has been achieved. A considerably more ambitious project involves modeling not merely the world's economy but all of the major variables of world society, including wealth, population, pollution, food, and resources. The first serious project of this kind originated with Jay Forrester (1971) at MIT and produced a sequence of models of increasing complexity culminating in WORLD 2 and WORLD 3. Part of this work was sponsored by an organization known as the Club of Rome. The models have become known under various names, including that of the sponsors, Limits to Growth, and World Dynamics. The modelers included several control engineers, and this fact has effected both the approach used in forming the model and the language describing it. The goals were described in one account by the modelers in the following terms,

Every physical quantity growing in a finite space must eventually exhibit one of three basic behavior modes: a smooth transition to a steady state, oscillation around an equilibrium position, or overshoot

235

and decline. The WORLD 3 model was designed to investigate which of these behavior modes is most likely to characterize the evolution of population and capital on this finite earth and to identify the policies that would increase the probability of an orderly transition to global equilibrium.

In forming the model, emphasis is placed on the interrelationship between the major variables. The world society is considered to be a closed system, so that feedback relationships can be found between many variables. For example, the rate of increase of population could depend on pollution levels, but pollution depends on production and production on population. The main feedback loops of the two WORLD models are shown in Fig. 11.1. The boxes represent the main subsystems of the world system. The arrows show the assumed causal links between them, and the broken arrows show links included only in WORLD 3. Some of the causal relationships are positive, so that an increase in capital investment leads to increased living standards and an assumed increase in population, and some are negative so that pollution leads to a reduction in population. The relationships may involve lags and many are taken to be nonlinear. Each of the main subsystems of population, pollution, geographic space, agriculture, nonrenewable natural resources, and capital investment are modeled separately and may involve several variables. The following are the main assumptions in each of the subsections:

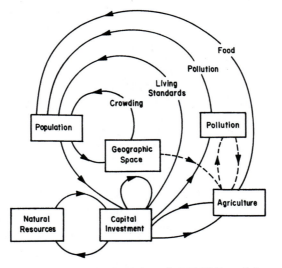

Fig. 11.1 Major feedback loops in WORLD models.

(i) Nonrenewable resources. On aggregate, the world has a 250 years supply of minerals, at current consumption rates, the minerals are perfectly substitutable, and the economic cost of exploiting the remaining deposits will increase significantly.

(ii) Population. The difference between birth and death rates is negative for low per capita nonfood consumption, increases as consumption increases, and becomes positive just below 1970 world average levels.

(iii) The agricultural subsystem. Food is produced from arable land and agricultural inputs, such as fertilizer and seed; food output increases as these inputs increase, but there are decreasing returns; newly developed land is expensive to obtain but enters at the current average land fertility; arable land erodes due to intense cultivation; capital-intensive use of land leads to persistent pollution of the land; land yield is reduced by air pollution; and arable land disappears when built upon, a process occurring more rapidly as wealth increases.

(iv) Capital and industrial output. The average life of industrial capital now and for an indefinite period is assumed to be a constant, 14 years; the industrial capital output ratio is a constant with a value of 3 and diminishing returns will not affect investment in the industrial sector; finally, the marginal utility of food and services as a fraction of industrial output is also a constant and does not change over time.

(v) Pollution. The generation of persistent pollution is the result of industrial and agricultural activities: There exists a delay between the time a persistent pollutant is generated and the time it appears as a harmful substance; the time required to absorb a unit of pollution increases as the total level of pollution increases.

An example of the type of equation found in the model is

Change in population =
(birth rate) − (death rate)] × (present population)

where both birth and death rates are specific, nonlinear functions of material standard of living (nonfood consumption per capita), food production per capita, population density, and level of pollution. The forms of the relationships are not estimated directly from data but are selected subjectively both so that the views of the modelers are represented and so that if the model is run using starting-up values for 1900, the plots of the variables fit adequately well to what actually occurred from 1900 to 1970. Once the full set of equations has been set up, the starting-up values can be inserted and the "standard run" of the model is then observed, in which it is assumed that no changes in the equations occur in the future. The conclusions from the standard run of WORLD 3 suggest that population will rise to a peak of perhaps six billion in the year 2020 and will thereafter decline. This decline in population is caused by falling natural resources, which become increasingly more costly to extract as their quantity declines. This means that more capital has to be allocated to extraction of natural resources and less is then available to industrial output and food. Thus, both industrial output per capita and food per capita reach peaks at about 2000 and decline rapidly thereafter. Pollution levels increase steadily until just before the year 2000 A.D. They then increase dramatically to very high levels until about 2040, when they start to decline. By the year 2100, industrial output and food per capita will be below 1900 levels, but population level will be much higher as pollution and natural resources will be only about 20% of 1900 values. The plot of the WORLD 3 standard run is shown in Fig. 11.2. The reasons for this prediction of world cataclysm from the model are easily found. It is assumed that, if left unchecked,

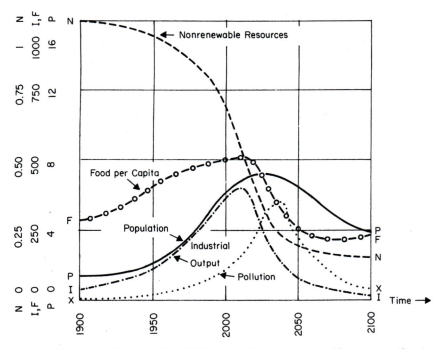

Fig. 11.2 Standard forecasts from WORLD model. *N*, nonrenewable resources (fraction remaining); *F*, food per capita; *P*, population (billions); *I*, industrial output per capita; *X*, persistent pollution.

population and capital levels will increase exponentially. However, such growth cannot occur because of the finiteness of the earth and its resources, the impossibility of providing enough food for the people and enough materials for the industrial processes, even if the latter are run cheaply by ignoring pollution problems. The physical limitations will constrain the exponential growth curves and, when the crunch does eventually occur, the controls on society act with such lags and inefficiency that production, for example, does not simply level off but actually crashes down from its peak value. If the assumptions about exponential growth in population and consumption are allowed to stand, it is easily shown from the model that a very similar scenario occurs, at only a slightly later date, if the assumed amount of available nonrenewable resources is dramatically increased or if some recycling of these resources is allowed. In general, the predictions from the model, all of which are strictly conditional forecasts, are very depressing and suggest that the human race as a whole is facing a desperate situation in the early part of the next century.

To prevent the predicted catastrophe, the model suggests that population control by itself may not be sufficient and that natural resource usage rate, pollution generation, food production, and gross investment will also have to be drastically reduced for a "global equilibrium" to be achieved.

11.2 EVALUATION

As might be expected the scientific community at large was hardly enthusiastic about the prediction of a doomsday so near in the future. There was an immediate dislike to the conditions of the model and the reality of its basic assumptions was attacked. There followed more careful analysis of the most important assumed feedback relationships, and some were found to be contrary to some empirical evidence or to modern theory. Finally, the whole system was run using rather different formulations to test the stability of its conclusions. Of course, the major problem with such models is to know how to evaluate them. An obvious start is to ask how realistic the assumptions are, how well it fits known data, and how sensible are the forecasts it makes. The economists, and particularly the econometricians, were most disturbed by the specification of the model and of the way it had been constructed. The fact that parameters had not been formally estimated from data was severely criticized, and the quality of the models was hardly enhanced by the remark by the original modelers that only 0.1% of the data necessary to build such a model from fact was actually available. The econometricians were also unimpressed by the size of even WORLD 3, which appeared very complex to the laymen, politicians, and media and yet only consisted of less than 50 equations, all of which were assumed to hold without error. It was argued that if it requires over 200 equations to properly model the economy of a single nation, it can hardly be possible to capture the true nature of the whole world society with just a few equations. The economists also found fault with the economic laws being called upon in the model. No price system was used to allocate resources and capital investment occurs in the model in a rather unconvincing fashion totally unrelated to potential rates of return. The implicit production function in the WORLD 2 model also had strange properties. It had a form such that if one were making pig iron and doubled both the number of blast furnaces and the number of ore fields, then the amount of pig iron produced would quadruple. Most economists would guess that in such circumstances, pig iron production would approximately double. The importance of this assumption is seen by noting that in the critical parts of the model forecasting period the above example is run backwards, so that a halving of both capital and resources divides output by 4. This pessimistic assumption obviously makes the system grind to a halt rather quickly.

One other important equation in WORLD 2 received a great deal of attention. It was assumed that as consumption per capita increased, so did the difference between birth and death rates and, conversely, as consumption decreased this difference also automatically declined. As was suggested in Chapter 9, the relationship between birth rate and the economy is by no means determined and is probably not a stable one. In any case, looking at current figures for birth rates in developed and undeveloped countries does not support the WORLD 2 assumed relationship. Some of these criticisms were partially met by altered specifications in WORLD 3 but many parts of the model remained controversial.

The results of running the models with different specifications did not resolve the question of their quality. Some workers found that the assumptions could be altered considerably without changing the conclusions appreciably. Others found the results much less stable, particularly if it is assumed that resources are recycled, population is controlled, and sufficient technological progress is introduced, the doomsday then postponed indefinitely. One group ran the model backward from 1900 and found that population should have been considerably higher in 1880 than it actually was, so that the model exploded when run in the reverse direction. There is considerable controversy about the appropriateness of such a test. It is certainly true that econometric models have not been subjected to such tests.

It soon became clear that most research workers who carefully investigated the MIT models found them flawed, and some highly critical remarks surfaced, such as "Malthus in, Malthus out," "Malthus with a computer," and the comment that the models are "bad science and therefore bad guides to public policy." In fact so one-sided did the discussion become that it turned from criticism of the actual models to worrying about whether it is even worthwhile trying to build quantitative models of world society. The discussion was not decisive but the most influential contestants supported the idea of attempting to construct such models. Even if the predictions made by the WORLD models are not accepted as being particularly realistic, the models have certainly forced consideration of the most important problems facing mankind. The more thought given to the problems of overpopulation, food and space shortages, and the repletion of resources, the more chance there is of reducing the impact of these problems in the future. The MIT experience has emphasized both these questions and the difficulties that will be encountered when worldwide models are attempted. The main difficulties are lack of knowledge about important social and demographic relationships, such as that between birth rate and the growth of the economy, and the problem of forecasting technological innovation and development, as has been emphasized in the previous two chapters. These difficulties will certainly not prevent other models being constructed and, one hopes, as knowledge is accumulated those models will evolve towards one that will provide both convincing forecasts and also useful policy suggestions.

11.3   FOOD FOR A DOUBLING WORLD POPULATION

The advent of the WORLD models has stimulated other models with wide scope. An example of a model that is less ambitious than those discussed in the previous two sections but which may well have greater impact is MOIRA — a Model of International Relations in Agriculture. It uses economic theory, plus some statistical modeling, to examine the effects of food production and of a doubling of world population over the period 1975–2010 and also to investigate what can be done to mitigate the problems that will obviously arise. It is based on such facts as that the industrialized nations have under 30% of world population but consume over half of the world's food supply, so that in the developing nations over 70% of the world's population have to survive on under half of the available food. Those that starve, or survive but are greatly undernourished, do so because they cannot afford food, not because it is not potentially available for them. Currently, there is sufficient food for everyone at an acceptable level if only it were distributed evenly. It has also been estimated that if all potentially productive land throughout the world were used in the most efficient manner possible, food production could reach 25 *times* present levels. Although such an increase could only be realized by considerable planning and huge inputs of capital, both physical and human, such figures do suggest that the population of the world should not face starvation problems due to an inability to produce food. The ability of most of the world to be able to pay enough to persuade farmers to produce the required food is a much bigger problem and is the main question that MOIRA investigates.

To simplify the situation, the model considers just consumable protein derived from vegetables, so that raising cattle is considered a protein loss or inefficiency in the production system. The world is divided into 106 geographic units but the results are then aggregated and presented for just ten world regions. Each unit is divided into twelve income classes, six in the agricultural sector and six in nonagriculture. The behavior of the food consumers are described in terms of a consumption function, so that demand for food is explained in terms of income and food price levels. The socialist block of countries is assumed to be neutral with regard to imports and exports. The exogenous variables, determined outside the system, are economic growth in the nonagricultural sector, population increase, income distribution within geographical units, and prices of agricultural inputs, such as fertilizers.

Assuming that population doubles over the period considered, that is, each region's population continues to grow at current rates and that there is also a steady growth in nonagricultural production, the model suggests that, while there will be the obvious increase in demand for food, production will not increase sufficiently to meet this demand, and so a relative scarcity will develop, driving up prices to two-and-one-half times as high in real terms by 2010. During this period the number of people who have less than the minimum necessary amount of food for a healthy life will quadruple to 1.5 billion — almost a quarter of the world's population. Members of the nonagricultural sector will be particularly affected. These consequences contrast with those for the wealthy countries, where food consumption per capita will increase, widening the present gap in standard of living between the countries that have and those that have not.

If nonagricultural production increases at a slower rate than assumed in the above scenario, MOIRA suggests that food production will double along with the population, but the number starving will also increase because of the assumed rigid income distribution.

The objective in building such models is not really to make forecasts but to check out the effects of alternative policies that might be attempted to alleviate the world's food shortage problems. A number of policies are considered, including measures to achieve redistribution of the available food in the world, such as a decrease in food consumption by the wealthy countries, food purchases by an international food aid organization financed by the wealthy countries which would distribute this food to the underfed population groups, measures to control world food prices, and measures intended to stimulate food production in the developing countries. These policy measures were first considered individually and then in combinations. If applied individually, a reduction in food consumption by wealthy countries has bad effects on total food production due to reduction of demand, but an aid program has great temporary benefits, although in the long term it may not encourage sufficient development in food production in the poorer countries. Stabilization of the world market price at a relatively high level does enable a gradual improvement of the food supply per capita of poor countries, but the extent of hunger is not very sensitive so such a policy. Regulation of the world market does not render food aid unnecessary, but seems to be better than a complete liberalization of international trade in basic foods, since in this latter case food production in the developing countries will grow more slowly than if policies remain unchanged. The most effective policy is to encourage more efficient food production throughout the world, so that the wealthy countries should provide suitable encouragement in terms of capital inputs, research, and know-how, combined with some price maintenance and food aid in the early part of the period. If the model is correct such a policy, together with further attempts to control population growth, should reduce the problem of undernourishment of a large proportion of the world's population, although part of the problem will remain.

MOIRA can be criticized in various ways, particularly for some of the assumptions made, but initial reaction to the model is that it is basically sound and the doubtful assumptions are not of considerable importance and can be fairly easily circumvented in later, improved versions of the model. It seems very likely that models of this kind will eventually have considerable impact on the form of international agreements and therefore be highly relevant for long-term forecasting.

Certainly the problem being considered is of considerable importance. Recent estimates are that 35,000 people a day are dying of hunger in the world, which is about 13 million a year. However, this figure was estimated to be about two million a year higher in 1977, so the efforts of the various world agencies do seem to have been somewhat successful. It is important to realize that many are dying not because there is no food available but because they cannot afford to buy the food. The problem is as much an economic one as a production one (see Sen (1981)).

11.4   ENERGY IN THE WORLD FUTURE

In the late 1970s an ambitious and scientifically sophisticated model for future world energy needs was constructed at IIASA (International Institute for Applied Systems Analysis) in Austria. Experts from most major countries were involved. To describe large quantities of energy, special units of measurement are required, one to describe *amounts* of energy and another to describe *rates* at which energy is supplied. For amounts, the unit used in the study is the tera-watt year (TW yr) which is 10^{12} watt-year. This is a very big unit, one tera-watt year is roughly equivalent to one billion tons of coal per year or 14 million barrels of oil per day, which is greater than the oil production currently considered to be possible for Saudi Arabia. Rates of energy are measured in tera-watt year per year (TW yr/yr). In 1975 the total world energy use was 8.2 TW yr/yr. The average use per capita was 2 KW yr/yr but this ranged from 11.2 KW yr/yr per capita in the U.S. and Canada to 0.2 KW yr/yr per capita in central Africa and southwest Asia. About sixty percent of the world's population used less than half the world average energy use rate per capita. It is clear that further energy will have to become available for worthwhile economic growth for much of the world.

The model divides the world into seven regions:

Region I   (North America) is rich in resources and has developed, market economies.

Region II   (Soviet Union, Eastern Europe) is also rich in energy resources and has developed, centrally planned economies.

Region III   (Western Europe, Australia, Israel, Japan, New Zealand, and South Africa) is developed but is less well off in energy resources.

Region IV   (Latin America) is a developing region with market economies.

Region V   (South and Southeast Asia, sub-Sahara Africa), developing area generally with few resources.

Region VI   (Middle East, Northern Africa) oil and gas rich, transitional economies.

The model is concerned with the period 1980 to 2030 and assumes a standard and fairly conservative growth curve for population, rising to eight billion by the end of the period. Two scenarios of world economic growth are considered. The high scenario has world growth in GNP starting near historical level (5%) and slowly declining to 2.7% in the period 2015 to 2030. The low scenario has a quick decline in growth rate in GNP to 3.6% and drops further to 1.7% by 2030. For both scenarios, growth rates are assumed to be substantially greater for the developing and communist regions (II, IV, V, VI) than the other developed regions (I, III). This assumption was made both for political reasons and because it is hoped there will be substantial development in the less developed regions.

The model is formed by first estimating demand for each region, by taking the projected growth and the energy requirements for country at that level of development, and then considering the various alternative supply possibilities to meet that demand. The full range of possible sources of energy are considered, and a method of supply is found that is both efficient and attainable and can match demand.

The division of energy needs between the primary sources found by the model under the two scenarios is shown in Table 11.1.

The solution shown in the table is thought to be both price efficient and the most achievable. There are a number of important points that arise from this table. If the world's economies are to achieve the fairly modest growth rates assumed in the scenarios, oil production will have to increase substantially, gas and coal production will have to increase very substantially, nuclear reactors will need to make a very large contribution, and solar and other sources, including biogas, geothermal, tides, and commercial wood will make a useful contribution, but this will be small compared to the total needed. To achieve these production figures huge amounts of new capital will be required and prices will have to adjust to ensure that the major oil, gas, and coal producers will increase their output, but these prices will not prevent developing countries from buying sufficient energy to allow economic growth. It appears to be clear that many developing countries will have to rely on nuclear reactors to produce their energy to achieve the assumed levels of growth. This will pose a difficult choice for some of these countries, particularly those short of land, of whether to have economic growth and nuclear power stations or to forego growth until fusion power becomes commercially viable, possibly in the middle of the next century.

TABLE 11.1

Primary Energy Sources for World Growth (TW yr / yr)

Primary Source	Base Year 1975	High Scenario 2000	High Scenario 2030	Low Scenario 2000	Low Scenario 2030
Oil	3.83	5.89	6.83	4.75	5.02
Gas	1.51	3.11	5.99	2.53	3.47
Coal	2.26	4.94	11.98	3.92	6.45
Light Water Reactor	0.12	1.70	3.21	1.27	1.89
Fast Breeder Reactor	0	0.04	4.88	0.02	3.28
Hydroelectric	0.50	0.83	1.46	0.83	1.46
Solar	0	0.10	0.49	0.09	0.30
Other	0	0.22	0.81	0.17	0.52
Total	8.21	16.84	35.65	13.59	22.39

Source: Energy in the Finite World, IIASA Report, page 145.

A further problem is the strong desire for the convenient oil as a fuel, but this will become more expensive to extract from increasingly marginal sources. There is plenty of coal and natural gas, but their conversion to oil is not easy or cheap and can lead to extra air pollution. Oil is also a major source of the fertilizers that are required to increase food production.

The report indicates the kinds of bottlenecks that the world faces if both population and standards of living are to grow. The need for extra energy will require large capital inflows, and this can take capital growth away from agriculture and thus hold back increases in food production. Altogether, it seems clear that it will be very difficult for the world to handle a large increase in population, produce sufficient food for this population, and also achieve worthwhile increases in standards of living for most of the people of the world unless some extraordinary technological advance occurs within the next twenty years or so.

Since the appearance of the IIASA report a number of important changes have occurred, although some of these may be only short-run. Population growth has slowed somewhat; oil prices have fallen substantially and production levels are not a constraint; demand for energy has declined in developed countries; and the risks of nuclear power have been dramatically illustrated. If such changes continue, developing countries would have inexpensive oil available and need to look less towards nuclear energy. On the other hand, research into new energy sources, particularly the potentially vital fusion power, will be slowed, delaying the availability of those less risky and low pollution alternatives.

FURTHER READINGS

Anderer, J. *et al.* (1981) *Energy in a Finite World* IIASA, Ballinger Publishing Co., Cambridge, Mass.

Bruckman, G. (1976). "A Pre-evaluation of Moira." *Technological Forecasting and Social Change* **10**, 21–26.

De Hoogh, J. *et al.* (1976). "Food for a Growing World Population," *Technological Forecasting and Social Change* **10**, 27–51.

Forrester, Jay W. (1971). *World Dynamics*, Cambridge, Massachusetts: Wright-Allen Press.

Meadows, D. H. *et al.* (1974). *Dynamics of Growth in a Finite World*, Cambridge, Massachusetts: MIT Press.

Semitechnical and detailed accounts of the world dynamics models.

Nordhaus, W. D. (1973). "World Dynamics: Measurement without Data," *Economic Journal* **83**, 1156–1183.

Severe criticism of the economic content of the models.

Sen, A. (1981). *Poverty and Famines: An Essay on Entitlement and Deprivation*, Oxford: Oxford University Press.

Sussex Science Policy Research Unit (1973). "Malthus with a Computer," and other chapters, *Futures*, Volume 5.

Wide ranging criticism of many aspects of the models.

CHAPTER

12

Techniques Old and New

I always avoid prophesying beforehand because it is much better to prophesy
after the event has already taken place.

Winston Churchill

Prophesy is a good line of business, but it is full of risks.

Mark Twain in Following the Equator

12.1 FORECASTS FROM THE PAST

It has probably always been realized that the person who can somewhat
predict what is about to occur will have an advantage over those who
cannot correctly forecast. Examples of these forecasts, or prophecies, are
found in written records from the earliest times. Probably any intelligent
person can provide forecasts of some quality, but in an attempt to get a
further edge some very curious information sets have been utilized. The
haruspex looked into animal's entrails, the palmist at hands, and the astrol-
oger at the stars. Other methods have included cartomancy, using playing
cards or the more powerful Tarots; numerology, which manipulates numbers, letters, and words; crystallomancy, whose proponent goes into a
trance and looks into a crystal ball; geomancy, done by throwing dice,
small bones coins, match sticks, or dominos; and taseology, which uses tea
leaves, coffee grounds, or even sand or pebbles. Spiritualists have used
various mediums, such as a planchette or ouija board, while others have
looked into ancient books, such as *I Ching* or the *Bible*, or even at the
pyramids. Such methods of sirying not only are from the past, but are arts
still practiced and apparently still believed in. Many people believe those
techniques are merely superstitious mumbo jumbo, while others plead that
such judgments should not be made without a proper attempt at evaluation. Astrologers, for example, point out that a study made by Gauquelin
in 1966 of 25,000 prominent citizens of Western European countries

found that significant numbers of scientists, doctors, athletes, and executives were born during the rising and setting of Mars and extra politicians and writers during the moon period. They ask if it is merely coincidence that two Nobel prize winning physicists, Albert Einstein and Otto Hahn, were both born on the 14th of March 1879, that two similar Irish writers, James Stephen and James Joyce, were both born at 6:00 A.M. on the 2nd of February 1892, and that two of the New York Metropolitan's famous tenors, Beniamino Gigli and Lauritz Melchior, were both born on the 20th of March 1890. There is ample evidence that one's birthdate partly determines a person's academic achievements, since a class will include students with almost a whole year's difference in maturity. A somewhat different example comes from the observation that during the Vietnam war men born earlier in the year had almost twice the probability of being drafted than those born later in the year, due presumably to an error in the selection procedure. Whether or not such facts are sufficient for an approach such as astrology to be taken seriously has to be a personal judgment. The majority of those taking a scientific approach appear not to be convinced. To properly evaluate any such technique a correctly designed experiment needs to be conducted in which a sequence of forecasts is made, measured against what actually occurs and compared with forecasts from other techniques, if possible.

A careful scientific study of astrology has been conducted and reported in Carlson (1985). Using an experimental design accepted by astrologers and using leading astrologers and their charts, the ability to determine the psychological properties of a number of subjects was tested. No evidence was found that the methods used by astrologers was useful in predicting the personalities of the subjects. The experiment was not specifically concerned with forecasting the future, but it does not suggest that astrology will be helpful in such forecasting.

The accumulated prophecies from the past do appear to give us plenty to evaluate. Some of the prophecies made are quite impressive. For example, Mother Shipton of Knaresborough, in England, was apparently making prophecies in the early fifteenth century, and her work was certainly known by 1641. One of her more famous pieces goes

> Carriages without horses shall go
> And accidents fill the world with woe.
> Around the earth thoughts shall fly
> In the twinkling of an eye.
> The world upside down shall be
> And gold be found at the root of a tree.
> Through hills man shall ride
> And no horse be at his side.

Under water men shall walk,
Shall ride, shall sleep, shall talk.
In the air men shall be seen
In white, in black, in green.
Iron in the water shall float
As easily as a wooden boat.
Gold shall be found and shown
In a land that's not now known.
Fire and water shall wonders do,
England shall at last admit a foe.
The world to an end shall come
In eighteen hundred and eighty-one.

Apart from the final lines, where she becomes more specific about timing, the statements are fairly unambiguous and could apply to the early twentieth century.

A second famous piece by Mother Shipton has

Over a wild and stormy sea
Shall a noble sail,
Who to find, will not fail
A new and fair countree
From whence he will bring
A herb and a root
That all men shall suit
And please both the ploughman and king,
And let them take no more than measure
Both shall have the even pleasure
In the belly and the brain.

It is easy to associate "a noble" with Sir Walter Raleigh, the country with America, the "herb" with tobacco, and the "root" as the potato.

Most of the famous forecast producers are much less easily interpreted. The sayings of the oracle at Delphi are famous for their ambiguity. The most famous and prolific prophet was probably Nostradamus. He was born in St. Remy, France, in 1503, and produced hundreds of prophetic quatrains in his 63 years. Books are still continually being produced attempting to interpret the statements. The interpretations given often reflect the interpreter's own background. For instance, in a book published in the United States the quatrain

The populous places shall be deserted
A great division to obtain fields
Kingdoms given to prudent incapable
When the great brothers shall die by dissension

is thought to refer to the Civil War in the United States, while writers in other countries could think that it refers to their own civil wars. Nostradamus seems to be frequently concerned with wars, plagues, fires, and other unpleasant events, and he is very rarely specific about when these events are to occur. An exception is the statement that "In the year 1999 and seven months, from the skies shall come an alarmingly powerful kind," which is certainly precise enough. A "forecast" that some event will occur, but at a totally unspecific time is of very little value. If one adds difficulty in interpreting exactly what the forecast means, the value is reduced even further. These difficulties are found in most of the ancient prophecies, which makes their evaluation so difficult. Further, only the apparently more significant or successful prophecies have been remembered and the rest have been forgotten and discarded. This bias has to be remembered when an apparently impressive example from the past is presented. In more modern terminology, it is unclear if the prophecies are actually forecasts or merely scenarios.

There are plenty of examples of specific forecasts made in the distant past which are now easily evaluated and there are plenty of examples of very unsuccessful predictions, including one by an Astronomer Royal that space travel is impossible made just a few years before the first moon walk, or older ones that humans could never survive speeds of greater than 25 miles per hour, which was a concern before the first passenger trains started to run. Other forgettable forecasts include that by the historian Henry Adams made in 1903, fixing "1950 as the year when the world must go smash," and a statement in the 1899 Literary Digest that the automobile or horseless carriage "is at present a luxury for the wealthy: and although its price will probably fall in the future, it will never come into as common use as the bicycle," an error compounded in 1902 by Harpers Weekly in saying that "the actual building of roads devoted to motor cars is not for the near future, in spite of many rumors to that effect." It is natural to wonder which of the futuristic statements being made currently will provide similar examples of totally incorrect forecasts in a text written 50 years hence.

Finally, it might be noted that many of the techniques developed for forecasting can equally well be used for backcasting, that is, for estimating the state of the world before the earliest data in the information set. One of the most famous backcasts, and certainly the most precise, was the estimate made by Archbishop James Ussher, a seventeenth century Irish churchman, who after studying the Bible decided that the earth was created in 4004 B.C., on Sunday, October 23rd at 9:00 A.M. More recent estimates put the creation at least four billion years earlier, which suggests the Archbishop produced a forecast error of record size.

12.2 CHOOSING METHODS

The preceding chapters have introduced a variety of forecasting methods, usually the best known and most respected. There are plenty of methods that have not been discussed and new ones are being proposed regularly. These alternatives range from the highly sophisticated to the very unsophisticated, from the sublime to the ridiculous. An example of a method at one of these extremes is known as the "one-percent method." Suppose that you want to forecast the GNP of Mexico but find the task difficult. The one-percent method suggests that you find a component of the variable that represents about 1% of the total and which is fairly easy to forecast, then make a forecast of this component, and finally, multiply your forecast by 100 to get a forecast value for the whole variable. There has been no serious attempt to evaluate this procedure, but its quality can be anticipated. Some other methods are based on more sophisticated statistical or economic techniques, such as Markov chain models or input—output matrices. The first of these is most relevant for event forecasting and is analogous to using an AR(1) model, while the second may be thought of as an alternative to econometric modeling, as it does interrelate various sectors of the economy, though generally ignoring many important sectors, such as the financial and monetary, and using few, if any, lags.

Some current developments, with clear potential for producing improvements in forecasts, are the following:

(i)   Multivariate generalizations of the Box-Jenkins type of statistical modeling described in Chapter 3, using just the data to pick a model rather than some causal theory, such as would be provided by an economist. Automated methods are already being introduced as commercial services to build univariate ARIMA models, and doubtless these will be generalized to deal with two or a few series. Other methods of dealing with several series try to simplify the situation by representing these series in terms of just a few others, using procedures such as principal components and factor analysis.

(ii) Nonlinear statistical models, both univariate and multivariate. The real world is almost certainly nonlinear and so one would expect nonlinear models to be necessary to properly model it. One problem is that the class of nonlinear models is immense, but for analysis, or identification, of a model a limited class is required. A class which involves a certain amount of nonlinearity, but is capable of analysis and has been shown to produce improved forecasts on occasion, is that of the bilinear models, an example of which is a series generated by

$$x_t = \varepsilon_t + a\varepsilon_{t-1}x_{t-2}.$$

One surprising feature of some model of this class, including the example just given, is that they identify as white noise, using the methods discussed in Chapter 3, and yet they are forecastable from their own past, although in a nonlinear manner.

(iii) Changing parameter models. The models discussed in earlier chapters generally assume that the parameters do not change through time, which means that the series are stationary. In the real world, an assumption of stationarity is unlikely to be true: Relationships between variables change over time and parameters will probably change. If they change slowly, or smoothly, it may well be possible to model this and produce a more complicated but more realistic model. In some cases, the parameters may alter in accordance with the value taken by some other variable. If the actual form of the model is known, the changing parameter model can be efficiently estimated and forecasts formed easily using an algorithm known as the Kalman filter. The main difficulty is selecting the proper model.

(iv) Improved modelling of the long-run components of series and particularly the relationships between the long-run components of several series. These lead to a concept known as cointegration in which several ARIMA $(p,1,q)$ series (see section 3.7.1) have linear combinations that are ARMA. If series are cointegrated, there exists a model, known as error-correcting, which can potentially improve short-run forecasts but which particularly affects the quality of long-run forecasts. More effort is also being put into more sophisticated methods of trend fitting and extrapolation.

(v) More attention is being paid to providing superior interval forecasts, both by combining interval forecasts and by using models to forecast variances of errors. It has been found from the residuals from ARMA, that regression on econometric models have variances that are not constant through time, as assumed in earlier chapters, and that these variances are forecastable. Some of the models designed to forecast these variances are called ARCH models in the literature.

All of these developments are discussed to some extent in Granger and Newbold (1986).

A professional forecaster clearly cannot rely on just a single technique and should both be aware of several current methods and also attempt to keep up, at least somewhat, with new developments. The only problem with knowing many alternative forecasting techniques is that one has to choose between them. Few people would want to apply every known technique to each forecasting problem they face. To help decide which method, or small group of methods, to employ, the overall decision can be broken down into a series of smaller and, hopefully, easier decisions. At each decision stage, the main possibilities can be listed to help selection. When all these subdecisions have been made, many possible forecasting techniques will have become irrelevant and one can list those that do remain available. In technological forecasting, this technique is known as morphological analysis. The various stages in the analysis of forecasts, together with the available choices, are shown in Table 12.1. Most of the entries should be self-explanatory given the contents of the preceding chapters, but in some cases some amplification is required. The types of information sets considered are (i) single series, in which a series is forecast just from its own past; (ii) noncausal, in which the series is forecast also from other series which are not really causal but may help predict, such as

TABLE 12.1

Forecasting Morphology

---

1. *Recognition of type of forecasting problem*

Timing   Event   Point   Trace

2. *Preanalysis decisions*

Information set
(i) Length		short series		long series
(ii) Depth	One series	Two series	Few series	Many series
(iii) Type	One series	Noncausal	Causal	Enhanced causal
Horizon	Short term	Middle term	Long term	
Cost	Low cost	Medium cost	High cost	

3. *Analysis decisions*

Trend	Trend	No trend
Seasonal	Seasonal	No seasonal
Transformation	Transformation	No transformation
Form	Linear	Nonlinear
Stationarity	Time invariant	Time-varying parameters
Analysis	List techniques available	
	(alternative identification, estimation methods)	

4. *Synthesis decisions*

One step   Two step   Many step

5. *Post analysis decisions*

Updating	None Occasional	Continual
Tracking	Automatic monitoring	No automatic monitoring
Evaluation	None Casual	Intensive

TABLE 12.2

Examples of Decision Sets and Resulting Techniques

Information set	A	B	C	D	
				D1	D2
(i) Length	Short series	Long series	Long series	Long series	
(ii) Depth	One series	One series	Many series	One series	
(iii) Type	One series	One series	Causal	One series	
Horizon	Short term	Short term	Short/middle term	Short term	
Cost	Low cost	Medium to high cost	High cost	High cost	
Trend	Trend	Trend	Trend	Trend	
Seasonal	Seasonal	No seasonal	Seasonal	No seasonal	
Transform	No transform	No transform	No transform	No transform	
Form	Linear	Linear	Linear	Linear	Nonlinear
Stationary	Time invariant	Time invariant	Time invariant	Time varying	Time invariant

Alternative Techniques

Methods available	Naive models
	Adaptive methods
		Automatic AR models
		Automatic ARMA models
		Stepwise autoregressive
		Box–Jenkins ARMA models, etc.
		Estimated by:
		  search estimates
		  maximum likelihood estimates
		  Bayesian estimates
		  robust estimates
			Econometric
			Factor-analysis time series
			Automatic AR models
			Many estimating techniques
			Time series–econometric
				Kalman filtering
				Time-varying AR
				Harmonizable
					Bilinear
					Bounded processes

Synthesis	One step	Two step (combining)	Synthesis (TSAR)	One step	One step
Updating	No updating	Occasional updating	Occasional updating	Continual updating	Occasional
Tracking	Trigg track	No automatic tracking	No automatic monitoring	No monitoring	No monitoring
Evaluation	No evaluation	Intensive evaluation	Casual	None	Casual

leading indicators; (iii) causal, which involves series that do cause according to some theory or statistical test; and (iv) enhanced causal, which uses both causal and other variables, such as anticipations data. The decision concerning "transformation" is whether to analyze the raw data or whether the data should first be transformed, by using the logarithm of the data or in rate of return form, for example.

If several different methods of forecasting are available, a decision has to be made about synthesis. By "one step" is meant just using whichever single method seems best; in "two step" a second round of analysis is considered, such as combining the consistent forecasts; and by "many step" synthesis is meant a deeper analysis of the relationships between methods, such as applying single or multiple time series modeling techniques to the residuals from econometric models.

The postanalysis decisions include the problem of how frequently to update one's model as new information becomes available, whether a track is kept automatically of the type and size of forecast errors being made, and how intensively the forecasts are being evaluated.

Table 12.2 shows some examples of different decision sets and the consequential alternative techniques that are available. Example A shows a low cost, single-series situation with few data, B is a higher cost, single-series case and leads to the ARIMA models, C is a multiseries situation with few or no data or cost limitations, and the two sections of D have either time-varying parameters or nonlinearity. Some groups of decisions lead to cases where there are probably no methods available. For instance, if one specifies that there is little data, requires low cost, and suggests that non-linear, time-varying models are most appropriate, then he should be not surprised that the cupboard is bare.

Although morphological analysis does help with the choice of a method, there still may remain a few alternative methods available. It will be up to the individual to use the techniques with which he is most comfortable or several methods together with a combining procedure. It is certainly true to say that not all forecasters will reach the same conclusion or the same model, so the possibility that experience, ability, or good luck will allow an individual to produce a better forecast than his competitors still remains.

12.3   THE MANAGEMENT OF FORECASTS

Forecasts are made to be used. In most companies or organizations there are the producers — the forecasters — and the users — who may be called the management — who incorporate the forecasts in their decision making process. There is often some tension in this situation. The producers may feel that management is unappreciative and makes insufficient use of the forecasts, whereas the managers may think that the forecasts are insufficiently accurate and can be easily improved. The tension can often be reduced by extra communication and by some knowledge of the other group's tasks. Management should be aware of the information set being utilized and have some appreciation of the techniques being used. The forecaster should be aware of how his forecasts will be used and of the inherent difficulties in the decisions to be made. It is also important for the forecaster to give some indication of the uncertainty attached to his figures, and he should resist the temptation to be overly optimistic in his estimate of the confidence bands around the forecast. It is equally important for management to supply the forecasters with all relevant information for incorporation into the forecasts rather than retaining some pieces for their own use. The most important thing of all is for both sides to agree on precisely what is being forecast and why.

Both groups do have certain responsibilities to ensure that good quality forecasts are produced. The forecasters have to be aware of the properties of the data being used, such as the precise definition, whether, and how, it has been seasonally adjusted, and how it is upgraded as new information becomes available. It is also necessary for the forecasters to attempt to keep up with new developments in the field. Management has to provide the environment and facilities to ensure that the forecaster operates as effectively as possible, known technically as prophet maximization.

QUESTIONS

1. How true is it to say that the more data analysis attempted, the better the quality of the forecasts achieved, in general?

2. A company director wants to employ you to forecast the monthly inventory levels for the firm, which manufactures a single product. However, he is unclear what facilities to provide you with, this being the first formal forecasting project undertaken by the firm. Discuss the kinds of decisions that need to be made, including those about what information to utilize and how much money to spend, and the implications of these decisions.

FURTHER READINGS

Carlson, S. (1985). "A Double-Blind Test of Astrology," *Nature* **318**, 5 December.

Granger, C. W. J., and A. P. Andersen (1978). *An Introduction to Bilinear Time Series Models,* Gottingen: Vandenhoech and Ruprecht.

Granger, C. W. J., and P. Newbold (1986). *Forecasting Economic Time Series,* (2nd edition) New York: Academic Press.

APPENDIX

Some Basic Statistical Concepts

A.1 POPULATION AND SAMPLE

The scientific field of study known as Statistics is concerned with uncertainty, how it can be measured and characterized and how data can be organized to quantify uncertainty. Suppose that a research worker stands on a street corner and measures the height of passing pedestrians. Now consider a variable defined as the height of the next person measured. It is impossible to know precisely this next height, and so the variable is called a *random variable,* as its forthcoming value is uncertain. By looking at the data gathered on previous heights it will be possible to make statements about the next height. It is important to know how to use this data; merely listing the data is likely to be too confusing. By properly looking at the data, one may find patterns that are helpful in saying something about the next height. Thus, one might notice that women are generally shorter than men, so that this does say something useful about the next height if it is known that it will be a woman.

If the symbol X is used to denote a random variable, it may be thought of as the outcome of an uncertain experiment, such as measuring heights. A useful abstract concept is the list of all the values that would arise from all possible experiments, called the *population.* In the height experiment, the population consists of the heights that would be measured if all the people in your region walked past your location and were measured. In practice it would be too expensive to measure everyone, so instead a representative group is used — called the *sample.* The statistician has to use the information available in the sample to imply properties of the population.

A particularly important concept in characterizing a random variable is that of *probability.* A probability is a number lying between zero and one that measures the likelihood of some uncertain event occurring. For exam-

259

ple, one could say that the probability of the next height being between 5′4″ to 5′7″ is 0.3. One might interpret such a statement as meaning that of all the people in the population, 30%, have heights in that range. If one can give probability values to every range of possible values, the random variable X is fully characterized. One way to do this is by using a function $F(x)$, called the distribution function, defined for any x by

$$F(x) = \text{Probability } (X \le x)$$

so that $F(\infty) = 1$. It is found that

$$\text{Prob}(a < x \le b) = F(b) - F(a),$$

so that knowing $F(x)$ allows a probability value to be put on the event that X lies in the range (a, b), for any values a, b. A second function is used more often, the probability density function $f(x)$, defined by

$$f(x) = \frac{dF(x)}{dx}$$

(assuming differentiation is possible). The probability of X lying in some small interval $(a, a + \delta)$ given by $f(a)\delta$. An example of a probability density function (pdf) is

$$f(x) = c \exp\left(-\frac{(x - m)^2}{2\sigma^2}\right)$$

with $c = 1/\sigma\sqrt{2\pi}$, called the *normal pdf*. All $f(x)$ functions are positive (or zero) for all x, and the area beneath the curve is equal to one (corresponding to $F(\infty)$). For the normal curve this last property is ensured by the value of c indicated above. The normal distribution is thought to be likely to occur in practice because of various technical properties of sums of random variables, and it often assumes to be the distribution of data found in the real world.

A.2   MEAN AND VARIANCE

For a sample, which is just a list of numbers, it is convenient to summarize the information in the sample by two numbers: one measures the middle (or typical value) called the location, and the other measures the variability of the data around the middle. The usual measure of location is the mean (or "average") of the sample, if the numbers in the sample, which contains n members, are denoted $x_1, x_2, \ldots, x_n$ where x_1 is the first measurement, x_2 the second and so forth, the sample mean $\bar{x}_n$ is defined by

$$\bar{x}_n = \frac{1}{n} \sum_{i=1}^{n} x_i \qquad \text{(A2.1)}^1$$

In some cases, the sample mean can be given a simple, useful interpretation. Suppose we chose n people at random from a town and measure their incomes x_1, $i = 1 \ldots n$. ["At random" means that each person in the town is equally likely to be selected for the sample.] Then $\sum_{i=1}^{n} x_i$ is the total income of the people in the sample, and $\bar{x}_n$ is the amount of income each person would receive if all incomes in the sample were redistributed equally. Clearly, when heights are being measured, this particular interpretation is not relevant. Nevertheless, the mean height suggests where a typical height might be. The mean height of a sample of men would be expected to be larger than for a sample of women. As the sample size n gets very large $\bar{x}_n$ will tend to the *population mean m*, which is defined as

$$m = \int_{-\infty}^{\infty} xf(x)\, dx. \qquad \text{(A2.2)}$$

For any n, $\bar{x}_n$ is an *estimate* of m, so that the sample is being used to suggest properties of the population. Naturally, one would expect that the larger n, the sample size, is, the better an estimate of m is $\bar{x}_n$.

A useful measure of variability is s, the sample standard deviation, where s^2 (the sample variance) is defined by

$$s^2 = \frac{1}{n} \sum_{i=1}^{n} (x_i - \bar{x}_n)^2. \qquad \text{(A2.3)}$$

A numerical example is given in Section A4. The larger the variability in the sample, the larger the value taken by s, so that if there is no variability, with all $x_i = \bar{x}$, then it will be zero. As n becomes large, s^2 tends to be the population variance, σ^2, given by

$$\sigma^2 = \int_{-\infty}^{\infty} (x - m)^2 f(x)\, dx.$$

As might be expected from the notation used, the normal probability density function has mean m and standard deviation σ. It is often convenient to assume that a random variable has a normal distribution. In this case, if X has such a distribution, then the scaled variable $Y = \dfrac{X - m}{\sigma}$ has a normal distribution, with mean 0 and standard deviation 1. Tables for the

[1] The notation $\sum_{i=1}^{n} x_i$ equals $x_1 + x_2 + \cdots + x_n$

probability that Y lies in some region (a, b) are readily available in statistics textbooks. In particular, it is found that

$$\text{Prob}(-1.96 < Y \le 1.96) = 0.95$$

and

$$\text{Prob}(-2.60 < Y \le 2.60) = 0.99.$$

It follows that with probability 0.95, X lies in the region $(m \pm 1.96\sigma)$, and with probability 0.99, X lies in the region $(m \pm 2.60\sigma)$.

These properties become important when one is discussing the estimated mean $\bar{x}_n$ from a sample $x_1, x_2, \ldots, x_n$, each component of which comes from some distribution with mean m and variance σ^2. Because different samples give different values, $\bar{x}_n$ is a random variable, but it can be shown that, generally and for n large, $\bar{x}_n$ will have a normal distribution with mean m and variance σ^2/n. It follows that with 99% probability $\bar{x}_n$ lies in the region $(m \pm 2.6\sigma/\sqrt{n})$, which is seen to become a very short region centered on m as n becomes large. These results are used in Chapter 4 when the topic of confidence intervals for forecast is discussed.

A.3 STATISTICAL RELATIONSHIPS

If one measures a pair of random variables, denoted by X and Y, for each individual or unit in the sample, there may be a tendency for the two to be related but for the relationship to be not exact. For example if one measures the heights and weights of a randomly selected group of adult men, it is to be expected that tall men generally weigh more than short men. However, there is no exact relationship between heights and weights, so that knowing a man's height does not provide a perfect forecast of his weight. Nevertheless, knowing the height, one can give a better estimate of the weight than if one did not know the height.

These ideas can be expressed graphically. Suppose that a plot is made with height measurement drawn vertically and weight measurement drawn horizontally. Thus, the height and weight of any individual man will be a point on the plot. The sample of men will produce a group of points. An example is shown in the next section. If there is a positive relationship between heights and weights as we expect, the points will lie *around* an upward increasing straight line but they will not all lie exactly on the line.

Statisticians use a measure of the closeness of the points around this line, called the correlation coefficient. For a sample $x_i, y_i, i = 1, \ldots, n$ this is defined by

$$r_{xy} = \frac{1}{n} \frac{\text{sum}(x_i - \bar{x})(y_i - \bar{y})}{s_x \cdot s_y} \tag{A3.1}$$

where s_x is the standard deviation of the xs, s_y is the standard deviation of the ys and the sum is over i from 1 to n, i.e. is $\Sigma^n_{i=1}$. If n is large, the correlation coefficient is interpreted as follows:

(i) r near one, the points lie tightly around an increasing straight line, a large x corresponding to a large y and vice versa.

(ii) r near zero, the points are diffuse, lying around no line, just spread evenly over the graph.

(iii) r near minus one, the points lie tightly around a decreasing line, so that an above average x generally corresponds to a below average y and vice versa.

From its construction, the correlation coefficient has the property that its value always lies in the range minus one to plus one. A further important property is that every x_i (or y_i) can be replaced by $x'_i = c + dx_i$ for any pair of constants c, d and the value of r is unchanged. For example if x is a temperature measured as $°C$, it can be replaced by temperature measured as $°F$ without the value of r being affected.

When the points do lie about a line, given by the equation

$$y = a + bx,$$

the obvious question to ask is how to estimate the coefficients a, b from the data. To start, one needs a criterion to decide which line to select amongst all the possible ones. One measure of the distance from a point to the line is shown here in

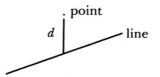

and $d_i^2 = (y_i - a - bx_i)^2$. The coefficients a, b are chosen to minimize the sum of the d_i^2, and are called the "least-squares" estimates. It can be shown that these estimates are given by

$$\hat{a} = \bar{y} - \hat{b}\bar{x}$$

and

$$\hat{b} = r_{xy} \cdot \frac{s_y}{s_x}$$

where r_{xy} is the correlation coefficient, s_x, s_y are the (sample) standard deviations of x, y respectively, and $\bar{x}$, $\bar{y}$ are the sample means.

The line can be used to perform a simple type of prediction; given a value of x and the coefficients of the line, an estimate of y is obtained as $\hat{y} = \hat{a} + \hat{b}x$. If the actual value of y is known, the residual or prediction error is $y - \hat{y}$. For the points in the sample one can write

$$y_i = \hat{a} + \hat{b}x_i + e_i$$

where e_i is the residual. The set of residuals e_i, $i = 1, \ldots, n$ will have mean zero and variance

$$\text{var}(e) = \text{var}(y) - (\hat{b})^2 \, \text{var}(x).$$

A measure of the goodness-of-fit of the line is

$$R^2 = 1 - \frac{\text{var}(e)}{\text{var}(y)}.$$

A value of R^2 near one suggests that the points lie near the line, so that fit is high, but a value of R^2 mean zero suggests that the fit is small. A little algebra shows $R^2 = r_{xy}^2$, which indicates why this interpretation is correct.

A computer program which performs this least-squares regression will also provide "t-values" for each coefficient, which are used to decide whether or not the coefficient is significantly different from zero. Any standard statistics text will discuss this test. Very crudely, a value of t over two in magnitude suggests that the coefficient is significant.

The line discussed so far uses x to explain y, so that y is called the dependent variable and x is the explanatory variable. The relationship can also be run in the reverse direction, the changes in the equations being clear.

More ambitious and complicated relationships will involve several explanatory variables. A model then takes the appearance of

$$y_i = c + d_1 x_i + d_2 z_i + d_3 w_i + \cdots + \text{residual}.$$

The coefficients can be easily estimated using a computer and the least-squares criterion, but their formulae are too complicated to discuss here. Each coefficient will have a t-test associated with it to help judge its significance, and R^2 is defined as before. A "corrected" R^2 is also available, as defined in Section 5.6 of this test, to allow for possible overfitting of a model when the number of parameters becomes large.

The discussion so far has been about relationships for a sample. There are naturally corresponding quantities for the population. If X, Y is a pair of random variables, let A and B be intervals, so that A is the interval $\underline{a}$ to $\bar{a}$, B the interval $\underline{b}$ to $\bar{b}$. If X lies in A and Y in B, a particular *event* will have occurred, such as a man's height being in A ($5'3''$ to $5'8''$) and his weight in

B (153 lbs to 168 lbs). The properties of X, Y are said to be characterized if the probability (X in A, Y in B) is known for all possible events. These probabilities can be found once the bivariate distribution function $F(x, y)$ is known, defined by

$$F(x, y) = \text{Prob}(X \le x, Y \le y),$$

as $Prob(X$ is A, Y is $B)$

$$= F(\bar{a}, \bar{b}) - F(\bar{a}, \underline{b}) - F(\underline{a}, \bar{b}) + F(\underline{a}, \underline{b}).$$

The bivariate probability distribution function is

$$f(x, y) = \frac{\partial^2 F(x, y)}{\partial x \, \partial y}$$

and

$$f(x, y) \, \delta_1 \delta_2 = \text{Prob}(X \text{ in } (x, x + \delta_1), Y \text{ in } (y, y + \delta_2))$$

for small δ_1, δ_2. The population correlation coefficient is defined by

$$\rho = (\sigma_x \sigma_y)^{-1} \int \int (x - m_x)(y - m_y) f(x, y) \, dxdy$$

where the integral is over the full plane

$$(-\infty < x < \infty, -\infty < y < \infty).$$

The random variables are said to be independent if

$$F(x, y) = F_1(x) F_2(y)$$

or equivalently

$$f(x, y) = f_1(x) f_2(y),$$

i.e., the distribution function is just the product of the individual distribution functions. This says that the probability of the event X in A, Y in B is just the product of the individual probabilities, prob(X in A) $\times$ prob(Y in B). Thus, the value taken by one variable does not influence (or is unrelated to) the value taken by the other variable. If, say, I.Q. and height of a man are independent, then knowing his I.Q. does not help predict his height. If X and Y are independent then $\rho = 0$. However, the reverse is not necessarily true, as ρ can be zero but X, Y not independent.

A.4   NUMERICAL EXAMPLES

To illustrate some of the formulae given above, the first example is a very simple one. Suppose that the height (in inches) and weight (in pounds) of four men are measured:

name of man	height	weight
Jim	73	210
Jack	62	165
John	67	179
James	70	202

The mean height is (using equation A2.1)

$$\bar{h} = \tfrac{1}{4}[73 + 62 + 67 + 70]$$

$$\bar{h} = 68 \text{ inches} \qquad\qquad ,$$

and the mean weight is

$$\bar{w} = \tfrac{1}{4}[210 + 165 + 179 + 202]$$

$$\bar{w} = 189 \qquad\qquad\qquad .$$

The sample variance for heights is (using A2.3)

$$S_h^2 = \tfrac{1}{4}[(73 - 68)^2 + (62 - 68)^2 + (67 - 68)^2 + (70 - 68)^2]$$
$$= 11.5,$$

giving a sample standard deviation for heights

$$S_h = \sqrt{S_h^2} = 3.39.$$

However, statistical theory suggests that for small samples a better estimate of the standard deviation is

$$S = \sqrt{\frac{n}{n-1}\,S^2},$$

which, in this case with $n = 4$ gives

$$S_h = 3.92.$$

Similarly for weights

$$S_w^2 = \tfrac{1}{4}[(210 - 189)^2 + (185 - 189)^2 + (179 - 189)^2 + (202 - 189)^2]$$
$$= \tfrac{1}{4}[1286]$$
$$= 321.5,$$

giving an estimate of the standard deviation

$$S_w = \sqrt{\frac{4}{3} \cdot 321.5}$$

$$\underline{S_w = 20.70}.$$

The sample correlation coefficient (using equation A3.1) has numerator

$$N = \tfrac{1}{4}[(73 - 68)(210 - 189) + (62 - 68)(165 - 189)$$
$$+ (67 - 64)(179 - 189) + (70 - 68)(202 - 189)]$$
$$= 285/4 = 71.25$$

so that

$$r_{xy} = \frac{N}{S_h S_w}$$

$$= \frac{71.25}{20.7 \times 3.92}$$

$$= 0.878.$$

Turning now to a real and thus more interesting example, the following table shows the rates of marriages per thousand population (denoted as the variable MAR) and the rates of divorces per thousand (denoted DIV) for all of the states in the U.S., (excluding Nevada) plus Washington D.C., for the year 1983. The data is taken from the *Statistical Abstract of the U.S. 1987*, page 81 Table 124. The figures for Nevada are added to the end of

TABLE

State	MAR	DIV
Maine	10.9	5.2
New Hampshire	11.5	5.0
Vermont	10.7	4.9
Massachusetts	8.5	3.2
Rhode Island	8.4	3.7
Connecticut	8.6	3.8
New York	9.2	3.6
New Jersey	8.3	3.6
Pennsylvania	7.7	3.4
Ohio	9.3	5.0
Indiana	9.9	6.2
Illinois	9.0	4.4

TABLE (*Cont.*)

Michigan	8.7	4.2
Wisconsin	8.6	3.5
Minnesota	8.7	3.6
Iowa	9.2	3.6
Missouri	10.7	5.2
North Dakota	8.8	3.4
South Dakota	11.5	3.7
Nebraska	8.6	3.9
Kansas	10.7	5.0
Delaware	9.2	5.0
Maryland	11.1	3.8
District of Columbia	8.7	4.9
Virginia	11.1	4.6
West Virginia	8.1	5.2
North Carolina	8.6	5.0
South Carolina	16.5	4.2
Georgia	12.8	5.8
Florida	11.1	6.6
Kentucky	10.1	4.6
Tennessee	12.1	6.3
Alabama	12.0	6.4
Mississippi	10.4	5.2
Arkansas	12.9	6.7
Louisiana	9.7	3.6
Oklahoma	13.3	7.2
Texas	12.6	6.2
Montana	9.9	5.6
Idaho	13.6	6.3
Wyoming	12.0	7.7
Colorado	11.5	6.2
New Mexico	12.8	8.5
Arizona	10.4	6.7
Utah	11.4	5.3
Washington	10.8	6.4
Oregon	8.8	6.1
California	8.8	5.1
Alaska	13.6	8.1
Hawaii	13.8	4.5
(Nevada)	(120.5)	(15.0)

the table. It seems that the figures vary quite widely across the states, with marriage rates of 8.5 in Massachusetts and 16.5 in South Carolina, for instance and divorce rates going from 3.2 in Massachusetts to 8.1 in Alaska. The Nevada figures are seen to be quite different from all of the others due to special circumstances and so may be treated as "outliers." It is perhaps interesting to ask if there is any statistical relationships between the figures in the two columns? If one excludes Nevada the summary statistics are

	MAR	DIV
No. in sample	50	50
Smallest	7.7	3.2
Largest	16.5	8.5
Mean	10.524	5.176
Standard deviation	1.902	1.364

The correlation coefficient is 0.520 and a regression using MAR as the dependent variable gives

$$\text{MAR} = 6.775 \qquad + 0.724 \text{ DIV}$$
$$(t = 7.367) \quad (t = 4.212)$$

$$R^2 = 0.27, \; R_c^2 = 0.255$$

Standard deviation of residuals $= 1.642$.

Similarly, using DIV as the dependent variable gives

$$\text{DIV} = 1.254 \qquad + 0.373 \text{ MAR}$$
$$(t = 1.326) \quad (t = 4.212)$$

$$R^2 = .270, \; R_c^2 = 0.255$$

Standard deviation of residual $= 1.078$.

Figure A1 shows the plot of the data. There does appear to be a relationship between the two variables MAR and DIV, but it cannot be interpreted as a causal relationship. The relationship can probably be explained using age, wealth, religious, and institutional differences between states.

It should be noted that the mean number cannot be taken as representing that for a randomly selected 1000 people in the U.S. as states vary in the size of their populations, so that one is more likely to select people from California or Texas than from Idaho or Rhode Island.

If the Nevada figures are added to the data set, the summary statistics become

	MAR	DIV
No. is sample	51	51
Smallest	7.7	3.2
Largest	120.5	15.0
Mean	12.658	5.369
Standard deviation	15.516	1.978

Correlation $= 0.753$

$$MAR = -19.835 \qquad + 6.057 \ DIV$$
$$(t = -4.597) \quad (t = 7.999)$$

$$R^2 = .566, R_c^2 = 0.557$$

Standard deviation of residual $= 10.32$

$$DIV = -4.183 \qquad + 0.094 \ MAR$$
$$(t = 17.915) \quad (t = 7.999)$$

$$R^2 = .566, R_c^2 = 0.557$$

Standard deviation of residual $= 1.282$

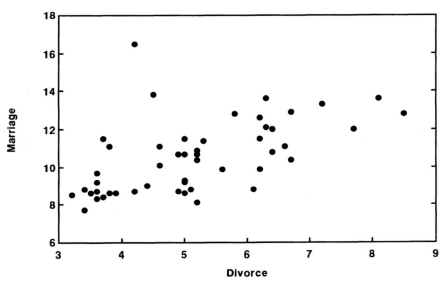

Fig. A.1 Plot of marriage and divorce rates.

The single outlier from Nevada has made a big difference in the statistics and models; means and standard deviations are larger, and t-statistics and R^2 values are larger. However the most relevant statistics are the standard deviations of the residuals from the regression models, which increase substantially when the Nevada figures are included, suggesting that the usefulness of the model as a predictor declines. Not all outliers should be excluded from analysis, but if they greatly increase the standard deviation of residuals, it is generally a good idea to remove them.

Index

W

weather forecasting, 2, 222
white noise, 47ff
Wiener, A. J., 233
Wiener, N., 212
Wilkinson, M., 161
Wold's Theorem, 66, 105
world dynamics, 235
WORLD models, 235

X

X-11 seasonal adjustment, 99

Y

Yule – Walker equations, 70